"Beverley Costa uses 30 years of professional experience to help all who foster understanding, as their work or through goodwill, to enable disparate groups to communicate honestly, safely and effectively in an ethical framework."

Neil Kinnock

"This is the type of book I want to have on my desk and look through it every now and then, to remind myself, to reassure myself, and to look for ideas."

Zora Jackman, *MCIL CL MITI DPSI,Tutor on the public service interpreting programme, Cardiff University*

"At a time when division and disconnection are increasingly visible, the book offers something both modest and radical: a workable approach to collective reflection that supports professional integrity, resilience, and ethical judgement, while helping groups remain engaged with difference, disagreement, and complexity in ways that deepen understanding and sustain meaningful change."

Professor Andrew Reeves, *Emeritus Professor in Counselling Professions and Mental Health*

"*The Art of Group Facilitation: Difficult Conversations and Reflective Practice* is an exceptional guide for any group facilitator interested in holding difficult and deeply reflective conversations."

Mamood Ahmad, *UKCP Psychotherapist, tutor and author*

"The sense of a lifetime of crafting is palpable in the writing. It helps the reader to face many things in the world right now that are completely alarming."

Professor Teresa Murjas, *Department of Film, Theatre & Television, University of Reading*

"*The Art of Group Facilitation* is full of well-grounded practical wisdom that is also strongly rooted in knowledge of group dynamics, leadership and reflective practice. There is a wealth of clinical illustrations throughout the book – highly recommended!"

Dr. Aisling McMahon, *Assistant Professor in Psychotherapy, Dublin City University, Ireland, and co-author of* Supervision in the Helping Professions, 5th ed.

"This book's exploration of how languages, minoritised experiences, identities, cultures, and other considerations feed into the power dynamics of a group is vital. It dismantles their impact in a way that I know rings true for a range of my peers in various contexts. Beverley's sharing of her own doubts and uncertainties are invaluable in modelling the self-honesty that a facilitator needs in this work. This is powerful, It serves as an invitation to the reader to bring the same self-honesty and curiosity to how they relate to situations like this."

Sumaya Bakhsh, *Journalist*

ROUTLEDGE

The Art of Group Facilitation

Difficult Conversations and Effective Reflective Practice

Beverley Costa

The Art of Group Facilitation

In this insightful book, Beverley Costa explores the crucial role of the group facilitator in shaping reflective groups that can move beyond disorganised and stagnant group dynamics, contain anxiety and foster meaningful change.

How can we create spaces where people can truly think together – especially when emotions run high, voices are unequal, and disagreement feels risky? Facilitating such spaces requires skill, ethical courage, attentiveness to power and boundaries, and a willingness to stay present when conversations become difficult. This practical, ethically grounded guide shows how reflective groups can be facilitated with care, confidence, and fairness, even in complex or divided contexts. Drawing on real cases examined from multiple perspectives, it invites readers to reflect on voice, power, positionality, and collective responsibility. Not everyone in a group feels equally entitled to speak. Some hesitate, unsure whether their voice is welcome; others may assert a strong right to be heard. These dynamics influence whose knowledge is valued and how power takes shape. The book explores how such tensions can be recognised and worked with compassionately, without reinforcing inequality. Groups tend to return to familiar ideas, mistaking repetition for insight. *The Art of Group Facilitation* shows how facilitators can raise awareness of this drift, hold uncertainty, and keep reflective practice alive.

Drawing on decades of real-world experience, the book offers clear frameworks, case examples, and practical tools for professionals in education, healthcare, social care, law, journalism, community and humanitarian work, and other relational fields – anyone who recognises the power of people thinking together.

Beverley Costa is a psychotherapist, trainer, supervisor, and founder of Mothertongue and the Pásalo Project. For over three decades she has facilitated reflective groups, pioneering therapeutic work across languages, and training thousands of professionals internationally. She is a senior practitioner fellow at Birkbeck, University of London and a senior visiting research fellow at the University of Reading.

The Art of Group Facilitation

Difficult Conversations and Effective Reflective Practice

Beverley Costa

Routledge
Taylor & Francis Group
LONDON AND NEW YORK

Designed cover image: Getty https://www.gettyimages.in/detail/illustration/abstract-asymmetrical-circles-seamless-royalty-free-illustration/1089785122/ Andrey Kozhekin

First published 2027
by Routledge
4 Park Square, Milton Park, Abingdon, Oxon OX14 4RN

and by Routledge
605 Third Avenue, New York, NY 10158

Routledge is an imprint of the Taylor & Francis Group, an informa business

British Library Cataloguing in Publication Data
A catalogue record for this book is available from the British Library

ISBN: 9781041112334 (hbk)
ISBN: 9781041112310 (pbk)
ISBN: 9781003658924 (ebk)

DOI: 10.4324/9781003658924

Typeset in Times New Roman
by Taylor & Francis Books

In memory of Mrs Paige – never seeking the spotlight, always bringing the light

Contents

Illustrations

Figures

Preface

Confucius is believed to have said: "There are three paths to wisdom. first, by reflection, which is noblest; second, by imitation, which is easiest; and third by experience, which is the bitterest." You may have no experience (bitter or otherwise) of facilitating groups. You may be an experienced facilitator. Or maybe you are somewhere in between. You may want to set up a support group for practitioners who do not have formal clinical supervision structures in place, or for practitioners from minoritised communities. Or you may want to have difficult conversations where you are not labelled a difficult person. Maybe you want to know how to recognise good facilitation when you join a group. This book is for anyone who wants to explore the fundamentals of facilitating groups well so that difficult conversations can happen. So that change, real change, can happen. You may be a care worker, a teacher, a case worker, a lawyer, a health and social care worker, a humanitarian worker, a journalist, an interpreter, a researcher, a psychological therapist, or any other practitioner. Although there is a particular focus on reflective practice groups, the facilitation skills explored are equally applicable to other groups that use reflection as a method of thinking about our private, professional, and public lives.

A book is an offering. You can choose to read it or not. You may choose to read all or parts of this book, agree or disagree with it, act on it or ignore it. My hope is that the book will help to build the confidence of those who want to, or who are already facilitating or participating in reflective groups. In the book I will give some information about research findings and theoretical ideas which underpin the core tasks of facilitation, together with many illustrations from my own practice and experience.

I am writing this book partly because I would have appreciated some form of guidance when I was starting to facilitate groups 30 years ago. Partly, because I have an irrepressible urge to pass on whatever I have learned to the next generation so that the learning isn't wasted. In fact, that is why I set up an organisation called Pásalo (www.pasaloproject.org), which means *pass it on* in Spanish. And last but not least, I want to write this book because I know that facilitating groups, especially facilitating groups that engage in difficult conversations, can feel lonely at times. The role of the facilitator is crucial in reflective groups. And yet a facilitator is often at their most effective if you don't even notice they are there. One participant of an ongoing group I facilitated called me their pizza base. She said that the cooked dough enabled sumptuous and varied toppings (the group participants) to show themselves and enjoy each other. It was lovely to be recognised and it was a very good metaphor for what I was trying to do. Still, a pizza base? It's not very glamorous. Neither is holding the frame for a group, much of the time. But it is essential. In this book the frame, and the process of holding the frame, are examined in detail so that we can work out the ingredients and assemble a recipe and method of working.

Whoever you are and whatever your professional background, if you feel that you and your peers could benefit from the type of support reflective practice groups or other reflective groups can give, I hope this book will be useful for you.

Acknowledgements

I am deeply fortunate to have so many people to thank. Over more than thirty years, I have worked with and facilitated reflective groups across a wide range of contexts. The people I have met during that time have shaped this book in countless ways, many without ever realising it. It was, in fact, the spoken language interpreters I worked alongside who first made it clear to me that this book needed to be written.

I want to thank everyone I encountered at Mothertongue Multi-Ethnic Counselling Service – clients, volunteers, interpreters, health and social care colleagues, research colleagues, funders, and membership organisations. Mothertongue was more than a workplace. It was a collaborative and compassionate community, where shared learning profoundly informed my thinking and practice.

I have had the privilege of being supervised by exceptional supervisors. I am particularly indebted to Patricia Sutcliffe for her wisdom, grace, and her outstanding modelling of the support–challenge continuum. Patricia's presence is alongside me in every group I facilitate.

My thanks go to all those who placed their trust in me as a facilitator of their groups. These include the Multilingual Reflective Practice Groups; the Reflective Practice Groups for caseworkers at the health rights charity Medical Justice; the Postgraduate Reflective Practice Groups at Birkbeck, University of London; the Reflective Practice Groups for psychosocial workers and lawyers at StARs, Egypt; the Reflective Practice Groups for Talking Therapies within the NHS, UK; and the Reflective Practice Support Groups for Doctors of the World in Bosnia. Each of these groups taught me something essential about reflective practice, collective wisdom, and the power of careful and caring action.

I am extremely grateful to those who generously read drafts of the manuscript and offered thoughtful, challenging, and insightful feedback. My thanks to Aneta Pavlenko, Sally Cook, Sumaya Bakhsh, Teresa Murjas, Mamood Ahmad (#TADF), Jude Boyles, Steve Page, and Zora Jackman. Readers may not realise just how much stronger this book became because of your contributions.

Thank you also to Alice Maher, my editor at Routledge, for her enthusiasm, patience, and insightful guidance.

My deepest thanks go to Phil – commenter-in-chief, indefatigable encourager, and steadfast champion. This book would not exist without your belief, patience, and unwavering support.

And finally, my everlasting gratitude to Sam and Rafe for everything they taught me about how to be a human being with other human beings.

Chapter 1

Introduction

I once asked a member of my family for their reflections about a troubling encounter I had had with a work colleague earlier in the week. This is what he said: "Perhaps you just realised that, like everyone else, you have the potential to be destructive in relationships."

The family member was my younger son. He was 17 years old at the time. It was difficult feedback to hear. But he was right. I'd been focussing on my work colleague's behaviour. It was easier than thinking about my own. The feedback wasn't a surprise though. I'd been thinking for many years about why humans (including me) are prone to difficulty and destructiveness with each other. It's so hard to shift ourselves, to role-reverse and take another person's perspective.

The title of this book is *The Art of Group Facilitation: Difficult Conversations and Effective Reflective Practice.* Most of the case examples demonstrate the facilitation of reflective practice groups for practitioners who work in relationship-intense professions. Fundamentally, though, the book is about facilitating meaningful conversations in small groups, of between four and ten people. In a world marked by division and uncertainty, this book offers a framework for connection – enabling professionals, communities and any groups to transform difficult conversations into collective understanding, mutual support, and meaningful change.

Reflective conversations can be supportive. Often they are challenging. It can be difficult to talk about issues where there are different priorities, values and beliefs in a group. You might fear you will be judged. It's lonely when everyone else in a group disagrees with you. It can feel exposing, shameful, and frightening when you are in the minority. It can feel that people are not just finding your views difficult. They are finding *you* difficult. Difficult conversations need to take place. They can be painful, dangerous or illuminating. But difficulties don't just disappear if we don't engage with them. One to one we find many ways not to understand each other, not to connect. It's a situation that gets magnified when we are in groups. Groups contain a shifting kaleidoscope of emotions. Groups like individuals can generate destructive experiences. With different conditions and contexts though, the collective spirit, wisdom and supportive insight of groups can be a powerful agent of

DOI: 10.4324/9781003658924-1

change. What makes the difference? That is the central question I ask in this book. To find the answer I look closely at the frame that surrounds and holds a group. I also reflect on the preparation, skills, qualities, and courage the group facilitator needs to hold the frame, so that difficult group conversations can become productive experiences.

I have now had plenty of experience of facilitating groups and I agree with Confucius. Imitation, or learning from modelling is easiest. The training I deliver in facilitation skills follows a four-step structure. It starts with participants observing my facilitation practice. I model facilitation and trainees then deconstruct my practice, question me and challenge me about my decisions. They then try to put what they have learned from that activity into practice. In this book I share what I have learned about group facilitation through three of the four steps of the training structure: *show, deconstruct*, and *reflect*. I hand over to you for the fourth step: *practice*.

What Are Reflective Practice Support Groups?

Reflective practice support groups serve at least two functions. They support practitioners firstly to repair from cumulative, challenging and stressful experiences from their practice. Secondly the groups can be viewed as continuous professional development that supports practitioners to be reflective about their practice which, in turn, maintains the quality of their work. Reflective practice support groups are a non-clinical activity.

When reflective practice is conducted within a group it helps group members to take a broad view of a problem or issue, hear other perspectives, be accountable and develop critical reflexivity. In the preface I said that reflective groups are suitable for a range of practitioners who work in emotionally intense contexts where relationships with other people are central. The examples I gave included care workers, teachers, humanitarian workers, lawyers, journalists, interpreters, and psychological therapists. The shared, relational learning in groups can transform knowledge into practical, useable wisdom.

Social Relevance

A recurring theme throughout this book is the vital role that reflective groups can play in offering safe enough spaces for practitioners who are marginalised and minoritised within their professional contexts. These groups offer structured support to trainees and practitioners from underrepresented communities, enabling them to build confidence, strengthen their professional identities, and articulate issues relating to marginalisation more clearly in their practice.

When practitioners from these communities are trained to become group facilitators the impact extends further. Their increased confidence equips them to guide groups in examining how oppression, inequality and intersectional identities shape both the work and the group's internal dynamics. This creates opportunities for courageous conversations, shared learning, and more equitable practice.

While it is often easier to talk theoretically about inequality and oppression, exploring and putting into practice these issues interpersonally and relationally, is far more complex and can feel exposing (Kuznietsova et al., 2024). Reflective practice groups – when facilitated with attention to safety and inclusion – provide a setting where participants are supported to take risks, challenge assumptions and dare to transform theory into practice. In a world fragmented by social division, the opportunity to share, reflect and learn together in groups has seldom been more necessary.

The whole or parts of this section may be used in funding bids to build the case and demonstrate the clear need for reflective practice groups. Reflective practice groups are not optional add-ons. They are integral and necessary components of effective projects, practitioner development, and equitable service delivery.

Facilitation by Non-psychological Therapy Specialists

This book is aimed at people who are not psychological therapy practitioners as well as those from the psychological or psych professions. It is aimed at anyone who is interested in facilitating difficult and reflective conversations with groups. It is especially aimed at people who work in relationship-intense professions supporting people through painful times in their lives. Psychological practitioners usually have support, often known as clinical supervision, embedded into their professional structures. Psychological practitioners also sometimes provide supervision (or reflective practice consultations) to other professions or community groups. Let's look at the pros and cons of facilitators from psych and non-psych professions.

The pros for facilitators from psych professions are their preparation in terms of training and experience to run groups, to work with group and interpersonal dynamics and personal disclosures ethically, and to create psychologically and emotionally safe environments. The cons are that they are unlikely to have the subject knowledge and experience of other professions. They may not have current experience of changes in practice, institutional issues, specific ethical codes etc.

The pros for facilitators from non-psych professions are that they have in-depth knowledge and experience of their professional contexts, the current issues, ethical codes and professional policies and practices. Resourcing and training non-psych practitioners from other professions or community groups to provide reflective support intra-professionally can build capacity and resilience. It provides additional opportunities for the development of those professions and their practitioners. A reflective group facilitated by someone who is your peer supports professional agency and contextual decision-making. Group support can build professional and community solidarity. The cons are that facilitators from non-psych professions are unlikely to have knowledge and experience of running experiential groups, managing group dynamics and creating and offering ethically and psychologically safe environments. Recognising that this may be new terrain for non-psych practitioners, I have included compendium entries of specialist terms and concepts in several chapters.

Despite the cons I have just mentioned, I believe that non-psych practitioners can be trained to become ethically sound and effective group facilitators. The training model I describe in this book for facilitators is explicitly transparent about the limits of the facilitator role and about how to provide sufficient safeguards for emotional well-being. This democratises reflective support and recognises it as an asset that everyone can access. It enhances sustainability, and strengthens intra-professional development. Facilitation of reflective groups need not be the preserve of psychological therapists. Other professions and community groups can do it for themselves.

Application of Group Facilitation

I have observed that groups really can be agents of change if they are facilitated well. We are living in a fractured world with physical, attitudinal and values-based battles being fought on multiple fronts: political, environmental, racial, cultural, economic. The list goes on. Written in 1919, these words from W. B. Yeats's poem "The Second Coming", could have been written today: "Mere anarchy is loosed upon the world". We feel that "the centre cannot hold" (Yeats, 1956, p. 211). Yeats reminds us that "things fall apart" if they are not held well. A group can fall apart if it is not held well. We need good group facilitators more than ever.

At the beginning of this century, political theorist Chantal Mouffe led the call for a system of radical democracy that embraces conflict and disagreement. She argues that consensus is often artificial when people's passions run high about many issues. It is more productive for groups to engage with their dissenting voices rather than aiming to neutralise them (Mouffe, 2000).

Reflective practice support groups are mainly about improving practice. And yet, the skills of reflective group facilitators can be applied to other group conversations. A skilful facilitator creates the conditions for *safe enough* conversations that embrace conflict and disagreement and which can lead to healthy, rather than potentially destructive outcomes. This type of space aligns with the process of non-violent communication (at its simplest, a form of conflict resolution) described by Marshall Rosenberg (1999). A safe enough space is one in which risk is not completely eliminated but there is still a responsibility to do no harm.

The role of the facilitator in creating and holding a safe enough space is crucial for group communication that can stay with dissent and disagreement long enough for new solutions to old problems and adequate solutions to new problems to emerge. Even though the focus, in this book, is on reflective practice support groups, the skills of facilitation are transferrable to other group contexts. I will return more specifically to the wider application of these ideas in the concluding chapter.

The Role of the Facilitator

It seems that some groups achieve important, positive aims and aspirations, while others just don't. The facilitator is crucial to the success (or not) of the reflective practice support group experience. But what does the facilitator actually do?

A facilitator's role has a few things in common with being a clinical supervisor or a teacher, but reflective groups are different – they're not about therapy or following a set curriculum. Because of that, facilitators need a slightly different set of skills. Facilitators I have trained are very clear about the responsibilities and what falls outside of the scope of their role. That clarity is a key safety feature when training non-specialists to run groups. For someone to finish their training and safely lead a group, they need to be comfortable with their ethical responsibilities *and* the limits of those responsibilities. They also need to know how to signpost group members towards appropriate support if that is what they need.

In the chapters that follow, we look at how a facilitator creates a space that feels psychologically safe enough for everyone; how they invite and encourage discussion of ethical dilemmas; how they help contain participants' anxiety or fear of making mistakes or being judged; how they model and encourage thoughtful, intelligent empathy; how they balance support with challenge; how they facilitate group conversations about difficult and uncomfortable topics; how they address and handle possible triggers; and how they guide the ongoing cycle of experiencing, learning and applying.

In group analytic psychotherapy the therapist who leads the group is often referred to as the conductor (Foulkes, 1986). Foulkes refers to the meaning of a conductor as a substance that allows energy (electricity) to flow. I like that idea but I prefer the term facilitator. I understand it to mean someone who guides the group through a process. They make it easier and safer for the group to work together effectively. A conductor can also refer to the conductor of an orchestra. A facilitator, not unlike the conductor of an orchestra, allows all voices (instruments) in the group to be heard. To do that they need to manage their own anxiety, hold and maintain the frame lightly yet firmly enough so that the group is effective and dynamic, not ineffectual and stagnant. What makes the difference can feel like a mystery. To demystify the role of the facilitator the book explores and illustrates how to embody and enact the role. More about the qualities and attributes of a group facilitator are included in Chapter 5. A list of skills a trainee facilitator develops in training is included in Chapter 11.

However, competencies and skills only get you so far as a facilitator. I suggest that the personal qualities of the facilitator are also significant, most importantly the facilitator's motivations for facilitating groups. Why and how do we approach the formidable task of facilitating powerful, productive and transformative groups?

Group facilitation is not an easy task. You might wonder why some people choose to do it. You might want to ask me why I do it. I will try to shed some light on my motivations and drivers by telling you a bit about myself.

My Background

I am a psychotherapist, clinical supervisor, and trainer. I grew up in a multilingual and multicultural household and family. When I was still young, I became interested in groups and in the power of groups. Why was I included in some groups and not in others? Who made the decisions? Who had decisions made for them?

Back in 2000, a few months before I had finished my training, I set up Mothertongue, a free counselling and psychotherapy service in Reading, UK. We offered therapy in people's preferred languages, including through trained interpreters, and we worked with some of the most marginalised people in the community – survivors of torture, trafficking, gender-based violence, and people seeking asylum.

Although Mothertongue was technically a service, we tried to operate like a reflective practice support group, albeit on a larger scale than the kind of groups I focus on in this book. We aimed to approach every element of our work reflectively. We offered multiple spaces and groups for people working in the organisation to reflect together – including therapists, interpreters, administrators, volunteers, arts facilitators and English teachers. We also tried, at any meeting, to behave according to the working agreements we had for our reflective practice support group sessions: to be considerate towards each other, and to behave with honesty and transparency. Having reflective spaces helped us to be critically reflexive at Mothertongue. We tried to increase our self-awareness – recognising our assumptions, and how these impacted on the ways we behaved and made decisions.

At Mothertongue, we worked very closely with interpreters and even offered them supervision groups – something they often don't get. Hearing their stories made me wonder: *could interpreters be trained to run their own reflective groups?* It could give them more confidence, connection and agency.

This idea led me to create a simple, practical training programme in reflective group facilitation for people who aren't psychologists. This approach works especially well in mixed professional groups because everyone brings something different. As one participant said, "Mixed professionals together can make this world a better place." Idealistic maybe, but worth holding onto.

Once I started thinking about training interpreters as facilitators, I realised that this type of role, and training for the role, could be valuable in any profession where relationships are central. Several of the characteristics facilitators need overlap with the profile and skills of educators, support and case workers, legal professionals, journalists, applied artists, and many others.

The experiences I have had in groups, both good and bad, have shaped me as a facilitator. In fact, I have sometimes learned more from what I didn't like than from what I did. As you read this book, I invite you to notice if you don't agree with any of the practical suggestions and to ask yourself why, and what you would do differently. I've found that one of the best ways of learning.

And with that invitation to use your reflections to structure a response to my practical suggestions, it is probably a good moment to consider the structure of *the frame* and why I suggest it's so crucial in group facilitation.

The Frame

An overly tight frame gives you no room to manoeuvre. A frame that is too loose can lead to disintegration. The frame for groups varies depending on several factors. One factor is the purpose or the agreed task of the group. What have people come together to work on? Other relevant factors include participants' familiarity with reflective practice support groups; the preference of group members for more support than challenge or vice versa; the stage of the group; and the capacity of group members to tolerate placing collective needs above individual needs.

As you read this book, you will see I have used different metaphors. Some feature plants, fire or pizza. Or jelly. Let's look at how jelly can illustrate the form and function of the frame and the facilitator's relationship with it.

When you make jelly, you pour the loose gelatinous fluid into a mould and you wait for it to cool and to set. If you remove the mould too early, before the jelly has set, the jelly collapses. It can't hold its form. However, when it is ready you can remove the mould and the jelly will maintain its form on its own and withstand some pressure (not too much) without collapsing. If we think about this in terms of a group, the mould represents a container that is the frame for the group. The facilitator's task is to hold the framing container with greater or less pressure according to the stages of the group. With a new group the facilitator needs to hold the frame more firmly than with a more mature group. The facilitator still has a role though, with a more mature group. The facilitator's role is to remain attentive to the maintenance of the frame so that it continues to serve its purpose. It's easy with jellies. It's not so easy with people in groups.

Institutions and organisations are structures. They provide a frame. Not all reflective groups take place within structures. My experience has been partly within statutory services. Mainly, though, I have worked in the third/

voluntary and humanitarian sectors and in private practice, running reflective practice support groups for psychologists and psychotherapists, spoken and sign-language interpreters, post graduate researchers in the humanities, teachers, humanitarian case workers and lawyers working with people who have experienced gender violence or who are from a refugee background. In this book I focus on groups in settings where there is very little institutional or external holding. As the facilitator in these settings, you bring your own jelly mould.

Theory and Practice

Plenty has already been written about groups and group dynamics, and we consider some of the theories later in the book. Yet, despite all the theorising, the poor group facilitator is often at a loss to know how to implement these ideas, when to draw from the theory or when the theory doesn't seem to help. More than anything else, the facilitator has to draw on themselves as the ultimate resource. But what does that actually mean in practice?

At the heart of all psychotherapeutic theories is the idea of relationship. The theories I refer to come from different therapeutic models including theories from individual and group psychoanalysis, person-centred therapy, systemic and family therapy and psychodrama. Groups are formed of people in relationship with each other. I share some ways of conceptualising groups, for example thinking about the *group-as-a-whole* (Bion, 1961), as well as thinking about individual group members.

Theory provides a way of making generalisations about the world based on observations from deliberate investigation or from reflections on professional practice. I agree with Schermer's view that "no single theoretical frame can explain group phenomena" (Schermer, 1994, p. 26).

In their paper "The Theory of Constructed Emotion: More Than a Feeling", the authors discuss the way in which research traditions may be valid for one period of human history. They may then need to be adapted according to changing contexts:

> A scientific research tradition, at its best, crafts a usable system of … concepts that works well enough for humans to act in the world, and even add to the world, in ways that interest them. Until it does not. And then it is time to entertain a different conceptual framework with an open mind.
>
> (Barrett et al., 2025, p. 410)

The same could be said for theories of psychology and other professional practices.

As far as reflective practice support groups are concerned there are many different ways to structure and facilitate them. I am informed by my experience and context together with some past theories, that have stood the test of time or have been adapted, and some newer theories which connect with the more recent ways of the world. My original training is as a psychodrama therapist. This essentially humanistic model has evolved into a more integrative model over time integrating elements of, for example, object relations, cognitive behavioural therapy (CBT), systemic theory, etc. I was trained in an integrative model, and that informs my way of thinking, but I don't propose to foreground that in the book. I refer to theories about groups broadly and flexibly.

Although theories may have their limits, we can't just act on intuition without having to account for ourselves. A theoretical underpinning to our work is important. However, casualties of rigid adherence to theoretical concepts are authenticity and spontaneity. I suggest using theoretical ideas like an anchor you drop to support and steady you, as needed, when you are facilitating groups. Like a boat though, a reflective practice support group you facilitate will float but it won't travel anywhere new, it won't make any discoveries, if you are not prepared to leave the harbour.

What Comes Next?

In a book like this there is an inevitable overlap of themes between the chapters. The themes of power dynamics, authority, safety, and the significance of the frame keep recurring. Hopefully, you will not find this too repetitive. Each chapter attempts to view themes through a different lens with examples from practice in diverse contexts.

I use my experience of participating in and facilitating groups, especially reflective practice support groups, to illustrate the ideas and concepts in this book. It is in the spirit of reflective practice that I share my practice and my reflections on it. Also, in the spirit of transparency and of sharing power I am attempting to "show my workings".

The examples are all based on my experience of facilitating or of training and supervising facilitators. They are amalgamated and fictionalised (although based in reality) to protect anonymity. In some chapters I use examples of different facilitators to represent different positions and contexts. In other chapters I use myself as the example. Sometimes the example features you, the reader!

Templates, models and tips are included. They are offered within a reflective process of deconstructing the kinds of activities, decisions and behaviour I adopt. I share my thinking behind my practice. This is the style I adopt in the facilitator training course I have developed and delivered over the past six years. The course is based on a creative apprenticeship model which is described in Chapter 11. The training model interweaves theory with practical demonstrations, experiential exercises and discussion. A similar combination is aimed for in all of the chapters.

The following chapters explore a group facilitator's position with regard to the frame, psychological safety, forms of leadership, power and authority, the life cycle of groups and ethical decision-making. The book introduces some attitudes and behaviours like *compassionate, connected inadequacy*, and *intelligent empathy*. These behaviours have helped me as a facilitator to respond to overwhelming need and distress. The final chapter considers the applicability of reflective groups and their relevance in today's polarised world. It suggests that by providing multiple opportunities for difficult conversations to become constructive discussions (Paredes et al., 2025) within numerous small, connected groups, transformational decisions and actions can emerge. Reflective support groups can be a force for change.

In the next chapter we begin by examining the nature of reflective practice in more detail, and the rationale for engaging in reflective practice in a group.

Who Is this Book For?

This book is a practical and inclusive guide. It offers a model of radical, reflective collaboration – one that empowers professionals and communities to transform difficult conversations into shared understanding, solidarity and change.

You may be some or all of these:

- An inexperienced or an experienced group facilitator.
- A care worker, a teacher, a case worker, a lawyer, a health and social care worker, a humanitarian worker, a journalist, an interpreter, a researcher, a psychological therapist, or any other practitioner.
- Someone with no experience of reflective groups.
- Someone who wants to have difficult conversations safely and productively in groups.
- Someone who wants to set up a reflective support group or who wants to know how to recognise good facilitation.

What Does the Book Offer?

What does good facilitation of reflective practice support groups look like? This book answers that question and offers guidance for how to become an effective facilitator. It aims to empower and build the confidence of those who want to or who are already facilitating reflective groups. It addresses the personal preparation of the facilitator, and how a facilitator can learn to offer and nurture spaces where difficult conversations can lead to meaningful change. As you read the book, it may come as a surprise that I pay careful attention to the administrative aspects of groups. I regard administration as dynamic (Follett, 1941). It is central to, not separate from the art of group facilitation. Dynamic administration facilitates group members to be interconnected, participatory and central to the coordination of the evolving nature of a group.

How to Use the Book

You may choose to read the book from beginning to end for a comprehensive view of what it offers. You may prefer to read parts of the book that are most relevant for you at different times. But just so you know, in order to avoid being repetitive, definitions of concepts are generally not duplicated across chapters although I cross reference to other chapters. The case examples can be used as a resource for your teaching. The templates in the Appendix may be useful, as you engage in your practice. My hope is that the book will help to build the confidence of those facilitating or participating in reflective groups where difficult conversations can happen.

Note

The ideas I share in the book come from the experience of using reflective practice in real-world group settings. Many of the principles in this book are included with reflective practice support groups in mind. But these principles also apply to any group meetings, where people want to create a reflective culture. I know my experience is limited, and I don't want to imply that only certain marginalised groups matter. The UK Equality Act of 2010 lists nine protected characteristics, and all of them are important. My hope is simply that people take ideas from my experience and adapt them to their own contexts.

References

Barrett, L. F., (2025). The theory of constructed emotion: More than a feeling. *Perspectives on Psychological Science*, 20(3), 392–420. doi:10.1177/17456916251319045.

Bion, W. R. (1961). *Experiences in groups*. Tavistock.

Follett, M. P. (1941). *Dynamic administration: The collected papers of Mary Parker Follett* (H. C. Metcalf & L. Urwick, eds). Harper & Brothers.

Foulkes, S. H. (1986). *Group analytic psychotherapy: Method and principles* (1st edition). Routledge. doi:10.4324/9780429475368.

Kuznietsova, E., McMahon, A., & O'Neill, R. (2024). Supervisees' perceptions of multicultural supervision in a historically monocultural context. *The Clinical Supervisor*, 44(1), 26–46. doi:10.1080/07325223.2024.2448954.

Rosenberg, M. B. (1999). *Nonviolent communication: A language of compassion*. PuddleDancer Press.

Mouffe, C. (2000). *The democratic paradox*. Verso.

Paredes, L. H., Riedy, C., Baumber, A., Robinson, H., Salignac, F., Matter, S., Spackman, C., Mason, S., Potts, M., & Wearne, S. (2025). Constructive discussion: Conceptualising a framework for productive communication across personal, conversational, institutional and cultural spheres. *Global Social Challenges Journal*, 4, 2. doi:10.1332/27523349Y2025D000000043.

Schermer, V. L. (1994). Between theory and practice, light and heat: On the use of theory in "Ring of fire". In M. Pines & V. Schermer (eds), *Ring of fire: Primitive affects and object relations in group psychotherapy* (1st ed., pp. 18–27). Routledge. doi:10.4324/9780203359402.

Yeats, W. B. (1956). *The collected poems of W. B. Yeats*. Macmillan.

Chapter 2

Reflective Practice

The Role of Intuition and Reflection

Case Example

> *Elias has been running a group for caseworkers who work with a client group of both victims and perpetrators of sexual violence. Although the caseworkers come from different organisations, the group seems to have gelled and people seem comfortable sharing experiences with each other. At the sixth session, one of the group members, Ana, shares that she has been offering a group (G) for perpetrators. It seems that she has created a space where the members of G feel they can talk about their past behaviour without feeling humiliated. Ana's voice wavers a couple of time. She says she has listened to some terrible stories. When Ana has finished describing the work, another group member, Teresa, wants to respond. She seems very upset. Teresa says she thinks that Ana's non-judgementalism is misplaced and she is angry that she isn't making the perpetrators accept their responsibility. There is an uncomfortable silence.*
>
> *Elias's intuition tells him to take a break. He feels he needs some time to think. He tells the group that they will have a ten-minute break.*

Einstein called intuition a sacred gift, and the rational mind its faithful servant. Intuition can help us to make sense of complex situations. However (and I don't like to contradict Einstein), intuition isn't always reliable. It is not bias-free. It can be influenced by strong emotions that cloud judgement. On the other hand, when it is balanced equally with reflective thinking, intuition can be an invaluable partner. Reflection frames intuition.

The illustrative cases in this book mainly draw on examples from reflective practice groups and reflective conversations more generally. It is therefore useful to include some background information about reflective practice now, as a foundation for the rest of the book.

Reflecting on our practice can help us to test our intuitive responses by thinking carefully, and by consulting available information. As a result, it may be that a *counter-intuitive* response is required. For example, it might make intuitive sense to match clients and practitioners from similar ethnic

DOI: 10.4324/9781003658924-2

and cultural backgrounds. Some clients might like it, but what if a client is trying to distance themselves from traditional cultural values and the practitioner is a person who follows traditional ways? The client might fear they will be judged by the practitioner. Not all clients welcome cultural matching, even though it seems intuitive. That doesn't mean though that there is always a simple way to resist making an assumption. A counter-intuitive response swerves assumptions. It involves a thoughtful process which can allow for a more nuanced response.

What Is Reflective Practice?

I view reflective practice as the chance to take some time to walk around my intuitions, my assumptions, ideas or aspects of my practice, and examine them from above, from below and from all sides. It is how I can take care of my practice, myself, my colleagues and ultimately, my profession. Barbara Bassot, in her comprehensive guide to reflective practice, reminds us that slowing down reflective processes and decision-making can help us to avoid mistakes. It is time well invested: "Taking time to analyse situations (what happened and why) …can prevent mistakes occurring in the future" (Bassot, 2023, p. 6).

When I use the term reflection I am referring to learning from the past. When I use the term *reflexivity* it is about looking inwards to understand, to attend to and to challenge underlying influences. When I talk about reflective practice I include both thinking outwardly and thinking inwardly.

Reflective practice involves engagement in a process of continuous learning (Schön, 1983). It combines a commitment to developing self-awareness, sharpening analytical processes, critically reviewing everyday assumptions and their impact on practice, and daring to imagine new responses to new situations. It can give our work and ourselves meaning, a sense of purpose and a sense of identity.

When we reflect *on* action, this involves thinking about past events and our own behaviour. It helps us to harvest the learning from both our good and bad experiences consciously. Reflection on action enables us to reflect *in* action, or to think on our feet. This involves us in thinking in the moment and applying what we already know, from theory and reflected-upon experiences, to the present situation. This is *thinking* which leads to *doing*. It's dynamic. It applies theory as a method of critical thinking, not as a way to mask poor practice. Reflective practice can be undertaken as an individual or as a collective experience. In the example at the beginning of the chapter Elias relied on his unexamined intuition to act. He called for a break. This wasn't reflection. It certainly wasn't reflection *in* action.

Here's what it might have looked like if Elias had examined his intuition and reflected in action. He might have noticed his own reactions and feelings first. He might have found that he was feeling uncomfortable, nervous about what to do next without behaving judgementally towards either Ana or Teresa, or indeed towards the whole group. He might have decided that on reflection, a break was a good idea. But, on reflection, he realised he needed to frame it more transparently. He might have said something like this:

> *This feels like an important moment for us as a group. The issues that Ana, you are bringing are very difficult and emotive and they have clearly and understandably affected you. Teresa has expressed some of the emotions that this brings up and looking around it seems that others may be feeling strong emotions. Can I suggest we take a X-minute break to notice our own emotions and to think about what, if any, meaning we can make out of what has just happened?*

You may well come up with much better responses than this. But I use this as an example to illustrate the difference between acting on unexamined, reactive intuition and acting on reflected-upon intuition. By modelling reflection in action, Elias provided an illustration and space for group members to reflect on their own immediate reactions and feelings and to formulate what they wanted to share with each other. The break he suggested now had a clear purpose. Reflective practice slows down processes. It gives people a chance to bring some light to difficult situations that can otherwise linger and stagnate or deteriorate in the shadows.

Reflective Practice and Supervision

Reflecting on our practice with another person or in a collective with others can be called *reflective practice support* or *reflective supervision*. Reflecting on our practice sustains professional quality and practitioner wellbeing. There do not seem to be any agreed distinctions between reflective practice support and reflective supervision. Here is a selection of points of view.

Supervision (as the term is traditionally used in psychological therapy contexts) can be regarded as a forum where supervisees reflect on their work in order to do it better (Carroll, 2007). Here's a more ample definition of supervision, in the context of supervision for sign language interpreters: "Supervision is defined as an intentional interaction between two or more practitioners, the goal of which is to engage in reflective practice, ensure quality services for consumers, and support the wellbeing of the practitioner" (Curtis, 2017: p. vii).

Reflective practice support shares features with reflective supervision such as a non-managerial, collaborative relationship, and the provision of a regular, agreed, safe space for reflection. Reflecting together with others enables people to take a broad view of a problem or issue (Bager-Charleson, 2010). Attending to others' perspectives on issues that arise in practice can develop critical reflexivity. This, in turn, increases awareness of how personal cultures and histories impact on, influence others and underpin taken-for-granted views of the world. Reflecting with others is a way of holding ourselves accountable. Like supervision, reflective practice helps us to stay energised and to resist unexamined habitual ways of doing things. (Carroll & Gilbert, 2011). It supports us to transform knowledge into practical, useable wisdom.

Why Is Support Needed?

> You can get home and it [the interpreting assignment] can impact on the relationship you have with friends and family. Because if you don't offload here [in the reflective practice support group] it's going to come out. And sometimes in the wrong situations.
>
> (Interpreter interviewed in Pásalo Project, 2017)

It's not surprising that interpersonal-focused professions are exploring this type of support. Listening to intense pain can cause vicarious trauma. Laurie Anne Pearlman and Karen Saakvitne define vicarious traumatisation as a transformation of the helper's inner experience, resulting from empathic engagement with a client's trauma material (Pearlman & Saakvitne, 1995). This is borne out by the evidence from research into brain activity (Singer et al., 2004) which suggests that brain regions involved in pain processing are activated, showing empathy for pain, when *watching* someone in pain.

Increasingly, support is recommended for people who work in difficult, complex, emotionally and ethically demanding roles where they may be listening to accounts of traumatic experiences. These are people in relationship-intense professions such as psychological therapists, practitioners and trainees, spoken and sign language interpreters (Anderson, 2011), teachers, postgraduate researchers, refugee support workers, humanitarian workers, journalists and lawyers and immigration case workers. Many professional practitioners are subject to vicarious trauma, compassion fatigue or burnout (Rothschild, 2007). Compassion fatigue is a result of emotional overload. Burnout is a response to chronic work stress. It is characterised by exhaustion, disconnection and negativity and can be produced by work overload, emotional labour, lack of autonomy and influence at work, ambiguity and role conflict, inadequate supervision and perception of injustice, lack of perceived social support and poor working hours (Edú-Valsania et al., 2022). Professional practitioners are also susceptible to moral injury. A term first used in military psychology, it is currently applied to a wide range of professional practitioners, including teachers. An article written by Glenys Oberg (2025) describes moral injury as occurring when "professionals cannot act in line with their values due to external demands". It is frequently regarded as a systemic condition caused by institutional oppression or failure rather than an individual psychological condition.

The Power of Groups

The practitioners I work with often feel quite isolated and vulnerable. They are unlikely to be offered forms of support like supervision which may be widely available for health and social care practitioners. Yet there is frequently a great need and appreciation for connection and for support. Social engagement and group participation have been identified (Folkman & Lazarus, 1984; Porges, 2017; Boukhaffa, 2024) as effective coping resources and self-care strategies. Self-care is seen, not as something done in isolation. Self-care connects an individual with their community and with social relationships. A review of group supervision conducted by John Cutcliffe et al. (2010) substantiates the view that groups which offer support are welcomed by practitioners who work alone. Another study of group supervision (Valentino et al., 2016) concluded that there were many benefits to supervision in groups including peer feedback.

Since the global COVID-19 pandemic of 2020–2021 isolation has become increasingly identified as a prominent symptom and cause of mental health issues. Practitioners of professions such as psychotherapy, spoken language interpreting, legal case work, journalism and other contexts already mentioned, frequently work in isolation. Groups provide a forum for them to listen to and share their experiences with each other. I have facilitated groups for people from single professional identities and for people from mixed professional backgrounds. The mixed professional groups I have facilitated frequently share similar experiences of compassionate engagement with people's distress accompanied by compassion fatigue and relentless pressures. They regularly express surprise at how rich and connecting an experience they find participating in a group with people from diverse professional practice backgrounds. Groups transform solitary reflection into shared, relational learning.

Elif Shafak is a Turkish-British novelist and activist, who was elected as the president of the Royal Society of Literature in 2025. Her book *How to Stay Sane in an Age of Division* was published in 2020. She writes about global anxiety, a social disease which she calls "contagious anxiety". Global anxiety riddles private and public life. Silence keeps us apart. One of Shafak's suggestions for how to counter anxiety and nurture wellbeing is to remember that sharing our stories brings us together.

Reflective Practice in Groups

Supportive groups play a vital role in enhancing resilience, confidence, and wellbeing.[1] However, support alone does not always lead to transformational learning. The group model I have developed combines support with reflective practice, creating reparative and reflective spaces for practitioners to share and reflect with their peers on work-related experiences and their emotional impact. Through collective reflection and thinking deeply together, new insights and responses can emerge.

According to the Health and Care Professions Council (which regulates fifteen health and care professions in the UK), facilitated reflective groups foster *collective wisdom* – the shared knowledge and creativity of a group. Group dynamics themselves provide valuable learning opportunities, revealing relational patterns that mirror those in professional practice (Marshall et al., 2022; Bassot, 2023). The homogeneous groups I facilitate include practitioners from a single discipline. The multidisciplinary groups bring together participants with diverse experiences and perspectives.

Participants in groups I facilitate consistently report that a supportive, blame-free environment, is crucial. They value the relationships within the groups. They say that reflecting on practice from multiple perspectives increases their flexibility, broadens their range of behaviours, their confidence, and their resilience. Several group members have commented that they find mixed-profession groups especially support adaptability and critical reflection. They feel the mixed groups develop their confidence to try out innovations in practice – echoing Thompson and Thompson's (2023) view that examining practice through varied frames helps prevent complacency. As Arabella Kurtz (2019) notes, reflective groups build peer support and foster a more reflective working culture.

Reflective group practice has been offered regularly to healthcare workers, for example through Balint groups (Balint, 1957) for doctors and Schwartz rounds (Farr & Barker, 2017), which are a type of reflective practice group, for clinical and non-clinical staff. Studies show that reflective practice groups can reduce burnout in healthcare workers (Neil et al., 2023; Davey et al., 2021) and enhance critical reflection and relational awareness in care (Dawber & O'Brien, 2013). Beyond healthcare, professions such as education are also adopting reflective models – such as the *ateneo* initiative in Argentina for teachers, which supports and develops professional identity, context-responsive teaching and professional agency (Banegas & Glatigny, 2021).

Representation and Systemic Change: Solidarity and Agency

It can be difficult to organise as a community in professions where people frequently work as freelancers (sometimes in competition with each other for work) e.g. interpreters, psychological therapists, contracted university lecturers, journalists, and arts practitioners working in health and social care (O'Connor, 2022). Groups can play a key role in achieving institutional change. It isn't easy to combine self-care with collective responsibility and systemic change. Reflective practice support groups help counter isolation by offering mutually supportive relationships. These relationships can evolve into solidarity at the personal/professional level. This is necessary if practitioners wish to have the collective power to take action and challenge oppressive practices and inequity.

My ongoing collaboration with arts practitioner Lisa-Marie Gibbs and journalist Sumaya Bakhsh led to the creation of an *Almanac* (Gibbs et al., 2025) clarifying key concepts in social justice work and social action projects. One concept – *representation* – is central here.

Representation is, of course, complex and layered (Younge, 2025). It involves power, fairness, and the distribution of agency in decision-making. As we say in the *Almanac*, redistributing power is not simple. It requires collective effort and an awareness of the historical conditions that produced existing disparities.

Systemic discrimination, as Ewart-Biggs (2022) describes, is a process that perpetuates privilege and dependency by maintaining in-groups and out-groups. While it may seem optimistic to suggest that reflective practice groups can help challenge these structures, I have seen them enable courageous dialogue and gradual change. It takes effort. And although it may seem very unfair, it requires an effort to be made by everyone: those who have been disadvantaged and those who have been advantaged by systemic inequalities. Though demanding, groups I facilitated that instituted and implemented changes in practice, were also energising, productive, and even enjoyable.

Addressing representation, discrimination, and power benefits all practitioners, especially those from underrepresented groups who often feel unseen, silenced, or misunderstood – experiences that erode confidence and professional identity. Reflective groups can offer what Paulo Freire (Freire Institute, 2025) calls *conscientização*, or consciousness-raising, supporting empowerment and collective agency (Boyles et al., 2022).

By providing protected space and time for dialogue and story-sharing, these groups allow practitioners to explore systemic structures and power relations, strengthen professional confidence, and articulate their knowledge. Such reflection can drive meaningful change in individual and institutional practice. I include examples throughout the book to illustrate this. One example, from my practice, is included at the end of this chapter.

Practitioner Stories and Testimonies: The Impact

The following accounts – drawn from different professional contexts – illustrate the value and impact of reflective practice.

We begin with perspectives from arts practitioners. In *The Work Hurts* (2022), Alison O'Connor reports on her research into the emotional impact on arts practitioners working in health, social care, and participatory settings, and on the potential role of supervision or reflective practice. One interviewee emphasised the importance of supervision:

> supervision needs to be valued and understood… it's not about just having a natter, it's actually needed to support your practice. It's not quite CPD but it underpins what you do and it's a cushion. And how on earth can you go around delivering some intensive projects without having that there for you?
>
> (O'Connor, 2022, p. 162)

A second perspective comes from a trainee psychologist who took part in a reflective practice group co-facilitated by Arabella Kurtz (2019). The trainee psychologist describes how the group's reflections influenced her therapeutic approach and impacted on her practice. The perspective of her peers helped her to gain distance from her immediate experience and find compassion for the client:

> I was coming at a different point from the rest of the group because I was so in it and they were able to take that step back … after I came back from reflective practice it's like another sort of filter had been put in those lenses … I could see her differently …which I think led to different things in therapy.
>
> (Kurtz, 2019, p. 73)

A longer version of this section, which includes insights from other professionals, including researchers and interpreters, can be found in the Appendix.

What Makes a Group Work?

Case Example

> *I have been facilitating a reflective practice group for multilingual practitioners for a year when, during a session, a group member called Frida asks to share an experience. She explains how in case conferences or with service managers she has to battle to get managers and colleagues to understand that language matching (between practitioners and clients) is more than a simple technical exercise. Frida says: "I have to explain that conducting a professional relationship in a language you have only used with your intimate family until you were an adolescent may affect your professional position and practice. I tell them that I agree that offering services across languages is potentially very beneficial for clients. I try to remind them though that the service has an ethical responsibility to support practitioners appropriately to do this demanding work." Frida then tells the group how much she appreciates the solidarity and support that the group has provided for her.*

The homogeneous group of multilingual practitioners helped her to build her confidence to articulate positions that are different from the mainstream perspective. Frida no longer feels that she gets passed over and treated as if she were invisible. She says she draws from the collective wisdom of the group. Collective wisdom, like clinical wisdom is pragmatic, balanced and paradoxical: "built upon kindness, humility, and a deep regard for the Other" (Baum-Baicker & Sisti, 2012, p. 13).

Another example of how reflective practice support groups can build the confidence of minoritised professionals in a safe and supportive space is provided by the Black, African and Asian Therapy Network (BAATN). On its website (www.baatn.org.uk) it says that one of its central goals is to support and encourage people of Black, African, Asian, Caribbean and People of Colour to engage proactively and consciously in their psychological lives enabling them to emerge from the effects of personal, internalised and institutional racism. BAATN facilitates supportive groups, or gatherings that create non-clinical spaces for mutual witnessing and being heard, while exploring the challenges of claiming space, sharing space, and resisting silencing.

The above two examples are of homogeneous groups which offer the opportunity to develop a sense of connectedness (or cohesion) relatively quickly. Additionally, if a safe enough space for exploration and connection is offered by a trained facilitator, groups of people, even those who have little in common, can achieve not just a sense of cohesion but of coherency – building bridges with each other across differences in order to work towards common goals (Ezquerro, 2010; Ezquerro & Cañete, 2024). The condition that needs to be met for this to happen is the safe enough space. That space sits within a frame.

At the beginning of Chapter 1 I asked the question "What makes the difference?" What makes the difference between those groups that collapse and even cause harm, and those groups that thrive and create new ideas, actions, products and even new ways of relating with each other as individuals, groups, institutions, and systems? I believe that the frame is key. In the next chapter we look at what it means for a facilitator to hold the frame in a reflective group.

Reflective Questions and Comments

Your Relationship with Intuition

- Think about your own relationship with intuition. When has it served you well? When hasn't it?
- What conditions made it reliable (e.g. experience, context)?
- When did emotion or assumption distort it?
- What do you think about the comment that intuition is not always bias-free? How might that impact on your practice as a facilitator?

Implications for Facilitation 1

- Think of an instinctual reaction to act in a group as a potential signal, indicating that you should slow down.
- Build an environment where group members are supported to test their intuitions through reflective questioning.

Developing Reflexivity

- Thinking *reflexively* about a situation can reveal something new about your assumptions and view of the world. How do you respond when you discover something new about yourself and your worldview?
- Do you resist the new knowledge? Do you welcome it? What feelings does it elicit in you?
- How could a group facilitator use their reflexivity to understand and challenge their own and group members' taken-for-granted influences?

Implications for Facilitation 2

- Reflexivity helps facilitators model openness and humility. This type of modelling is a necessary foundation if you are to challenge group members with integrity.

Facilitators and Representation

- "Representation is about power. Who makes the choice about what choices are available? Who is invited to choose from the selection on offer? Where is the power?" (Gibbs et al., 2025). How do these comments about representation make you feel?
- What preparation does a facilitator need to do if they are going to reflect on and address these questions with groups?

Implications for Preparing for Facilitation

Before engaging groups in dialogue about representation and power, facilitators need to:

- Be honest with themselves about their own relationship with positionality and privilege.
- Develop awareness of systemic structures that shape participation and voice.
- Go slowly. These conversations can bring up complex feelings and ethical challenges. If these conversations are going to be open and productive, group members need to have developed a level of trust in you and

the group. They need to feel confident that clumsiness and ruptures can be tended to with sensitivity.

Note

1 There are some overlaps between reflective practice conducted in groups and "communities of practice". Communities of Practice bring together practitioners from the same professional contexts, who share solutions for problematic situations (Wenger et al., 2002). For Reflective Practice Groups to be effective. they are facilitated by trained and supervised facilitators with clear contracts, boundaries and protected space.

References

Anderson, A. (2011). Peer support and consultation project for interpreters: A model for supporting the well-being of interpreters who practice in mental health settings. *Journal of Interpretation*, 21(1), 9–20. https://digitalcommons.unf.edu/joi/vol21/iss1/2.

Bager-Charleson, S. (2010). *Reflective practice in counselling and psychotherapy.* Palgrave Macmillan.

Balint, M. (1957). *The doctor, his patient and the illness.* Pitman.

Banegas, D. L., & Glatigny, R. (2021). The ateneo as an effective model of continuing professional development: Findings from southern Argentina. *Pedagogies: An International Journal*, 16(4), 363–377. doi:10.1080/1554480X.2021.1897012.

Bassot, B. (2023). *The reflective practice guide: An interdisciplinary approach to critical reflection* (2nd ed.). Routledge. doi:10.4324/9781003277699.

Baum-Baicker, C., & Sisti, D. (2012). Clinical wisdom in psychoanalysis and psychodynamic psychotherapy: A philosophical and qualitative analysis. *Journal of Clinical Ethics*, 23(1), 13–27.

Boukhaffa, A. (2024). *Self-care, translation professionalization, and the translator's ethical agency: Ethics of epimeleia heautou* (1st ed.). Routledge. doi:10.4324/9781032713557.

Boyles, J., Ewart-Biggs, R., Horn, R., & Lamb, K. (eds). (2022). *Groupwork with refugees and survivors of human rights abuses: The power of togetherness* (1st edition). Routledge. doi:10.4324/9781003192978.

Carroll, M. (2007). Coaching psychology supervision: Luxury or necessity? In S. Palmer & A. Whybrow (eds), *Handbook of coaching psychology: A guide for practitioners* (pp. 431–448). Routledge.

Carroll, M., & Gilbert, M. (2011). *On being a supervisee: Creating learning partnerships* (2nd edition). Vukani Publishing.

Curtis, J. (2017). Supervision in signed language interpreting: Benefits for the field and practitioners. Master's thesis, Western Oregon University. https://core.ac.uk/download/pdf/228830905.pdf.

Cutcliffe, J. R., Hyrkäs, K., & Fowler, J. (2010). *Routledge handbook of clinical supervision.* Routledge.

Davey, B. R., Byrne, S. J., Millear, P. M., Dawber, C., & Medoro, L. (2021). Evaluating the impact of reflective practice support groups for nurses in an acute hospital setting. *Australian Journal of Advanced Nursing*, 38(1), 6–17. doi:10.37464/2020.381.220.

Dawber, C., & O'Brien, T. (2013). A longitudinal, comparative evaluation of reflective practice support groups for nurses working in intensive care and oncology. *Journal of Nursing Care*, 2, article 138.

Edú-Valsania, S., Laguía, A., & Moriano, J. A. (2022). Burnout: A review of theory and measurement. *International Journal of Environmental Research and Public Health*, 19(3), article 1780. doi:10.3390/ijerph19031780.

Ewart-Biggs, R. (2022). Group and community approaches: A response to the barriers of institutional racism in the UK asylum system. In J. Boyles, R. Ewart-Biggs, R. Horn, & K. Lamb (eds), *Groupwork with refugees and survivors of human rights abuses: The power of togetherness*. Routledge. doi:10.4324/9781003192978.

Ezquerro, A. (2010). Cohesion and coherency in group analysis. *Group Analysis*, 43 (4), 496–504. doi:10.1177/0533316410380837.

Ezquerro, A., & Cañete, M. (2024). *The power of group attachment: John Bowlby revisited from a group-analytic perspective* (1st edition). Routledge. doi:10.4324/9781003271956.

Farr, M., & Barker, R. (2017). Can staff be supported to deliver compassionate care through implementing Schwartz Rounds in community and mental health services? *Qualitative Health Research*, 27(11), 1652–1663. doi:10.1177/1049732317702101.

Folkman, S., & Lazarus, R. S. (1984). *Stress, appraisal, and coping*. Springer.

Freire Institute. (2025). Concepts used by Paulo Freire. www.freire.org/paulo-freire/concepts-used-by-paulo-freire.

Gibbs, L.-M., Costa, B., & Bakhsh, S. (2025). *Almanac*. Colour Visions.

Kurtz, A. (2019). *How to run reflective practice groups: A guide for healthcare professionals*. Routledge. doi:10.4324/9781351112994.

Marshall, T., Keville, S., Cain, A., & Adler, J. R. (2022). Facilitating reflection: A review and synthesis of the factors enabling effective facilitation of reflective practice. *Reflective Practice*, 23(4), 483–496. doi:10.1080/14623943.2022.2064444.

Neil, S. T., Johnstone, M., Fox, K., Collins, R., & Mulligan, L. (2023). Staff experiences of reflective practice groups in a crisis resolution and home treatment team: A mixed methods service evaluation. *Reflective Practice*, 24(6), 736–748. doi:10.1080/14623943.2023.2264193.

Oberg, G. (2025, July 1). "It feels like I am being forced to harm a child": Research shows how teachers are suffering moral injury. *The Conversation*, 23 June. https://theconversation.com/it-feels-like-i-am-being-forced-to-harm-a-child-research-shows-how-teachers-are-suffering-moral-injury-258821.

O'Connor, A. (2022). The work hurts. *Journal of Applied Arts & Health*, 13(2), 153–166. doi:10.1386/jaah_00096_1.

Pásalo Project. (2017). Supervision of interpreters [Video]. www.pasaloproject.org/resources.html#SOI.

Pearlman, L. A., & Saakvitne, K. W. (1995). Treating therapists with vicarious traumatization and secondary traumatic stress disorders. In C. R. Figley (ed.), *Compassion fatigue: Coping with secondary traumatic stress disorder in those who treat the traumatized* (pp. 150–177). Brunner/Mazel.

Porges, S. W. (2017). *The pocket guide to the polyvagal theory: The transformative power of feeling safe*. W. W. Norton.

Rothschild, B. (2007). *Help for the helper: The psychophysiology of compassion fatigue and vicarious trauma*. W. W. Norton.

Schön, D. A. (1983). *The reflective practitioner: How professionals think in action*. Basic Books.

Shafak, E. (2020). *How to stay sane in an age of division*. Profile Books.
Singer, T., Seymour, B., O'Doherty, J., Kaube, H., Dolan, R. J., & Frith, C. D. (2004). Empathy for pain involves the affective but not sensory components of pain. *Science*, 303(5661), 1157–1162. doi:10.1126/science.1093535.
Thompson, S., & Thompson, N. (2023). *The critically reflective practitioner* (3rd edition). Bloomsbury Academic.
Valentino, A. L., LeBlanc, L. A., & Sellers, T. P. (2016). The benefits of group supervision and a recommended structure for implementation. *Behavior Analysis in Practice*, 9, 320–328. doi:10.1007/s40617-016-0138-8.
Wenger, E., McDermott, R., & Snyder, W. (2002). *Cultivating communities of practice*. Harvard Business School Press.
Younge, G. (2025). *Pigeonholed: Creative freedom as an act of resistance*. Faber & Faber.

Chapter 3

Holding the Frame

Introduction

A fireplace is a frame. Uncontained, fire destroys. The purpose of a fireplace is to contain fire and make its power usable. Groups, like fires, need frames. Without them, groups become overwhelmed by uncontained energy, or they burn out. With them, something sustaining can emerge. It is no coincidence that *focus* comes from the Latin word *focus*, which means the hearth, the fireplace, the home. A frame offers a focus. It draws in the attention, it maintains stability, and provides an opportunity to see, feel and work with what is temporarily within it.

The frame I use as a facilitator of reflective groups has been shaped by theories of group behaviour and psychological safety, as well as by what experience has taught me. Its primary function is containment: creating a boundary strong enough to hold uncertainty, difference, and emotion without extinguishing them. For reflective practice groups to work, participants need to feel safe enough - not protected from any possible challenge - but safe enough to stay present. They are warmed by the group experience, rather than burned.

A frame is never neutral. It is an intentional choice, and like any hearth, it requires care and maintenance if it is to continue doing its quiet, essential work. A frame needs to be held.

Case Example

> *A facilitated group, scheduled to meet for ten sessions, is meeting for the second time. The promotional and joining information about the group, sent out in advance to group members, was incomplete. Timings and arrangements for payment were missing. Group members are feeling confused about what is going to happen and what is expected of them. Just like the first meeting, the second meeting is taken up by several people expressing their frustration and anger. Monique is annoyed. It wasn't her job to send out the joining information and she feels let down by the people who had assured her they would do this. Monique doesn't want to criticise the organisers in front of the group. She does her*

DOI: 10.4324/9781003658924-3

best to finish the group in as positive a way as possible. The session ends. Monique, the facilitator feels relieved, but also pleased that, in her opinion, she contained the group.

Monique feels relieved. She feels she has contained the group. Maybe you also think she contained the group. I'm not so sure. Monique didn't help the group members to think about what was happening in the group and what was needed. Maybe she felt overwhelmed and preoccupied with the organisational process that had let her and the group down. Maybe she couldn't wait for the group to end. But containment is more than just getting to the end. It involves more than withstanding difficult experiences, waiting for them to run their course so that things can return to "business as usual". Group members feel contained when they are helped by the facilitator to understand and recognise difficult and uncomfortable feelings and experiences in the group, so they can regain the capacity to think and make considered decisions. They are supported to think about the capacity for the group to be destructive, without becoming overwhelmed or feeling they have to pretend that everything is ok. In the above example, the outcome of the session was that it just ended. Containment enables difficult conversations, with creative outcomes, to happen safely.

This case further demonstrates that dynamic administration, as introduced in Chapter 1, is central to the practice of group facilitation. I wouldn't describe myself as a natural administrator. It can be tempting to breathe a sigh of relief when someone else takes responsibility for the set-up and pre-group organisation, and to simply let them get on with it. However, experience has shown me that this is often a mistake. Pre-meeting administrative matters play an important role in holding the frame. They are systemic issues for which I need to take responsibility, and they require my active attention and collaboration.

Learning from Observation

I have participated in many groups: in-person, online, in training, as therapy, for personal development, for clinical supervision. However, the occasions when I have come away feeling satisfied with the experience have been few. Maybe I'm just fussy. Maybe I have unrealistic expectations. It's possible. But, in my defence, I do recognise when I have taken part in a group that has been facilitated well. There doesn't seem much to notice though. There's nothing fancy. Nothing (seemingly) out of the ordinary.

A few years ago I decided to observe more closely what good facilitators did and didn't do. As I was having more of the "not so good facilitator" experiences I decided to observe their behaviour too. I learned a lot. Good group facilitation isn't so ordinary after all. It's intentional. It won't be a surprise, given how I began this chapter, that I discovered that choosing and implementing a frame played a significant part in good facilitation. Not just finding a frame for the group experience but holding and tending to the frame too.

A frame helps a group to perform its stated task. The facilitator or supervisor needs to manage the group experience if learning opportunities in the group are to be effective (Valentino, et al., 2016). This involves carrying out advance preparation and employing the agreed frame to set the boundaries, to structure and create a supportive environment. Holding the frame nurtures trust, authenticity, growth and, above all, safety, within the group. Maintaining the frame supports the group's integrity and purpose and gives it the best chance of thriving.

We use the structure of a compendium of themes, terms, and concepts in this chapter. The compendium is followed by case examples which illustrate how the theory and concepts are implemented in practice. As you read this chapter, observe how you react to the descriptions of theory and the practical examples. How do you respond to the idea of a frame and of holding a frame? Is it a positive feeling? What does your reaction tell you about your facilitation style? What (if anything) are you learning?

Compendium of Themes, Terms and Concepts

Literature on facilitating reflective practice groups is limited. However, if the book is to be more than a compilation of my opinions and observations, it needs to be grounded in theory. The concept of a frame for a group derives from psychoanalytic theory, which is why I include some of the concepts from that theory here. This is not a comprehensive account of psychotherapy models. I have tried to include what is relevant to the frame for reflective practice groups.

1 Boundaries, Holding, Containment

A group is an entity in its own right. Bion calls this the *group-as-a-whole* (Bion, 1961). The facilitator supports group members to become a resource for each other, where they can draw on their collective, practical wisdom. A colleague, who is an interpreter and a group facilitator, refers to this in English as the "collective mind". *Boundaries, holding*, and *containment* create the conditions for this to emerge.

Boundaries, in a reflective group context, are the limits that offer protection from psychological harm. They are often expressed through ground rules that clarify expectations about behaviour, mutual respect and healthy relationships.

Holding is the process of facilitation and guidance that enables participants to feel safe, supported, and able to contribute.

Containment involves the twin processes of support and challenge. The purpose of containment is not to constrain, but rather to expand the frame safely so that difference, disagreement and complexity can be explored.

If individuals feel held and contained, it doesn't mean they are suppressed. It means they feel safe and that they feel seen and understood. For some groups, the support they receive from holding will be sufficient. For other groups containment will provide them with enough safety to stretch themselves and work with challenges, disagreements and divergent views that may expand their view of themselves and the world.

As we saw in the example at the beginning of the chapter, Monique, didn't seem to offer the space to explore and hold different perspectives that containment can provide. Perhaps she was absorbed in her own frustration. Perhaps she only had enough energy left over from managing her own frustration to get everyone to the end of the session. That is understandable. But it's not providing containment.

Containment and holding entail boundary setting and ongoing boundary *maintenance*. The practice of setting boundaries is of no use if the boundaries are not maintained, repaired and reviewed regularly. There is sometimes ambivalence about boundaries. They can be experienced as restrictive. But limits offer a protected space in which creativity and *spontaneity* can occur. In psychodrama, spontaneity is defined as a new response to an old situation or an adequate response to a new one (Moreno, 1964, 1987).

2 The External and Internal Frame for Groups

Containment takes place within a frame. Drawing on theory about the therapeutic frame (Gray, 2013), I distinguish between the external and internal frames.

The external frame is intentional and strategic (De Bruycker, 2016). It provides structure, clarity, purpose, boundaries and identity, distinguishing the group from other contexts. Over time, responsibility for maintaining this frame can be shared, though ultimate responsibility always rests with the facilitator.

The internal frame is fluid and responsive. It is shaped by group dynamics such as tension, rupture, repair, creativity and learning. The facilitator partly maintains the internal frame through metacommunication or *talking about the talking* – how everyone will talk, listen, agree, disagree, allow space for each other. The internal frame is also maintained through the facilitator's transparency about their decision-making. By sharing their thinking, the facilitator treats the group as a group-as-a-whole (Bion, 1961) and invites collective responsibility.

Both frames are essential. The external frame provides the stability that allows the internal frame to develop and become productive.

You may want to return to the case example in Chapter 2 for an illustration of the application of the external and internal frames. Elias's first response saw him rely on the external frame. He called a break. There was nothing wrong with that from a logistical point of view. Elias's second response gives an example of transparency about his decision to offer a break. He shared his concerns, and the reasons for his proposal about how the break could be used. with the group. This is the internal frame in action. It is flexible and fluid and it is shaped by the group's dynamics, not just logistics.

Both frames are needed for the group to thrive.

3 Holding the Frame: The Working Agreement

The core element of the external frame is the working agreement. Berne (1966) describes a contract as an explicit commitment to a defined course of action. In reflective practice groups, this usually takes the form of agreed guidelines that clarify expectations of behaviour, communication and collaboration with each other. Scheduled reviews act as a system of checks and balances. A set of terms included in a working agreement for a reflective group can be found in the Appendix.

For a working agreement to be viable, it must meet two criteria: group members must be able to accept it, and the facilitator must be able to uphold it with integrity. At the outset, participants decide whether the terms work for them. If not, they may choose to leave. This is a regrettable but often healthy outcome early in a group's life, when the stakes are low.

By agreeing to the norms, members explicitly lend the facilitator authority to maintain the frame until the group is ready to share that responsibility. As a facilitator, I make this explicit because I want to build trust and clarity: the group knows what to expect, and I commit to holding the frame.

4 Tension in the Frame

The frame helps contain group anxieties, often arising from the tension between the need to belong and the need to preserve individuality. This tension can surface in unhelpful behaviours if ignored. Hinshelwood (1994) notes that excessive fear undermines a group's capacity for reflection. As we saw in the case example at the beginning of the chapter, the capacity for reflection is further undermined if intrusive group dynamics are left unexamined.

The purpose of the frame is to create a supportive environment where trust, authenticity, growth and safety are nurtured. That doesn't mean though that "being lovely" should be an organising principle. Being "nice and polite" can shut down difficult conversations (Brown, 2018). A facilitator who wants to be liked by everyone and to comply with all demands may find that the frame becomes overextended and loses its functionality (like an overstretched elastic band). That doesn't mean that routinely refusing people's requests is recommended either. Equally, rigid adherence to the frame can cause it to snap under pressure. Effective facilitation requires discernment.

When requests stretch the frame, slowing the process down is often more useful than quick problem-solving. Instant problem-solving closes off any space for reflection. Holding the frame requires self-awareness, emotional strength, and sensitivity. When group members perceive boundaries as protective instead of restrictive, they are more likely to respond with creativity rather than resistance.

5 Holding the Facilitator

Facilitating a reflective, emotionally containing space is demanding. A facilitator needs to balance the firmness of stability and structure (external frame), with the lightness of candour and creativity (internal frame).

Facilitators should be able to rely on their own sources of support. Regular supervision provides containment, increases self-awareness and supports ethical, thoughtful decision-making. When facilitators feel held, they can contain the group more effectively. As a result, group members can relax into the process, trusting that their psychological safety is being attended to and that the frame is being held.

The following section gives practical examples which illustrate some of the compendium entries in action.

Preparing to Hold and Maintain the Frame

The way I prepare for building and facilitating a group, illustrates what I mean by *holding the frame.* As you can see from the following examples, thinking about the frame begins well in advance of the first meeting. In preparation for the first meeting, the facilitator draws on a combination of prior experience, empathic connection and an ability to conjure up an idea of the potential group in their imagination. Preparation includes administrative processes, clear communication and addressing possible anxieties. The preparatory phase can be conceptualised as *dynamic administration* (Follett, 1941). This phase consists of three components (which do not need to occur in sequence). The first is the core work: identifying and communicating about the task and purpose of the group including the working agreement. The second component is attendance: recruitment of group members; expectations about group attendance; the extent and limitations of the psychological depth and exploration of the group; alternative support structures available for those group members who require greater psychological depth and exploration. The third component concerns logistics: communication about dates and timings, venues or remote platforms for the meetings; whether or not there will be fees; whether or not a trial (or demonstration) session will be offered.

The following examples relate to each of the three components and how they are put into practice with reflective groups. The illustrations are presented as exercises with questions as prompts, and examples of how a facilitator might think about those questions and the solutions they opt for in practice. The practical situations are based on my experience of running reflective practice groups in a variety of contexts. To preserve confidentiality, I have changed identifying features in each example, (although the first two examples feature the same facilitator as they are about the same group). In other chapters I offer examples directly from my own practice, where I am identifiable as the facilitator.

In this book I am only including groups where participants attend voluntarily. Regardless of whether attendance is voluntary though, there always needs to be open and honest communication about desired outcomes with a commissioning body. Elsewhere (Kurtz, 2019), you can find examples of ways of providing reflective practice support groups, where attendance is mandated by statutory and other institutional organisations.

Core Work: The Task

Be clear about the task of the group.

Questions to consider: What is the aim? What's the point of the group? Is this a group you are setting up? If so, why? What needs are you meeting? If group members are doing clinical work, do they have supervision with someone (other than you) who holds clinical authority? Do you? When will its work be complete?

Notice the connections in this example between the compendium entries about the external frame and the facilitator's own supervision.

Case Example

> *Because of her specialist interest in multilingualism and therapy, a therapist and group facilitator called Maria is regularly approached by multilingual therapists for support. They tell her that the topic of multilingualism was neglected in their training and continues to be ignored or misunderstood in their clinical supervision. She decides to try to set up a time-limited reflective practice support group with the focus on multilingualism and psychological therapies.*

Attendance: Recruitment of Group Members

Questions to consider: Who is the group for? Have you been asked to run it by an organisation or is this your initiative? Do the potential participants want to attend? Do they know each other? What is the level and breadth of group membership e.g. trainee/qualified/single or mixed professional practice? What are the maximum and minimum numbers for a group to be viable? How many sessions will the group run for? Will the group be run in-person or online? Will this be a closed group, or will people be able to join the group once it has started? How will you target potential members? How much/what information do you need to give potential group members at this stage?

Case Example

> *Maria informs the people who have already contacted her about her proposal to set up an online reflective practice support group which focuses on the experience of multilingualism in psychological therapies. She also uses an established mailing list for trainee and qualified multilingual therapists and supervisors to send out a message asking if anyone would like to join this type of a group. She explains that there needs to be a minimum of four and a maximum of eight participants for the group to be viable. The response is positive. Eight people express an interest. Had there been more than eight people, Maria would have started a waiting list and begun a second group once there were enough people.*

Notice the connections in this example between the compendium entry about the external frame.

Logistics: Trial Session

Questions to consider: Are the potential group members familiar with the type of reflective practice support group you are offering? How psychologically robust/fragile are the group members? Is this a single level or mixed level group in terms of professional experience? Is this a group for under-represented practitioners, practitioners from mainstream backgrounds, or a mixture? How much challenge and how much support are the group members you are targeting prepared for? What will encourage and motivate group members to prioritise these group meetings and commit to regularly attending the group sessions? What is the level of psychological depth to be addressed in the group meetings? How much/what information do you need to give potential group members at this stage?

By a trial session, I mean a taster session where participants can experience being in a group. They don't bring their own material. I bring fictionalised case material. This is so that new group members can have an immersive experience of the group, they can see how case experiences are treated in the group, and they can assess whether or not they will be able to trust the facilitator with their own vulnerabilities. The idea of a trial session is supported by research on the experience of student nurse members of reflective practice support groups. The researchers recommend introducing new members to the ideas and processes involved, albeit in a more didactic format than a trial session: "Our results also suggest the possible benefit of engaging students in introductory sessions on the theoretical basis of the reflective learning methodology before …" (Fernández-Peña et al., 2016, p. 64).

Case Example

A facilitator called Hosam is about to start a new reflective practice group for transgender spoken language interpreters who work with refugees and asylum seekers. He decides to start with a taster/trial session. This is for a number of reasons. It is partly because this is a new initiative and because reflective practice support groups are often confused with supervision and other groups. It is also because the transgender spoken language interpreters who are joining the group have often experienced themselves as a minority, marginalised on their training courses and in the services for which they work. He is aware of the need to go slowly to build trust. The trial session uses a fictionalised real case, and Hosam runs the session as if it were a real session so that participants can experience the frame, the session structure, the working agreement, and the roles of the participants. He uses a fictionalised case (based on real experiences from elsewhere) for this session so that people can make mistakes, ask questions about the process, deconstruct the experience and try this out to see if this is something they want to commit to.

A trial session can be conceptualised as one component of the foundational *warm-up* phase, which is described in psychodrama theory. The warm-up phase in psychodrama involves any activities which build trust, safety and confidence in group members so they feel they can bring their vulnerability to the group, knowing they will be treated with compassion and respect.

Notice the connections in this example between the compendium entries about the external frame, the working agreement, and the internal frame (which supports making mistakes, questioning etc.).

Core Work: Communication

Questions to consider: What do you need the group to know before you begin? What do you need to know? How far in advance of the start of the group do you need to send out communication? How do you strike a balance between too much and not enough information?

Case Example

Shireen has been asked by her organisation to provide a reflective practice support group for psychosocial workers who work in a refugee support organisation in North Africa. Shireen is based in the UK. The group will be delivered online. She wants to let prospective group members know about what is helpful in terms of timings, internet platforms, joining from a confidential and quiet space, the need for good internet connectivity and for cameras to be functioning and turned on during the whole session. But before she does any of this, she checks with the refugee support organisation, for which the prospective members work, about how much of this is feasible in their context and what adaptations can be made so that the group can function adequately. She needs to assess whether or not a safe enough group offering will be feasible. Too many adaptations may lead to the frame being overstretched and that isn't helpful for a reflective practice support group. But some flexibility is possible (and desirable) especially if the organisation can help with some of the infrastructure issues. She also sends information to the group members about how the group will work and the preparation expected of them in terms of thinking of content. She wants to check that prospective group members are aware that this is not a psychological therapy group and that they have identified additional support structures for themselves, if necessary.

An example of a standard joining email is included in the Appendix.

Notice the connections in this example between the compendium entries about the external frame, the working agreement, containment, holding, and boundaries.

Logistics: Timings and Payment

Questions to consider: You will need to find a time and date for meetings that are agreed by all. First of all, what times work for you? (You need a time that you can commit to without too much difficulty.) Are you being paid to run the groups? Are you charging a fee? If you are asking people to make a commitment to prioritise the group, what is a reasonable initial commitment to request? If you have been commissioned by an organisation to facilitate a group, do you accept that you are accountable to the organisation? In the contract with the organisation and the working agreement with group members, what do you agree you will and won't do, and who will you talk to if you consider it necessary?

Case Example

Dmitri is starting a reflective practice support group for postgraduate researchers in the law department of a university. He has been commissioned to do this by the university. He decides to adopt a "three session plus review" format for the group. He thinks it is important for there to be consistent attendance if relationships of trust are to be formed. He is aware of an evaluation of reflective groups for children's social workers (Lees, 2017) which found that poor attendance limited the chance for development of trust and safety in the groups. He believes that asking people to commit to three sessions is a reasonable request. This is an initial commitment. Once the group has established itself, it may become an ongoing group, with subsequent blocks of three sessions, and maybe further regular sessions planned, for e.g. a whole year. Dmitri shares his thinking with the prospective members, explaining that they will need to attend all three sessions so that trust can be built between individuals and with the group itself. He says that at the end of the three sessions they will have an opportunity to review the three sessions together. Some members may want to continue. For others three sessions may be enough. Once the group has settled, they can contract for a longer period. Dmitri also explains to the university that he will invoice for blocks of three sessions in advance so that he can plan ahead.

Notice the connections in this example between the compendium entries about the external frame, the working agreement, holding and boundaries.

Core Work: Working Agreement (Set-Up and Maintenance)

Think about what you want to incorporate in your working agreement.

Questions to consider: Do you want the group to come up with its own working agreement? If so, how much time will you need for this? Will you include a commitment to regular review sessions? What will you do if consensus about the agreement can't be reached? What will you do if the group wants to include a guideline that you feel you cannot adhere to or deliver with integrity?

Case Example 1: Set-Up

Niamh is starting a group for school counsellors. She is going to begin by sharing a suggested working agreement. She has decided to use a draft working agreement that she feels aligns with her ethical principles. She also feels it can be more productive to start with an offering (of a draft working agreement) that people can build upon, rather than starting with a vacuum. But she wants to make sure that group members can reflect on the working agreement, ask for changes and for explanations. She also makes it clear that they will review the working agreement regularly, as part of a system of checks and balances, to see if it still fits their purpose or if amendments need to be made. Not only does she think it important to establish a working agreement, but she also knows that it will need to be tended and maintained. Like Arabella Kurtz (2019) she thinks that contracting can often be given too little time. Niamh wants to make sure she doesn't take a cursory or tokenistic approach to the contracting phase.

Kurtz talks about "tokenistic or overanxious contracting" (Kurtz, 2019, p. 51). The agreement phase is rushed over and "got out of the way". Issues like confidentiality are rightly considered to be important but there are several other issues about respectful communication, for example, that need careful attention and adequate time to explore so that truly informed agreement is given. Without that careful initial attention, when difficulties and anxieties arise in the group at a later date, they are difficult to resolve. The initial, hastily approved agreement, doesn't offer enough support for conflict. Working agreements (contracts) provide roots for groups. Without them the group structure can wither at the slightest provocation. It is worth taking the time at the beginning of a group to set up the agreement. However, establishing and agreeing to the working agreement are not enough on their own. To extend the plant metaphor, the working agreement needs tending to, if it is to develop and flourish. Holding the frame is like tending to the plants in a garden. Like plants, the working agreement requires ongoing care and attention.

Notice the connections in this example between the compendium entries about the external frame, the working agreement, tension in the frame, containment.

Case Example 2: Maintenance

What happens if the group seems to be moving away from the norms which had been agreed when the group began? Do you ignore this? Do you address it? If so, how? How might the review process help?

> *Dimitri has been facilitating another reflective practice group for the university, in the Faculty of Health Sciences. This time it is for lecturers. The group members are feeling overwhelmed by the increasing workload and work pressures. Two of the eight group members regularly bring case material to share. The other group members seem to find it all pertinent and useful. Dimitri wonders, though, what is happening to the shared responsibility, they had all agreed to in their working agreement, for bringing cases? Are some people scared to bring case material? Is something going on of which he is unaware? He suggests they set aside some time to explore what may (or may not) be happening to the group-as-a-whole.*

Notice the connections in this example between the compendium entries about the working agreement, tensions in the frame, spontaneity (or lack of), holding the frame.

Concluding Thoughts

I don't see the frame as a constraint. Just as I don't see a fireplace as a constraint. Although it offers protection, an effective frame does not suppress or fence people in. It offers a container that hopefully is safe enough for creative exploration to occur within it. In the next chapter we continue to explore the notion of psychological safety for different groups and the components of psychological safety. Can there be too much or too little safety for a group to be effective? We consider what a trial session of a reflective practice support group can look like in more detail, before moving on to the general structure for an individual regular group session.

References

Berne, E. (1966). *Principles of group treatment*. Grove Press.
Bion, W. R. (1961). *Experiences in groups*. Tavistock.
Brown, B. (2018). *Dare to lead*. Vermilion.

De Bruycker, I. (2016). Framing and advocacy: A research agenda for interest group studies. *Journal of European Public Policy*, 24(5), 775–787. doi:10.1080/13501763.2016.1149208.

Fernández-Peña, R., Fuentes-Pumarola, C., Malagón-Aguilera, M. C., Bonmatí-Tomàs, A., Bosch-Farré, C., & Ballester-Ferrando, D. (2016). The evaluation of reflective learning from the nursing student's point of view: A mixed method approach. *Nurse Education Today*, 44, 59–65. doi:10.1016/j.nedt.2016.05.005.

Follett, M. P. (1941). *Dynamic administration: The collected papers of Mary Parker Follett* (H. C. Metcalf & L. Urwick, eds). Harper & Brothers.

Gray, A. (2013). *An introduction to the therapeutic frame* (1st ed.). Routledge. doi:10.4324/9781315882185.

Hinshelwood, R. D. (1994). Attacks on the reflective space: Containing primitive emotional states. In V. Shermer & M. Pines (eds), *Ring of fire*. Routledge.

Kurtz, A. (2019). *How to run reflective practice groups: A guide for healthcare professionals*. Routledge. doi:10.4324/9781351112994.

Lees, A. (2017). *Evaluation of reflective practice groups project: Brighton & Hove Children's Services*. Centre for Social Work Practice. http://www.cfswp.org/paper-20-06-2017-evaluation-of-reflective-practice-group-project-brighton-hove-childrens-services-preliminary-report.php.

Moreno, J. L. (1964). *Psychodrama* (3rd edition). Beacon House Press.

Moreno, J. L. (1987). *The essential Moreno: Writings on psychodrama, group method, and spontaneity* (J. Fox, ed.). Springer.

Valentino, A. L., LeBlanc, L. A., & Sellers, T. P. (2016). The benefits of group supervision and a recommended structure for implementation. *Behavior Analysis in Practice*, 9(4), 320–328. doi:10.1007/s40617-016-0138-8.

Chapter 4

Psychological Safety

> The dark side of emotions is only where we begin. It cannot be where we end up.
>
> (Shafak, 2020, p. 64)

Case Example

It's the checkout at the end of a group session and I have reminded participants that this phase of the group is about closing and not opening things up for the group. Despite my reminder, in the checkout a participant called Petra says she is feeling very uncomfortable. She is uncomfortable about a comment another member of the group had made earlier about their own behaviour. Petra's statement is quite vague and non-specific. Some group members look confused. Petra says she doesn't want to say any more. Some of the group think they know what she is alluding to. Some members of the group are confused and think they have missed something vital. While setting up our working agreement we had already discussed the function and significance of boundaries. The set-up phase serves us well for a situation like this. Because, although it feels uncomfortable, we have to leave it like that as the group session has to end.

You too may be feeling uncomfortable reading this. It may not feel like a satisfying place to end this example. These are some reflective questions that might serve as a useful warm-up to what is coming next.

- How might you have felt if you were the facilitator?
- What would you have done in this situation?
- How does this relate to psychological safety and the responsibility of the facilitator?

We will return to this scenario and explore what happens in Part 2 of this chapter. Part 1 contains a compendium of themes, terms, theoretical concepts and explanatory models. Part 2 contains practical examples.

DOI: 10.4324/9781003658924-4

Part I: Themes, Terms, and Concepts

Introduction

Feeling safe is subjective. No one can *make* something feel safe for another person. How does a group facilitator foster the conditions for the *possibility* of a psychologically safe-enough environment? What is safe enough? What does safety, which is also dynamic, look like? Can there ever be too much safety in a group, and if so, what are the consequences for growth and learning? These are some pertinent questions we try to address in this part of the chapter, by examining some useful concepts and models. We start with a compendium of themes, terms and concepts that relate to psychological safety.

A group facilitator (co-)creates and maintains the potential for a safe enough space that is as shame-free as possible. In this, and other chapters, we think about how different groups require differing levels of facilitator and participant responsibility.

For groups with a specific task, the facilitator holds the space for the task to be carried out. For groups focused on the self-expression of participants, the facilitator holds the space for vulnerabilities to emerge and to be treated with respect. For groups exploring difficult issues and difficult conversations, safety may be created and held jointly by the group and the facilitator.

One of the common threads connecting these endeavours is a desire for change, for improvement, to create something new. While many groups share a desire for change and improvement, others may prioritise support and comfort, particularly those whose group members are feeling fragile or vulnerable.

Overview of the Compendium Entries

I have selected the compendium entries. They reflect my approach to psychological safety in groups considered from different angles. The recurring issues of power and authority inherent in the role of the facilitator are also reviewed briefly. For example, how a facilitator's choice of interventions about power differentials between minoritised groups and those from the dominant culture, impact on the sense of safety experienced by different group members.

If reflective groups are to be effective in bringing about change, group members need to feel confident to take risks. They need to feel they can express emotions safely, reflect on them, receive feedback, go at their own pace, make mistakes, be a bit clumsy – and ultimately learn and create. Not all people may be ready for, or welcome this kind of a dynamic group, straight away. We consider if there may be stages of *warming up* to participating in a dynamic reflective group. Some differences between in-person and online groups are included in this chapter. Finally, we consider the role of metacommunication in creating shared understandings about communication processes and cultures within a group.

In Part 2 of this chapter, we examine how the models and concepts in the compendium show up in practice.

Compendium of Themes, Terms, and Concepts

1 Safe Enough

The UK government Health and Safety Executive[1] recognises that while risk of harm cannot be eliminated there is still a responsibility to take action to eliminate a hazard, or if this isn't possible, control the risk. In the *Almanac* (Gibbs et al., 2025), which I mentioned in Chapter 2, the definition for *safe space* comes from a variety of sources including dictionaries, statutory service policies and procedures, and funders' priority statements. We summarise them all with this single definition in Section 2 of the *Almanac*: "A safe space is a place or situation in which you are protected from harm, (shame) or danger" (we address shame in Chapter 8).

The Almanac (Gibbs et al., 2025) extends this definition with examples from real-life situations. In the reflective practice support groups I facilitate, I also adopt a broader and more dynamic approach. The groups I run are not risk-free spaces, but *safe-enough spaces.* Although the ultimate responsibility lies with the facilitator, there is a group culture of interdependence; "everyone who participates tries to be considerate to each other. They also try to attend to their own self-care at the same time" (Gibbs, et al., 2025). We commit not merely to say the words *safe enough*, but to put them into action. Thus, *safe enough* is not just a phrase but a shared practice.

For the reflective practice support groups I run, I hold the ultimate responsibility for the space and for safeguarding. By participating in a facilitated practice support group, group members delegate temporary authority to the facilitator to hold the space safely enough. By lending the authority, group members invest trust in the facilitator for the duration of the loan period. The skill of the facilitator is in acknowledging the responsibility and managing that with the informed consent of the group members.

As I said in the introduction, feeling safe is subjective. A facilitator tries to optimise the chances of people feeling safe enough, but no one can make you feel safe. This is an even trickier undertaking for a group, as individuals may have very different prior experiences and toleration for varying levels of risk. I try to address this by building in regular, frequent review points throughout the life of the group to check perceived current safety levels and adjustments that need to be made. I aim to create an environment where small mistakes are welcome as an opportunity for learning. I try to be as honest as I can be about my own mistakes and about how I endeavour to accept my imperfection and inadequacy. Trust needs to be earned. As a facilitator, I am conscious that the pace of building confidence to trust in my facilitation may vary between group members.

2 Safety as a Dynamic Phenomenon

Groups can be so safe that nothing is allowed to change. But groups can also be unsafe. They can be destructive. In order for change to occur we need to feel safe enough (as a group participant) to relax but not so enmeshed with safety that (as a participant *and* as a facilitator) we can't let go of its comforting and powerful embrace.

Safety can lead to a sense of the preservation of the status quo. Sometimes that may be what is required. People may want to feel reinforced and they may not be ready for change. A support group may be able to offer them more of what they need. However, if people are looking for a reflective space, then too much safety can lead to stagnation, stifle spontaneity, difference and disagreement.

I call safety without challenge *single-dimensional safety*. However, a problem with this type of safety is that it can lead to groupthink or a club mentality where only certain views and values are allowed. Single-dimensional safety is appropriate, and probably necessary, for a group which aims to offer support only. But single-dimensional safety is too limited for a truly *reflective* support group.

Dynamic safety allows for a support-challenge dimension to be incorporated into the notion of safety. I call this *two-dimensional safety*. The model of single and two-dimensional safety intersects with a learning model of single-loop and double-loop learning (Argyris and Schön, 1978). Single-loop learning is explicit and confirms what we already know. Double-loop learning takes the explicit as a starting point and challenges its underlying assumptions. Sofie Bager-Charleson, in her book on reflective practice for psychological therapists, describes double-loop learning as an invitation to the practitioner. "It invites the practitioner to consider their own underlying assumptions behind their expressed goals and strategies" (Bager-Charleson, 2010, p. 24).

Reflective practice support groups provide opportunities for learning, for dynamic change and transformation, where differences can be thought about and gaps addressed. To achieve this, a reflective group facilitator has to be prepared to model dynamic safety through their own behaviour. For example, if they hold the agreed working boundaries of the group by intervening consistently and compassionately, whenever a boundary is contravened, this shows the group members that it is possible to support and challenge at the same time. An additional challenge for a facilitator is to hold and address the competing needs of group members for safety, trust, risk and innovation with fairness and in the service of the whole group. Balancing these needs is what ultimately shapes group cohesion. This brings us to *cohesion* and *coherency* in groups.

3 Cohesion in a Group

Cohesion occurs in a group when its members feel connected and trust each other through a shared sense of belonging and group identity. Members feel positively about each other and emotionally invested in the group. The existential group psychotherapist, Irvin Yalom, identifies cohesion as a significant factor in group development. Groups initially achieve cohesion through the sense of connection which holds the group together (Yalom, 1975). This is a good place for groups to start. Cohesion can give a sense of reassurance, that nothing unexpected will happen. However, cohesion also has risks. Cohesion can create echo chambers, where everyone thinks the same. They present us with what we already know, repeatedly. As Elif Shafak says, "repetition, however familiar and comforting, will never challenge us mentally, emotionally or behaviourally" (Shafak, 2020, p. 16).

4 Coherency in a Group

If a safe enough space for exploration and connection is offered by a trained facilitator, groups of people, even those who have little in common, can achieve not just a sense of cohesion but of coherency. Coherency occurs in a group when its members are able to tolerate, and regard as a positive feature, different perspectives and identities within the group. It functions by positively incorporating rather than by shunning differences, building bridges with each other across differences and working together towards common goals (Ezquerro & Cañete, 2024). The facilitator's role here, is to remain attentive and recognise both the differences within the group and the discomfort that surfaces when sensitive topics are raised. Rather than moving past the tension, they name tensions and invite the group to stay with them – to go slowly, remain open and interested, practise communicating across difference and learn together through the experience. A mature group can reach a stage of both cohesion and coherency, experiencing a sense of belonging and connectedness while simultaneously valuing difference and tensions as a source of learning. This may take time. We don't come into existence as mature beings. We warm-up to maturity through a series of experiences.

5 The Warm-Up Phase

Jacob Moreno (1937), the founder of the theory and school of psychodrama suggests that warming up creates spontaneity. A warm-up process is anything that helps people feel at ease. It reduces their stress levels so that they are not emotionally overloaded and they can entertain a range of ideas openly, without anxiety.

When I have set up groups for minoritised and/or marginalised group members, the group often feels quite vulnerable. Members come to the group feeling isolated and with a strong desire to connect and belong. That desire needs to be satisfied before they can feel ready to embrace external challenge and difference of views or values.

For some group members, being in a cohesive group may constitute a warm-up phase – a stage on the journey to being able to operate simultaneously at the levels of both cohesion and coherency.

6 Ethical Implications

The purpose of ethical guidelines and ethical practice in supporting professions is to address the differentials in power in the helping relationship and ensure that people are treated fairly. A reflective group facilitator may feel that they do not want to hold power or authority. They may favour a more collaborative approach. This can work in a simple, single dimensional safety-continuum group. For a more complex two-dimensional safety-continuum group there are more moving parts. For these to be contained safely, a facilitator who is able to contain and guide the group (like the conductor of an orchestra[2] who guides multiple instrumentalists to create music together) is required. Without a facilitator in a group of this type, the group can become chaotic and unsafe. Some facilitators may resist the idea that their role carries any authority. The resistance may be connected with the facilitator's own internal relationship with power and authority. Their own needs and anxiety may lead a facilitator to discount their power and their authority. Anxiety can make it difficult for a facilitator to attend to the needs of the group and the ethical responsibility which goes with their role. Discounting their power as the facilitator may also disadvantage less empowered members of the group who benefit from a facilitator who can challenge dominant members of the group. As the facilitator in a reflective practice group, I hold responsibility for safeguarding in the group. Although all the group members share in creating and maintaining a safe enough environment, ultimately the buck stops with the group facilitator. People with less power and less agency in a relationship need to be protected. This is relevant for reflective groups which reflect the wider social context where those people from traditionally less powerful sectors of society have not been heard (Gabriel & Reeves, 2024). They may never have had a chance to exert influence.

For facilitators to develop and maintain ethical awareness and integrity, ongoing activities which promote self-awareness are recommended. These activities and exploratory exercises help us to take care not to impose our self (needs, anxieties etc.) onto others. Care involves continuous ethical decision-making (D'Anselmi et al., 2013; Silverman, 2003). Ethical maturity for a reflective practice support group facilitator requires courage, accountability and the humility to accept and learn from mistakes (Carroll & Shaw, 2013). Ethical decisions require the facilitator to be able to hold the boundary under pressure. This will be covered more fully in Chapter 9.

7 Working Agreement

In previous chapters I have said quite a bit about the working agreement and how it is a central structure of the frame. A working agreement is a type of contract. An example of important elements of a working agreement is included in the Appendix. The working agreement facilitates fairness, transparency and trust – all three essential components of psychological safety and ethical practice. The working agreement I generally offer includes attention to *time boundaries* and how time boundaries contribute to psychological safety. Timings mark beginnings, endings and transitions. They help people have a sense of where they are. They provide a reliable anchor. To shift timings, to overrun or to begin late makes an anchor unreliable and unsafe. People generally say they understand the rationale and agree to the maintenance of the time boundary. But I have never been a member of, or facilitated, a group where there wasn't an attempt to breach the time boundary often several times within the lifetime of a group. I understand why. It can seem that adherence to a time boundary is rigid, controlling and, at times, uncaring. But a time boundary, if held with consistency is about fairness and equity for all. It acts as a marker for the group. A time boundary marks what is inside the frame and what is outside. In the practical illustrations included throughout the book there are examples of this type of challenge to the group's time frame.

8 Intelligent Empathy

Empathy is the ability to see things from another person's point of view and to connect with and understand another's emotional reactions. Compassion can move us to act on our empathy. This causes us to react, without cognitive engagement, probably feeling as overwhelmed by the emotions as the person with whom we are connecting. *Intelligent empathy* is a concept I have written about (Costa, 2026). It involves holding and attending to the tension between an emotional and rational response so that, when we act, our action is driven by both responses together. This aligns with the cognitive continuum theory (Hammond, 2000), which positions decision-making along a continuum between intuition and analysis.

Cognitively as well as emotionally connected, a reflective practice support group facilitator can respond rather than react, maintain boundaries, recognise others as distinct from themselves, avoid merging with them, and allow them their own autonomy and agency rather than feeling the need to rescue them. This is a process that requires practice and support.

As a facilitator I will often meet someone's story, once they have finished telling it, with an empathic, emotionally connected response. An example might be something like "It sounds like this had a bigger effect on you than you had expected." Or I might create a little bit of distance by putting the empathic statement into the third person. For example: "It is hard when you feel that no one else seems to be making an effort." You can see from these examples that they are light statements. This is not a psychologically invasive intervention. The aim is not to go too deep, but the statements still need to be emotionally true. However, empathy isn't always universally welcomed. Individuals may feel exposed or belittled if they feel ashamed and feel they have been found wanting (Cowan et al., 2013). I therefore try to keep my empathic statements both real and gentle, avoiding platitudes. In a group where members bring examples of their own experiences and cases, the person who shares their story is called the *sharer* and those who respond to the sharer are *participants*. The aim with an empathic statement is for the sharer to feel they are not alone and that the connections with the group have not been severed. In Chapter 11, I share an example of where I didn't fully engage my intelligent empathy. I failed to make a sufficient emotional empathic connection and stayed at the cognitive level. I missed the sharer in the process. In that chapter I explore the ensuing rupture and repair that occurred.

9 Safety in Online Reflective Practice Support Groups

In-person and online group settings are different but perhaps less different than people expect them to be. It can seem easier and quicker to establish trust and connection in person. However, in my experience, trust and connection can be achieved at depth with online reflective practice support groups. Online groups offer some advantages too, such as increased accessibility and the possibility for international groups. However, for an online group extra care needs to be given by the facilitator to the set-up, advance troubleshooting of technical difficulties and expectations, norms around confidentiality and privacy of space, and to the working agreement in general. The working agreement for online groups needs to cover additional norms about communication, specifically about turn-taking, the use of the chat/text function and the effects of eye contact online.

A facilitator of any type of group may fall into the trap of focusing specifically on one person in the group and ignoring the rest of the group. In an online group, everyone is expected to have their cameras turned on and to be visible to everyone all the time. This may help the facilitator to keep the group in their sight all the time. There may be other reasons why having cameras turned on is useful. But it is a crucial norm as far as safety is concerned. It ensures that everyone can be confident that the session is happening without anyone outside of the group being able to see or hear what is taking place. It maintains the external frame which is there to distinguish and protect the group session from anything external to it.

10 Metacommunication

Metacommunication is the last compendium entry. It is last, but certainly not least. I have already referred to it in Chapter 3, where I proposed that metacommunication provides structure for the fluidity of the *internal frame*. What does that look like in the context of psychological safety?

Metacommunication or *talking about the talking* is not always prioritised when thinking about psychological safety. For me it seems not only a feature of safety, but a crucial feature of equity. By *talking about the talking* in groups, I mean the process of exploring how communication works for a specific context. It includes thinking about how we take turns, how we limit interruptions and talking over each other, how we give space to one another. It includes how we respect that some people can't hold court without others being disadvantaged. This is a question of power. Thinking about the communication process also involves thinking about what is different about communication in groups as opposed to one-to-one communication. How are some people excluded, how are acts of disrespect (even if unintentional) handled? Members of a group who have been disenfranchised regularly in other group contexts may feel disempowered in groups where the communication is unbalanced. However, it's not straightforward. Sometimes, those who have felt disempowered elsewhere, experience a paradoxical sense of entitlement in the group, feeling a strong right to be heard wherever and whenever they choose. It is not so much about the quantity of interventions people make but about how long some people may speak when they have the floor. For those people who personally, politically or culturally find it difficult to have their voice heard, it can seem like there is no space for them in the group. Embarrassment about interrupting someone can get in the way of fairness.

In a reflective group, you can get going without delay, you can quickly run through a list of do's and don'ts about proposed conversational conventions, or you can take time to think about and question together the do's and don'ts so they belong to, and work in the best interests of the group. It not only saves time later, but it also avoids the avoidable cost to some group members of feeling poorly treated and disadvantaged. One of the ground rules in the working agreement I use in all groups (including with speakers of English) is that we avoid any conversations between two people, in any language, that exclude the rest of the group. I also compare the group session to a chaired meeting. This is sometimes a bit alarming for people who have had experiences of poorly chaired meetings. But a well-chaired meeting aims for fairness and equal opportunities to be heard. Fairness seldom happens by chance. If you are serious about fairness, you will be intentional about ensuring equity. I try to enact this intention with groups by asking people to indicate if they want to speak, asking them though, to wait to *actually* speak until they are given the floor. In online meetings this is often achieved relatively simply using the "Hands up" feature and for people to turn their microphones on or off. For in-person meetings it is tempting to be more informal. However, I have observed that the result of less intentionality is that opportunities to speak are often less evenly and fairly distributed.

I also discuss the following suggested ground rule with the group – that all of us speak as concisely as possible. It isn't always easy. I therefore provide opportunities for people to shape what they want to say by giving short periods of time for everyone to think, in silence, about how they can deliver their responses succinctly. This gives people time to think and time to formulate without distraction. Some people may benefit from these spaces more than others, so I keep the time frame for this exercise brief – sometimes as little as one minute. One minute is enough time to focus and to get one's thoughts in order. It is not too much time if you don't like the exercise. By committing to concise delivery where possible, it means that more people have a chance to speak, and a session is less likely to be dominated by a few individuals.

Having said that, I also need to clarify that it may seem I am ignoring the request for brief communication in the early days of the group. This is because I need to say a fair amount, at this stage, to establish how we are going to work together. But as the group continues, my input should diminish so that there is increasing time available for group members to use. This is a model that incrementally shares and hands over the responsibility for the group to the group members. The facilitator behaves in similar ways to a trainer of group facilitators. We will return to this model of *gradual release of responsibility* (Pearson & Gallagher, 1983) in Chapter 11.

Together with other aspects of the working agreement, it's a lot for group members to remember in the moment. Although it may be tempting to gloss over and ignore people's forgetfulness, as the facilitator, it is my job to gently remind them, if they forget, about what we agreed.

Given my interest in multilingualism[3] and the experiences of multilingual people in psychological therapies (Costa, 2020) it would be remiss of me to omit any mention of multilingualism and reflective groups. Whatever the agreed, shared working language is in a group, it is good practice to be aware and acknowledge that some people will be making more of an effort linguistically in the group than others. If the shared working language is English, for example, who in the group speaks it as their first language? For some people, English may be their second or third language. What impact does that have on the power dynamics in a group? I frequently facilitate groups where English is the shared language. It is my first language. It is the third, fourth or even fifth language for some of the group members. I am always grateful for the effort they are making.

For multilingual groups where some group members share languages that others do not understand, I ask people to be prepared to translate anything they say in the room that might otherwise exclude any other group member. This is a ground rule I adopt and adapt from my experience of interpreter-mediated communication: "Everything that everybody says in the room is translated out loud so that everyone understands."

Metacommunication provides the structure for the *internal frame* of the group. It is easy to ignore the importance and the power of metacommunication. Used wisely, though, it shoulders most of the work, helping to shape and sustain spaces that feel genuinely psychologically safe.

In Part 2 of this chapter, case examples illustrate the practical implementation of the themes, terms and concepts described in the compendium entries.

Part 2: Practical Examples

Introduction and Session Structure

In the following three examples from my practice, I illustrate some of the concepts I describe in Part 1 of this chapter. Again, details have been changed and all the people depicted are fictitious versions drawn from real experience. The first example is an introductory, trial/taster session. I offer an introductory, trial session for people who are unfamiliar with reflective practice in group settings. A trial or taster session warms people up to the process, cognitively and emotionally. In this way, participants get a taste of the reflective group experience. They learn about and can question the process, the structure and the rationale for the structure and boundaries. They get a glimpse of the emotional impact and processes that can be elicited in reflective groups. The trial session also provides an opportunity of assessment for both the group members and the facilitator. Sometimes a group member may decide, after a trial session, that a reflective group isn't for them. Similarly, if you are a facilitator, the trial session may give you information that leads you to conclude that this type of group isn't the best fit for a participant. This isn't an easy situation. I give examples of how this type of situation can be handled (and the potential consequences if it is not) in Chapters 9 and 11.

For the trial sessions I use fictionalised and anonymised case material based on real examples to ensure psychological safety. Participants can be free to try out responses on these types of case examples where real, personal issue aren't at stake.

This is what interpreters who attended a taster session in 2025 said:

> We, as interpreters (and as individuals), don't usually get the chance to be so open and upfront about what we think and how it makes us feel. I've found this session very interesting and I think it's a great initiative to prevent long term problems for interpreters. It reminded me of the

importance of having a safe space to reflect, and how valuable it is to pause, think, and process what we go through in our work. I would join a regular group like this, if it was on offer.

The second example illustrates dynamic safety: how a group moves from embracing the safety of support which reenergises them, to welcoming challenge and finding creative solutions.

The third example picks up the case we last saw at the start of Part 1 of the chapter. It is an example of an established reflective practice support group which has been meeting for several sessions. It presents and reflects on the closing moments of one of the group's sessions. It highlights the fragility of psychological safety, the impossibility of being prepared for all eventualities and the important role of a facilitator's self-reflection, and access to their own supervision. In the second and third examples, I describe some of the ways in which each group session and a course of sessions are structured, according to the following sequence.

This sequence of *share–connect–respond* contains these steps:

- Agreement and warm-up
- Selecting and scheduling cases
- Sharing
- Connecting and responding
- Last word from sharer
- Close.

1 Example of a Trial/Taster Session

> *I am invited by the director of an interpreting team within a statutory health and social care service to run an online reflective practice support group for their interpreters. The team members are aware that they are beginning to feel burned out and negatively impacted by the work. They have requested an intervention of support and I am satisfied that participation is voluntary. We agree that we will begin with three sessions, including a review structure. The team members have not participated in a reflective practice support group before and so I decide to start with a trial or taster session using fictional cases based on real situations, before starting the three-session programme. This is so that participants can familiarise themselves with the method and process before bringing their own material that they wish to talk about.*

Practising being in a group by using fictionalised cases demonstrates actively (learning by doing) what it is like to be in a group. The structure of the group and the concepts of *sharer* and *participant* are introduced. (The person who brings the case is called the *sharer* and the rest of the group are known as the *participants.*) I had already started my *warm-up* to the group with the following preparatory thinking. I sent a joining email (see an example in the

Appendix) to the group which was intended as an opportunity for group members to start their warm-up process. The email explained that for the trial/taster sessions fictionalised cases would be used. I also reminded the group that the reflective practice support groups are not clinical supervision sessions or personal therapy.

At the start of the taster session, I explain that there will be some time for introductions, reflections on a draft working agreement for the group, and presentation of the first one or two fictionalised cases to be discussed. There will also be time for questions and for closing at the end of the group.

This loosely follows the structure of a regular group session. In this group I know I will be working with interpreters who have very little voice professionally (they are the voice of others) and who come from cultures which have traditionally been marginalised. There is also a difference of professional experience in the group. Some of the group may feel inhibited to take the space from people who are their professional seniors. Thinking about fairness of *communication* processes will be crucial for these group members. For online reflective groups, attention to communication is always important if there is going to be an opportunity for all to contribute.

I want to attend to the metacommunication, or "talking about the talking". I decide to include an agreement, with this group, about all of us committing to be as concise as possible. I also receive permission from the group members to remind any member if they forget to be concise! I try to model conciseness in my own communication. I also make it clear that group members can remind me too if I forget. Despite meeting online, we want to have a real connection at depth with each other. For this reason, we agree not to use the chat function of the online platform except for administrative purposes. After agreeing to the working agreement, we check in with each other. Overall, we have 90 minutes with seven people attending the session. I want to make sure we hear from everyone but that we allow sufficient time for cases that people have brought to be attended to thoughtfully. So, we use the "One minute, one word" exercise.

I often use a "One minute, one word" exercise as a check-in. The one minute is a timed minute of thinking time during which no one speaks. For the check-in, the purpose of the minute is for people to scan themselves and choose a feeling that is around for them at the moment, and that they would like to share. I ask group members to try to find one word for the feeling and to share that without any comment. This exercise serves a number of purposes:

1. It slows things down. It gives people a focus. It connects them back in with the group of people they may not have seen for a while.
2. Everyone has the same amount of time to think. Some people are ready sooner than others but with one minute in silence for everyone it means that no one is rushed.
3. One minute isn't very long. It's not really long enough for most people to get bored. I am clear that I will time the minute carefully so that we all know when it will end. This is important for group members who might be uncomfortable with a prolonged silence.
4. There is thinking time but, by sharing one word only and not inviting comments we use the time (90 minutes is the fairly typical duration of a session) as efficiently as possible. One word lets us know a little about how people are feeling so we are aware of each other.
5. Adequate time is left for those people who are keen to use the session for its principal task – to think together about professional issues that are on our minds.

In a regular (non-trial) group, after the check-in, we find out who will be a sharer – who will bring a case or a question to discuss – so we can divide up the time appropriately. In the taster or trial group we imagine that someone is sharing the scenario I have prepared. Let's now look at the development process of a (non-trial) ongoing group.

2 Example of Dynamic Safety

This example of a group illustrates the movement from support only, to support and challenge.

> *The group is for casework practitioners, working for an organisation called Justice for Migrants that supports immigration detainees. The people they serve are often desperate, with no other recourse to support. The caseworkers recognise that they are tired. They are tired but not defeated. The group has been meeting regularly for five months. The group members feel that the experience of participating in the reflective group sessions helped them to understand the impact the work has on them. They feel* supported. *Gradually, they become more energised and eager to think about their own agency and how, if at all, it is possible to work in a way that gives them more compassion satisfaction and less compassion fatigue. They are ready and willing to be* challenged. *We look at scenarios together, from different perspectives, thinking about the fears they touch in the group members. They begin to think more reflectively about their practice. As the group progresses, a group member called Paquita, says that she is deepening her understanding, emotionally as well as cognitively, of the significance of compassionate boundaries in this work. Darius agrees and says that he has*

become more confident, in his practice, to hold the boundaries compassionately with the clients he is supporting. Holding the boundaries does not have the negative effect he had feared. The clients of Justice for Migrants still, understandably, want more. But the cost of giving more is often burnout and sickness and, ultimately, the unavailability of a caseworker if they need to take sick leave. The consequences of having no dedicated caseworker (even short-term) can be devastating for a client. The practitioners see, for themselves, their potential negative (although unintended) impact on clients. They start to view the benefit for clients of their own careful, preventative self-care strategies (such as compassionately holding the boundaries). Justice for Migrants adapts its training and induction methods to share this deeper understanding with new members of the team. Paquita makes this comment about the group: "I like being a part of this group. It is going somewhere."

The group moves from fragmentation (fatigue, burnout) toward integration by developing new understanding – self-care aligns with client care. Compassionate boundary-holding becomes an ethical stance.

REFLECTIVE QUESTIONS

What do you think about the idea of compassion satisfaction? What do you think of compassionate boundary-holding as an ethical stance? How can reflective practice groups contribute to practitioners' preventative self-care? If you were a member of a reflective practice group, would you welcome challenge as well as support? What would you need to be in place to feel safe in a group that was challenging? Why do you think Paquita says "I like being a part of this group. It is going somewhere"?

3 *Example of an Ending of a Session*

INTRODUCTORY COMMENTS

We return to the example which was at the beginning of Part 1 of this chapter. In this example I unpack an incident that happened in an ongoing group I ran, in some detail. My aim is to show what I do, why I do it, and what I am thinking at each stage. A case example can be presented like a whodunnit. It is satisfying to be able to solve the case. This example isn't like that. It's an example of trying to engage with the "mess" and of not giving up even if the story of the case and the process of the group are fragmented and unfinished.

Like the other examples, this case is based on amalgamated and anonymised experiences, for reasons of confidentiality. The session I describe occurs when the group has been meeting regularly on a monthly basis for twelve months. Participants have committed to attend for three months at a time. At each three-month point, there is an informal review. During the twelve months some people have chosen to leave the group and some have continued. A few new people have joined along the way after a review session. At the review sessions there have been small challenges and some adaptations have been made. The challenges have been, for example, questions about the rationale, or expressions of feeling about parts of the working agreement. Participants also say in the reviews, that they feel they have been heard and they feel connected to others in the group and trust that the group is safe enough for them. The current group members have all been part of the group for at least nine months and they have decided they want to move to a yearly contract, committing to be in the group for a year. At the first meeting, after the commitment to attend for a year, something challenging happens. It happens at the end of the session.

Closing Phase

As I have not yet addressed the final, closing part of the sequence of any session, I will make a few general points first. My rationale for the group *closing phase* is informed by a belief that group members are not passive observers. They are active participants who share, with the facilitator, the responsibility for the group's integrity and resilience. As the group analyst Arturo Ezquerro puts it: "Each member has a double function: being the recipient of the group processes but also an active supporter and vital link in the group structure" (Ezquerro, 2010, p. 499).

At the end of a group session, we try to help each other make the transition between the group and what we are moving on to when the session finishes. It is also an opportunity for people to name, notice and commit to something that they have received from the session. It is important, and we always make sure we have time for it. Even if it is brief, it needs to be meaningful.

I often employ the one-minute exercise for people to think about what they want to say. Depending on the time available we may do it as a one-minute, one-word exercise or we might all take responsibility for speaking within an agreed amount of time, dividing up the remaining time so that everyone has an equal amount of time available to speak. In the session I am describing, we have time to do the latter.

Example

It's the checkout at the end of a group session and I have reminded participants that this phase of the group is about closing and not opening things up for the group. Despite my reminder, in the check out a participant called Petra says she is feeling very uncomfortable. She is uncomfortable about a comment another member of the group had made earlier about their own behaviour. Petra's statement is quite vague and non-specific. Some group members look confused. Petra says she doesn't want to say any more. Some of the group think they know what she is alluding to. Some of the group are confused and think they have missed something vital. While setting up our working agreement we had already discussed the function and significance of boundaries. The set-up phase serves us well for a situation like this. Because, although it feels uncomfortable, we have to leave it like that as the group has to end.

What Happens Next

During the week after the session a couple of members of the group send me an email to ask if I am ok and if there is anything they can do. I reassure them that I am ok and I gently remind them of one of the terms in the *working agreement*. We had agreed that apart from communication about administrative or technical issues I would not engage in any communication outside of the group meetings. We had agreed to keep all our conversations about the group members or about the group as a whole, within the group. Conversations outside of meetings can quickly make those members of the group not included in these conversations feel excluded or even unwanted. The group starts to feel unsafe.

Although people agree, at the beginning of a group's formation, to terms in a working agreement about communication, there is sometimes resistance to them as the group gets going. The working agreement starts to feel like a constraint. But the agreement exists to provide a safety net to protect the group from becoming an anti-group (Nitsun, 1996) subject to insoluble destructive dynamics which attack it. If these dynamics can be caught by the safety net of the working agreement they can be recognised and explored reflectively and creatively. This is what I mean by *containing* a group. It goes beyond withstanding an attack. As the facilitator I have the task, in the service of the group, of tending to the agreement even if at times it makes me unpopular.

So, I remember that I have an ethical responsibility to hold the boundaries although at the moment it feels unsatisfactory. I wonder if the group doesn't feel contained or safe. Maybe that is why some of the members have sent me an email. Maybe they are checking to see if I am still able to hold the group. I think about this after the session has ended. I think about it a lot. I take it to supervision.

One of the most important things a facilitator of a reflective group can do to foster trust for the group and to help them feel that they are in safe hands is to act with honesty. Honesty with themselves and honesty with the group. This means acknowledging when you have made a mistake as a facilitator. This is essential. Wringing your hands is not. A mistake doesn't need to demolish you. You can make a commitment to learn from a mistake and you can demonstrate a commitment to make the effort and to be held accountable to the group for learning rather than repeating the same behaviour. A facilitator who models this kind of fallibility with integrity and authenticity will be respected, not idealised or idolised. They will deserve the trust of the group.

I try to be honest with myself. I can't see that I have made an obvious mistake in this instance but a variety of ideas and feelings swirl around in my head. I feel inadequate. I imagine that some of the group members are thinking I *am* inadequate. I feel annoyed with myself for being inadequate. I feel annoyed with Petra for bringing this messiness in at the end of the session when there was no time to understand what was meant. I know this introjected and projected annoyance can give me some useful information if I don't shy away from it. And I do try to shy away. There are plenty of things I can legitimately distract myself with. I can reflect on the fact that the move to a year's agreement had provoked strong unconscious feelings in Petra. But I know, interesting as that is (and it may well be what is happening for Petra), for me it will be a way of using theory to distract myself from myself. I may come back to the theory later, once I no longer need to hide behind it. So, I bring my attention back and I begin to reflect on my fears and my motivations. With the help of supervision, I think about how to take the temperature down for myself so that I don't inflame things further for the group. I remember my son's words that I quoted at the beginning of the introductory chapter: I, just like the rest of the human race, have the capacity to be destructive. Hiding away from that fact and distracting myself preserves an illusion and avoids reality. I start to try to understand my annoyance and anxiety so that I can regain my empathy for Petra and for the group as a whole. Once I can see both Petra and the group again it becomes clear to me what I can do next.

I regularly send an email after a group session, sometimes summarising key themes discussed and or/reminding about the date, time and venue for the next meeting.

> *I send the email and add a brief acknowledgement that we ended the group in what felt to me like an unfinished way. I suggest that if people feel it could be useful, we can start the next meeting by reflecting on what that was like and what we want to do next. I also acknowledge that some people may have felt confused about what happened and that we can also address that next time. I keep it brief.*

In this case the email is also metacommunicative: it addresses *how* the group is relating and processing, not just content.

Shortly after I send the email, I receive an email from Petra saying that she is no longer able to attend the group. A family emergency has occurred and she needs to attend to that. This doesn't necessarily explain the comment she made at the end of the last session but I remind myself that sometimes a group member needs to be a recipient of group processes (Ezquerro, 2010). They need to be in receive mode only. So, I don't ask any more of her. I reconcile myself to the fact that there probably won't be a neat ending to this story for me and for the group. Nor for Petra either, unless she returns to the group. I thank Petra for letting us know and check that she has some other source of support. She tells me that she has some good support for herself during this time.

> *At the next meeting I let the group know Petra's decision to leave and we have some time to process that information and, for those who want to, to process their own reactions about the ending last time. Some people want to say something, others don't. There's still some confusion but we have at least recognised it and made our peace with the lack of a tidy ending. Some group members say they are going to continue to explore their own reactions in their personal therapy.*

This part of the session is fairly brief. Of course, we could have attended to this experience at much greater depth. Groups mirror families of origin. Some groups may work with repetitive dynamics from people's families. We could have focused on those dynamics. But the decision for where to put the focus depends on the frame and the agreed task of the group. So, in a reflective practice support group which focuses on professional practice, we may notice dynamics and personal psychological processes but, as agreed in the working agreement, people use the support structures (such as psychological therapy) they have elsewhere if they want to explore those dynamics in depth. The limits of the group and of the facilitator's role are discussed further in the chapters on leadership.

And After That ...

> *After the processing time, the group feels ready to continue with the session and to work with professional issues that members have brought to reflect upon. There seems to be some relief that we can talk about difficulties and feel safe enough.*

The group continues to meet for two more years. One or two group members leave and others join. Petra doesn't return but most of the original members continue. The group could have been destroyed. But the effort of the group members to preserve something of value and to tolerate not having all the answers meant that connections and trust between us deepened. To quote Elif Shafak again: "the dark side of emotions is only where we begin. It cannot be where we end up" (Shafak, 2020, p. 64).

The group found that it could function at levels of both *cohesion* and *coherency*. In Part 1 of this chapter, I proposed that coherency involved the facilitator in recognising discomfort, naming the discomfort and inviting the group to stay with it, and learn together through the experience.

For myself, it was hard. I felt challenged and I hoped I could rise to the challenge without attacking and without justifying or defending myself. I wanted to be available for the group, rather than focusing on my own needs. My own needs were clamouring for attention very loudly at one point. Supervision of my practice was invaluable in helping me to attend to my needs in an appropriate place. Supervision helped me to disentangle my reactions, regain empathy and find a way forward that was appropriate for a reflective group.

Years later, writing now about what happened with Petra has got me thinking again. Was her ambiguous comment about a group member really about that group member? Was it a veiled attack on someone else, on me, for instance? It could have been an attack unconsciously aimed at me personally, or at the authority I held in the role of facilitator. Did the family emergency occur before the session, after the session, or did it occur at all? Was it the move to a year's agreement that had provoked strong unconscious feelings in Petra? These are all questions I could spend more time on. An unfinished story is seductive. But succumbing to that seduction wouldn't get us anywhere now. It wouldn't have got the group anywhere productive then either. I've been thinking about something else too, as far as this group is concerned. Did I rush the processing at the beginning of the session after Petra left? I could have offered more time as I would have with a psychotherapeutic group. But psychotherapy was not this group's core task. Hopefully, by acknowledging the unfinished feeling later, offering some space to talk about this unsettling experience, and by reassuring people that we could talk some more about this in the future if they wanted, felt emotionally honest and more like containment than suppression. Containment and emotional honesty are key ingredients of psychological safety.

Reflective Questions

How might you have felt in a group session that ends in an inconclusive and possibly confusing way? What would you need to feel psychologically safe in a situation like this? What did I do that contributed to psychological safety? What would you have done differently? In what ways does this example demonstrate dynamic safety, cohesion and coherency in a group? Do you think I rushed the processing and exploration of difficult feelings in the group? What might you have done differently?

Reflective Question for All the Examples

In what way do the three examples illustrate intelligent empathy, ethical decision-taking and metacommunication?

Summing up

Each of the three examples illustrates *intelligent empathy* – compassion balanced with reflective distance – and ethical decision-making aimed at preserving both individual safety and group integrity. We began Part 1 with an excerpt from the third example and the question "How does this relate to psychological safety and the responsibility of the facilitator?" The example reveals something crucial about the stance a facilitator must take. A facilitator is not simply another group participant. A participant can become completely absorbed in the impact the group is having on them; a facilitator, while still aware of their own feelings, cannot afford to be consumed by the moment. If they are, they step out of the role – and out of the responsibility – that the group has entrusted to them.

A facilitator must continually scan the horizon. They monitor themselves while paying close attention to what is unfolding in the group. Groups can behave predictably or unpredictably. They can leave people confused or unsatisfied. There may be no neat conclusions, no discoveries or elegant resolutions. Being able to tolerate confusion, ambiguity and unfinished stories goes with the role of the facilitator. It is always tempting to tie things up neatly or deliver a breathtaking final line. Psychological safety – *safe enough* – may seem dull by comparison.

Yet beneath the surface of dynamic psychological safety, you will see a facilitator acting with humility and a blend of honesty, and compassionate toughness with themselves, and with the group. You will see intelligent empathy at work – cognitive clarity combined with emotional attunement. You will see a facilitator who believes in the values of the boundaries the group has asked them to hold, and who works to maintain those boundaries ethically, with integrity, and sometimes even with flair. What you will *not* see is a facilitator succumbing to the pull of their own ego, trying to dazzle the group like a magician producing a rabbit from a hat in the final minute, as though they alone could conjure order from chaos.

Psychological safety may appear ordinary. There may be no rabbit. But there is still a great deal happening under the hat.

You may disagree that the examples at the beginning and end of this chapter illustrate the facilitator's responsibility for psychological safety. You may feel uneasy about the level of responsibility placed on the facilitator to lead and to create the conditions for a *safe enough* environment. If so, consider the following reflective questions: What, exactly, makes you uncomfortable? How do you feel about leading? About authority? About leading *with* authority? Have you been on the receiving end of oppressive leadership? These questions will return, in different forms, throughout the coming chapters.

In the next chapter, we look more closely at the role of the facilitator – and at the nature of leadership and facilitation itself.

Notes

1 https://www.hse.gov.uk/
2 With thanks to Nathalie Talbot for this metaphor.
3 A holistic approach to multilingualism defines all speakers with knowledge of more than one language as multilingual (Dewaele, 2015).

References

Argyris, C., & Schön, D. A. (1978). *Organizational learning: A theory of action perspective.* Addison-Wesley.

Bager-Charleson, S. (2010). *Reflective practice in counselling and psychotherapy.* Learning Matters.

Carroll, M., & Shaw, E. (2013). *Ethical maturity in the helping professions: Making difficult life and work decisions.* Jessica Kingsley Publishers.

Costa, B. (2020). *Other tongues: Psychological therapies in a multilingual world: A guide for qualified practitioners, trainers and supervisors.* PCCS Books.

Costa, B. (2026). The impact of interpreters' emotional involvement on interpreters' health and wellbeing: An overview across modes, modalities and settings. In A. Amato & G. Mack (eds), *Interpreters' health and wellbeing: An overview across modes, modalities and settings.* Routledge. doi:10.4324/9781003586647.

Cowan, E. W., Presbury, J., & Echterling, L. G. (2013). The paradox of empathy: When empathy hurts. *Counseling Today*, February.

D'Anselmi, P., & Di Bitetto, M. (2013). Micro-ethics. In S. O. Idowu, N. Capaldi, L. Zu, & A. D. Gupta (eds), *Encyclopedia of corporate social responsibility.* Springer. doi:10.1007/978-3-642-28036-8_688.

Dewaele, J.-M. (2015). Bilingualism and multilingualism. In K. Tracy, C. Ilie, & T. Sandel (eds), *The international encyclopedia of language and social interaction* (pp. 1–11). Wiley. doi:10.1002/9781118611463.wbielsi108.

Ezquerro, A. (2010). Cohesion and coherency in group analysis. *Group Analysis*, 43 (4), 496–504. doi:10.1177/0533316410380837.

Ezquerro, A., & Cañete, M. (2024). *The power of group attachment: John Bowlby revisited from a group-analytic perspective* (1st edition). Routledge. doi:10.4324/9781003271956.

Gabriel, L., & Reeves, A. (2024). *Navigating relational ethics in day-to-day practice: Working ethically in the counselling professions* (1st edition). Routledge. doi:10.4324/9781003354970.

Gibbs, L.-M., Costa, B., & Bakhsh, S. (2025). *Almanac.* Colour Visions.

Hammond, K. R. (2000). *Judgments under stress.* Oxford University Press.

Moreno, J. L. (1937). Inter-personal therapy and the psychopathology of inter-personal relations. *Sociometry*, 1, 9–76. doi:10.2307/2785258.

Nitsun, M. (1996). *The anti-group: Destructive forces in the group and their creative potential.* Routledge.

Pearson, P. D., & Gallagher, M. C. (1983). The instruction of reading comprehension. *Contemporary Educational Psychology*, 8(3), 317–344.

Shafak, E. (2020). *How to stay sane in an age of division.* Profile Books.

Silverman, M. (2003). A personal journey in rural Ireland, 1980–2001. In P. Caplan (ed.), *The ethics of anthropology: Debates and dilemmas* (pp. 115–132). Routledge.

Yalom, I. D. (1975). *The theory and practice of group psychotherapy.* Basic Books.

Chapter 5

Leadership and Facilitation

Introduction

An effective and ethically mature leader in any setting, is driven not by status, but by their own vulnerability and courage. Brené Brown (2018) sees the role of an effective leader in organisational settings as someone who takes responsibility for developing potential in people and processes. She believes that daring leadership is "about serving other people, not ourselves" (Brown, 2018, p. 69).

A facilitator of a reflective group is a type of leader. Their role is to help the group members engage in the task they have set themselves. Not to do the task for the group, or direct them, or have the answers, or provide solutions that save the day. A reflective group facilitator guides the group's process so that group members can fulfil the task. For instance, for a reflective practice group, the task is to think about participants' work from a variety of perspectives (their own, their clients' and the wider sociopolitical context), in order to maintain and improve the quality of their practice. Facilitation for any kind of reflective group requires a light form of leadership, but it is still leadership. It is leadership conferred by the group.

A group facilitator helps the group to manage and make sense of group dynamics, keeps the group focussed on the agreed task, and adapts their position as the group evolves and its needs change. A facilitator moves between a directive, a non-directive and a supportive leadership stance. The stance a facilitator chooses relates to the stages, task and processes of a reflective group. It also depends on something else.

When I deliver training in facilitation skills, I am often intrigued by the response I get when I introduce this "something else". It is the notion of *authority*. Authority can be held lightly in an authoritative way or tightly in an authoritarian fashion. A facilitator can be authoritarian. A facilitator can be authoritative. What is the difference? An authoritarian facilitator asserts their power and demands compliance. An authoritative facilitator offers appropriate guidance and support as needed, responsibly enacting the authority the group has placed in them.

DOI: 10.4324/9781003658924-5

Frequently, however, people associate authority only with authoritarianism. Even thinking about the word authority brings up strong feelings for many people. Is that the same for you? If you take a moment and think – what does the word *authority* elicit in you?

An important section of this chapter deals with people's previous experiences of and relationships with authority at the micro, macro, and systemic levels (e.g., interpersonal authority figures, cultural norms and expectations, and formal institutions). These experiences intersect with how they hold a leadership role and their personal motivations for facilitating groups. I suggest that an effective facilitator needs to have examined their own relationship with authority and to have developed a compassionate relationship both with their own vulnerability and with their own authority. If they haven't been able to do that, what will they do when their (perceived) authority is challenged?

There are two chapters dedicated to leadership and facilitation. This chapter and the following chapter are about the type of leadership and facilitation that are suitable for reflective practice support groups and other groups that engage in challenging conversations. This chapter covers theory and includes a compendium of themes, terms and concepts. The next chapter contains several examples from practice which illustrate the compendium entries.

The compendium entries address our personal and social relationships with authority and power, the triangle of power and the drama triangle, a spectrum of leadership styles, a model of supportive leadership in groups, ethical positioning, getting out of the way as a facilitator, personal characteristics and attributes of group facilitators, and co-facilitation.

Compendium of Themes, Terms, and Concepts

1 Authority

"In contemporary times authority has a very bad press" writes the sociologist Frank Furedi (2023) in "Why Is Authority Always a Problem?". Authority's poor reputation is hardly surprising given (a) the increasing revelations of abuses of power by those in positions of authority, and (b) the ineffectual behaviour of those in power to address global health, environmental and financial issues, among others. And yet, as Furedi (2023) also says, "The fear of authority inescapably leads to the problem of trust."

If authority has a bad press, what does it take for authority and power to be regarded as trustworthy and benign?

A note about power. I talk a lot about personal power. That is power for and with yourself. It is different from the notion of power defined by Max Weber (1978) as power *over* people, or the ability to achieve one's will whether or not people accept it. Legitimate authority on the other hand, enacted on behalf of others, is power that is considered as just and appropriate by those who accept it. Doreen McCalla (2002) writes about power in the context of schools' decision-making processes. She regards power as benign when it serves a collective purpose and when it upholds the values of democracy, and social justice. If we translate this to the context of the reflective practice support group, we could say that power or authority are benign when they serve the group's agreed primary task and when they are not oppressive. Authority exercised with firmness around the external frame and lightness within the internal frame enables spontaneity and creative solutions to emerge from the group: "In reflective practice support groups the supervisory resource is the group rather than an individual supervisor" (Kurtz, 2019, p. 35).

2 Personal Relationship with Authority

Our relationships with authority, power, and control begin when we are babies and children. Because as human infants, if we are to survive, we have a protracted, dependent infancy ahead of us (longer in some societies than others). Those experiences have a lasting impact.

We learn about power in our family systems of origin, not just with our parents but with siblings (Adler, 1927; Adler & Fleisher, 1988). Some people may have had experiences within their families, or family-like systems, where that power was abused. Many people continue to learn about power in another common group experience – at school, both primary and secondary school. For some people, school can be an oppressive experience where power is abused. For other people, school may be an opportunity to experience authority exercised well.

I was lucky. I had teachers who cared, who were interested in us, interested in their subject matter, and who wanted us to reach our potential. I trusted them. They were good role models. I was well equipped to tell good leadership from bad.

If you have had a bad experience of education and of teachers, you may be motivated by a desire to offer others something better than the experience you had. Although that is a kind and humane intention, it can be enacted in an unexamined, reactive way ("I will never behave like teacher X") rather than a compassionately assessed and reflective way ("I think this would have been a better way for teacher X to behave. I will try it and see what happens, and I am open to the possibility of being wrong").

Our motivation – examining why we want to be a group facilitator – matters. In a recent interview (Kochetkova-Korelova, 2025), the Russian group psychotherapist Elena Rechkina suggests that facilitators need to have the courage to ask themselves why they are leading the group, what needs they are satisfying, and what they are getting out of it.

Why do people want to be group facilitators? As you are probably already aware, the role of a facilitator of reflective groups is demanding. Why do it unless you believe that groups can be a profound source of creativity, learning and healing? For me, although I know that groups can be destructive in professional settings (Nitsun, 1996) as well as family settings (Brown & Errington, 2024), I also have the experience of being in groups which are positive, bringing out the very best in people.

Even if you haven't personally had good experiences of groups, you may be motivated to facilitate them. If that is the case, it is a good idea to seek out satisfactory experiences of groups first. Those experiences can be a resource which accompanies and guides you. It is also a good idea to engage in personal awareness work that helps you to reflect personally on your position with power and authority as a facilitator. These questions may be useful.

Reflective Questions

Think about your own history with authority, with teachers, leaders, or parents. Who, if anyone has been a model of empowerment rather than of oppression? What did they do? What did they not do?

Why do you want to facilitate reflective groups?

Do you think that sometimes you try to mend or reverse your own negative experiences of being oppressed through your facilitation? Why is that a good thing? Why might it be problematic?

3 Aspects of Power

You may be a person who likes power and attention. Or you may be shy. You may resist the limelight. Maybe you feel that your voice has been ignored because of your cultural and political heritage. I have found the triangle of power (Hawkins & McMahon, 2020, p. 125) very useful in helping me to reflect on my various and fluid relationships with power.

The triangle represents three aspects of power: personal, cultural and role power. People have different emotional and cognitive relationships with cultural and personal power as a result of personal, cultural and political experiences in life. The triangle of power has helped me to think about the fluidity of the relationships I have with authority and to decide whether or not I accept the role and the authority inherent in a leadership role, such as a facilitator. If I do accept it, and I want to occupy the role with authenticity and integrity, I need also to accept parts of myself personally and culturally that do not feel so authorised. This was the process I followed when I was deciding whether to take on the role of director of Mothertongue. I had to reconcile two demands. Firstly, my personal desire (combined with cultural messages I'd absorbed) to keep a low profile and avoid drawing attention onto myself. The second demand came from the role, which was to represent the organisation and be its visible face at public events. It was a challenge for me to trust, allow and accept my vulnerability and let it give me valuable information. Attending to the vulnerability meant drawing on courage. I decided to become the director, I took on the authority as required by the role.

In her book about workplace dynamics called *All That We Are*, Gabriella Braun refers to the work of Obholzer et al. (1994) on authority, power and leadership. She refers specifically to the idea of authority from within: "if we cannot find authority within ourselves, we won't be able to use the authority conferred by others" (Braun, 2023, p. 250). In other words, if we don't trust in our own authority others won't be able to trust us.

Reflective Questions

The following question is one I return to regularly. How do I find a way to be confident enough in myself to access the authority from within? That is quickly followed by another: How can I be authoritative and not fall into the trap of being authoritarian? What would your answer be to those questions to yourself?

4 Personal and Social Power: Micro and Macro Systems

The triangle of power (Hawkins & McMahon, 2020, p. 125) is a useful frame through which to consider the role power, personal power and cultural power held by a leader or facilitator. We are now going to think about power within the system, at the *micro and macro* levels.

By the *micro level* I am referring to the personal dynamics that occur within the group. We will think more generally about group dynamics in Chapter 8. For now, the spotlight is on the facilitator's position of power and what that elicits in others. The facilitator can find that their own (perceived) power or authority is challenged by the group. That can feel frightening and lonely. It is easy to rely instinctively on our habitual stress responses. We may, for example, go into fight mode or we may freeze.

The family, or family-like systems in which we grow up are our first experiences of groups. These early experiences provide a blueprint for how we experience other groups throughout our lives and how we respond to them. If you take a moment to think back to other groups you have participated in during your life as an adult, how many seem to repeat your own family's relational dynamics? I know for myself, that although I may justify and resist recognising these repeated dynamics, if I pay close attention I can see patterns, often veiled, with group facilitators or with my fellow group members which resemble my early relationships with siblings and parents. They often don't seem to be obvious to other people (who may, of course, be absorbed in observing their own repeating patterns). They can trigger my familiar and unexamined stress reactions (of fight or flight, for me) if I stop being reflective.

You may think of yourself as a supportive facilitator. You may believe that you use your power in the service of the group, that your authority is benign. However, as a figure of authority the facilitator of a group is often a magnet for all kinds of projections which arise from relationships with other authority figures in group members' lives. These projections can manifest as covert attacks on a facilitator's authority and they can be easy to miss. The problem with missing a projection is that you react rather than reflect on how to respond.

As I said, you may think that you use your authority benignly. But as we saw in an earlier section of this chapter, not everyone trusts in the benevolence of authority. For many people who may be thinking about or who are currently running groups, the spectre of inhumane authority hangs over them. This spectre often has a long history. It has its roots in *macro level* systems, which are bigger than family systems. Sociopolitical dynamics, at the macro level and outside the group, can get played out within the group.[1] Groups may be comprised of participants who have experienced different levels of sociopolitical power. Some members in a group may come from sectors of society associated with influence, advantage and wealth. Others may come from traditionally marginalised sectors of society where their voices are seldom heard and they have had little chance to influence social structures and policies. They may have experienced prejudice and discrimination. These dynamics can find their way into the group, in relationships between group members, and between group members and the facilitator. The process can be productive. It isn't always.

Reflective Questions

Have you ever been in a group where the facilitator acknowledged systemic and interpersonal power dynamics (e.g., race, neurodiversity, gender)?

How well was the intervention handled?

What aspects of the facilitator's behaviour contributed to it going well/not so well?

5 The Leadership Spectrum

Leaders of groups are known by different titles according to the theoretical models and practices that inform their work. A group analyst is often referred to as the conductor of a group (Foulkes, 1986). In supervision groups, the group leader is known as the supervisor (Proctor, 2008). In reflective practice groups for teachers (*ateneos*) the group leader is referred to as the tutor (Banegas & Glatigny, 2021). The guiding figure in an encounter group is known as the facilitator (Rogers, 1971). Facilitator is also the term used for the person who runs a reflective practice support group (Kurtz, 2019). They may all be conceptualised as trusted and supportive leaders, although they occupy different positions on the continuum of helping behaviours (Downey, 2024).

The *helping continuum*, like its clinical parallel the beneficence – autonomy continuum (Beauchamp & Childress, 2013), depicts a range of helping behaviours. These are the types of behaviours displayed by practitioners who work in contexts such as health and social care, education, and emergency services. They correspond to different leadership styles on the *leadership spectrum*. At one end of the helping continuum are directive behaviours, displayed for instance by an expert taking control and making decisions about other people. A firefighter in an emergency situation is a good example of an appropriate role and situation for a directive approach. They could be classified as a directive leader on the leadership spectrum. At the other end of the helping continuum are non-directive approaches: people are regarded as autonomous agents. In practice, non-directive facilitation, which is rooted in the work of Carl Rogers (1951) in the field of psychological therapies, is considered an attitude or stance, rather than a behaviour (Tudor & Merry, 2002).

Another facilitation approach is situated a little way before the non-directive end of the leadership spectrum. This is a style of *supportive leadership*, and it is guided by the needs of the group. It is leadership conferred on the leader by the group it is leading. A facilitator who adopts a stance of supportive leadership constantly assesses themselves, checking their own needs and anxieties, together with the needs of the group. In this way a facilitator, as a supportive leader, can lead on behalf of the group.

Reflective Questions

Can you think of any good experiences you have had in groups? Was there any leadership? Can you imagine anyone for whom the group experience, that was positive for you, might not have been positive? What influenced or informed your answer to the last question?

What do you think of the approach of *supportive leadership*?

6 The Drama Triangle

In practice, we can tie ourselves up in knots trying to work out which position to take on the helping continuum, and leadership spectrum. When we work with people's vulnerabilities we can feel pulled to protect and save people from their pain. It might be right to intervene. Or we might inadvertently get in the way. The line between empowering people to find their own solutions and solving their problems for them, can be very thin. As facilitators, we know we need to keep developing and monitoring our self-awareness to check that we are not imposing our own needs and anxieties onto group members. However, this is not as easy as it may sound. We may

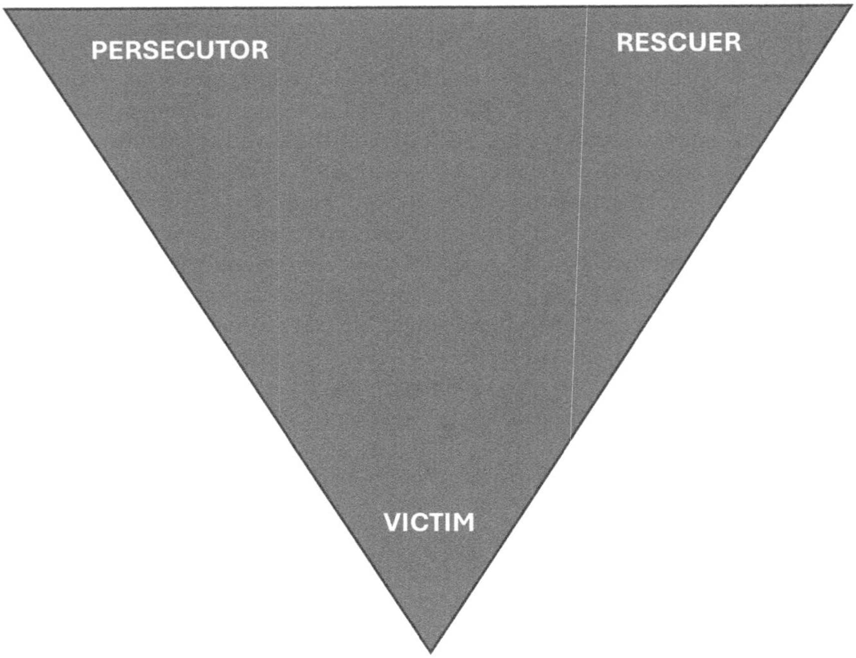

Figure 5.1 Karpman's drama triangle
Source: Karpman (1968); drawn and captioned by the author.

find ourselves unconsciously slipping into the role of the rescuer as illustrated in the drama triangle (Figure 5.1).

The three roles in the triangle can be enacted by each of the participants. As a rescuer, we can feel good, convinced that it is our moral duty to rescue. Compassionate engagement may inspire us to take action on another's behalf. But inadvertently we may be taking away a person's autonomy and agency. This behaviour, motivated by compassion, may bring about unwelcome and unexpected results, referred to in systemic therapy as ironic consequences (Byng-Hall, 2008). Suddenly we can find we have become the persecutor for the person we were trying to help. Even though only one position is called the victim, all three end up feeling like a victim.

Reflective Questions

How easy/difficult do you find it to resist the pull to solve problems *for* the group?

How easy/difficult do you find it to trust a group to find their own solutions?

Have you ever been in a situation when you thought you were being helpful and you ended up being perceived as a "persecutor"?

How can facilitators hold a safe enough space and support the group without removing their agency?

7 *Supportive Leadership*

At the early stages of most groups, the facilitator may find themselves leading more actively with a view to stepping back and getting out of the way when the time is right and the group culture has matured. For groups that address difference and challenge, an active facilitator who takes a supportive leadership stance, may be more suitable than a non-directive facilitator, even after the group is established.

Paradoxically, non-directivity can be experienced as oppressive by some group members. It may feel quite liberating for those group members who are used to belonging to dominant groups in society e.g. male, neurotypical, white etc., to have a non-directive facilitator who leaves the group to manage itself. But for those from less empowered social and cultural groups, a facilitator who takes responsibility for challenging the status quo, especially at the early stages of a group, may be experienced as more empowering and more containing. People from minoritised groups may not initially feel empowered to make that type of challenge for themselves. A facilitator who is a supportive leader can demonstrate that these inequalities of power have been seen and are regarded as significant and challengeable. By making a challenge themselves, the facilitator models the containment and safety of the group. It is not completely straightforward, though. How much does the facilitator actively engineer things so that dynamics are made explicit or indeed reversed? If the facilitator intervenes too much, there is a danger of acting like a saviour, getting in the way, and taking the opportunity away from people to exercise their own agency. The facilitator's job as a supportive leader is to keep the frame safe enough and model boldness so that if people want to, they can take up opportunities at a time that is right for them. It's not easy. It requires a sensitive and dynamic relationship with authority. A facilitator, acting in a supportive leadership capacity, strives to be authoritative rather than authoritarian.

Reflective Questions

Can you think of times when you have been in groups that felt supported and well-facilitated?

Have you been in groups where power dynamics in the group ever challenged?

What did the facilitator do/not do in those groups?

8 Supportive Leadership and the Group

A participatory group involves compromise and negotiation. It has to be able to survive and thrive in the face of shared vulnerability and challenge. To achieve this, an effective group creates a culture of interdependence where the group can count on the mutual support of its members. Without connection and compromise, interdependence is not possible. Have you ever been in a leaderless group which has managed that kind of compromise, connection and commitment? It may be possible, but I think that connection and compromise generally require work and maintenance. A group which strives for this level of commitment and mutual support benefits from a structure which is held by a trusted facilitator who acts as a *supportive leader*. But how does the facilitator nurture and maintain the trust of the group? Maintenance of trust is a long-term, rather than a short-term activity. Trust involves not only connecting and intervening with integrity. It also involves knowing when to step out of the way and when to let go.

9 Leading and Getting in the Way

The primary resource for reflective groups is the group itself. A group can be a powerful resource but this may take time to achieve. The group facilitator allows space for a group to develop, stepping in when the group lacks clarity, safety, or direction, and stepping back when the group shows readiness to use its own resources.

Groups, like individual humans, go through different stages of development. One of the most influential models of group development was proposed by psychologist Bruce Tuckman in his 1965 essay "Developmental Sequence in Small Groups". He identified five stages through which groups typically evolve: *forming, storming, norming, performing*, and *adjourning*. Groups begin and end, and in between they interact, resist, adapt, and sometimes struggle before – hopefully – achieving the tasks they were created to tackle.

A sensitive facilitator recognises the stage and function of a group and adjusts their approach accordingly. This is rarely straightforward. Facilitators can easily impede a group's development, especially given the strong pulls of Karpman's Drama Triangle (1968). The task is to judge when to step into a leadership role and when to step back so the group can use its combined knowledge, experience and perspectives - its collective wisdom (Uricchio & Cizek, 2022) - and exercise its own agency. If a facilitator doesn't make this assessment, they are in danger of replacing the group's wisdom with their own.

That assessment is fundamentally an ethical one. A facilitator shifts continuously between stepping in and stepping back, based on observation and ethical judgement, shared transparently with the group. One question I return to repeatedly is: "Is the group is ready to cope with the task I am asking of them?"

Reflective Questions

How might you convey authority without becoming authoritarian?

Where might power dynamics – hierarchy, experience, identity – shape your choices?

Have you been in a group that demonstrated its collective wisdom? If so, what did that look like?

Have you ever been in a group where the facilitator did *less* when they should have done *more*? What was that like? What might you have done differently?

What learning about yourself is emerging throughout this chapter?

10 Ethical Positioning

Learning to inhabit the role of a facilitator in a way that is empowering, ethically anchored and with ethical maturity is a continuous task. The three main ethical preoccupations in psychotherapy relate to trust, caring and power. They are also three of the major ethical preoccupations for reflective practice group facilitators.

In the book so far, the roles of safety and containment in creating trust and care in a group have been explored. Sharing transparently – through metacommunication - about the pushes and pulls you experience with a group can help to share the power in a group, if done appropriately. Instead of rushing to provide a solution, you might first transparently share the dilemma of wanting to provide a solution. This helps to slow the process down so that problem-solving can be shared by the group.

For example, listening to a sharer's story during a group I facilitated, I was pulled in not just by compassion but by the story itself. It wasn't only me who felt the pull; I could see that there were lots of people who wanted to hear more. The seductive power of stories can pull the listener, unawares, off course. So, first I reminded myself that the sharer wasn't there to entertain me with her story. My need; not hers. I shared with the group that I had felt the captivating pull of the narrative. I reminded us all that we needed to respond as the sharer had requested (unless the sharer's need had subsequently changed).

Transparency and openness lead to trust and a cooperative way of behaving. They maintain the flexible, internal frame. As transparency becomes the custom and culture of a group over time, the group moves from dependence on the leader to interdependence with each other, working together collaboratively to achieve the purpose of the group.

Reflective Questions

What do you think are the pros and cons of transparency in a group?

Can there ever be too much transparency?

Can you think of examples of when transparency has been used to positive effect?

Can you think of examples of when you witnessed transparency resulting in a negative outcome?

11 Personal Characteristics and Skills of Facilitators

Before we consider facilitating with another person, let's look at the individual, personal characteristics and attributes desirable in group facilitators. The list is long. No one is likely to have all of the attributes, but to be an effective facilitator you need to have or be prepared to develop as many as possible. The following list draws from various sources. The three main sources are firstly, Bridget Proctor's (2010) chapter on training for the supervision alliance, included in the *Routledge Handbook of Clinical Supervision*. The second source is from the Circling Institute.[2] The third source is from my organisation, the Pásalo Project.

Personal characteristics and attributes of group facilitators:

- clear communication
- negotiation skills
- humour
- listening
- not making assumptions
- authoritative (as opposed to authoritarian)
- non-defensiveness and ability to withstand challenge
- non-judgemental
- respectful
- co-managing agreements
- patience and presence
- courage
- adaptability and flexibility
- commitment to connection
- authenticity – walking the talk
- personal integrity
- creativity
- being psychologically minded and psychologically mature Ringer (1998)
- self-awareness and self-honesty
- maintaining a work-life balance
- humility
- broad-mindedness
- ability to tolerate not knowing.

There are also many similarities between this list and the list of desirable personal qualities of a group analyst or group conductor identified by S. H. Foulkes in a chapter titled "The Conductor as a Person and His Training" (Foulkes, 1986, pp. 157–159). The task and the purpose of the group will require varying styles of facilitation as reflected in the list.

Reflective Questions

Which characteristics/skills do you already have?

Which three characteristics/skills do you most want to develop?

12 Co-facilitation

With so many desirable personal attributes and characteristics it might seem a good idea to pool your efforts with someone else and jointly facilitate group sessions. It might seem that co-facilitating with someone else will automatically lighten the load of holding the space for people who are burdened by the pain, violence and sorrow they witness in their practice. Certainly, when you first start to facilitate groups, you might find it useful to team up with a more experienced facilitator who can take the role of primary facilitator while you are the assistant facilitator. It is of course important that you spend time preparing together beforehand so that you are clear about your own and each other's roles. This includes: the extent and limitations of each co-facilitator's roles and responsibility, how you will manage misunderstandings between each other in the sessions, the processes you have for reflecting together after the group on your process, and identifying an external consultant who can help you think through potential difficulties if you need another perspective. It is also important to think about how you are going to present the facilitator relationship to the group. Working in this way can be valuable for both the primary and assistant facilitator. You can give each other feedback and learn from each other. You have the mutual responsibility of helping each other to develop as facilitators. This is a fairly clear partnership with specific roles which are not weighted equally.

Co-facilitation with two facilitators whose roles carry equal weight and responsibility builds on the process described in the last paragraph, but it is more complex. There are parallels between co-facilitation and collaborative parenting. Both activities involve communication, a commitment to helping each other to develop in the role, teamwork, accountability, giving and receiving feedback, shared values and respect for each other. However, co-facilitators, like parents, can engage in unhelpful behaviours with each other, such as: competing for a child/group member's affection, withholding information, being dismissive, excluding each other from interactions with a child/group member, and more.

Co-facilitators need to dedicate time and space to think and talk to each other about the process, outside of the group. Co-facilitation can work well, but it requires a commitment to work hard on the process. I give an example from my practice, of co-facilitation that worked well, in the next chapter. The group my colleague and I co-facilitated was for people working in a very tough context. I think that having two co-facilitators was just what they needed. Two people, who collaborated and supported each other, meant that an almost uncontainable situation could be contained. There were certain conditions that were met in that example which made the co-facilitation a constructive experience. The most significant condition was the lengthy amount of time my co-facilitator and I dedicated to pre-group reflective conversations. post-group de-briefs, and general preparation. Although we didn't need to use it, we knew that there was external support for us if we needed help in getting untangled from some of the dynamics that co-facilitating can give rise to. Even though co-facilitation can be a hugely effective and satisfying experience for all concerned, it is not a simple option. I would recommend that equally weighted co-facilitation is something to aim for once you have had a chance to go solo for a while. It is good to have established your own style, to have made your own mistakes, found ways of making repairs, and achieved some confidence. Being an assistant facilitator with a more senior primary facilitator can though, be a very helpful first step.

Concluding Comments

If you have been a member of a group that you found to be effective, supportive and progressive, you might consider yourself lucky. The chances are that the group was facilitated by someone who regarded their continuous self-awareness as a vital component of their leadership role.

In any groups, fears and vulnerabilities can surface for all the participants, including the facilitator, at any time. If you are the facilitator, you have a responsibility to manage your fears with an open heart. This requires a commitment to continuous learning. Fears manifest in varied ways. You may fear your own authority, or others' authority over you. You may fear that people will make the wrong decisions for themselves and for others. We all know fear and we have all carefully developed our coping mechanisms over years. Those coping mechanisms become automatic, unexamined forms of protective behaviour. Fear breeds mistrust. Fear shuts down spontaneity: the ability to think creatively with an open mind. What might you discover if you reflect on your coping mechanisms from time to time, and ask this question: "Are they suitable for what I am trying to achieve, now?" You might find that sometimes they aren't. If you are a reflective group facilitator you might find that sometimes your coping mechanisms are serving *you* well enough, but they aren't serving the people you are supporting. Facilitation is a relational and dynamic process with others and with oneself. Here are some reflective questions to ask yourself regularly.

Reflective Questions

What are my default coping strategies I tend to rely on when I feel I am losing control?

Am I acting from fear or courage?

Is this intervention in the service of the group or to ease my own discomfort?

The next chapter includes a range of practical examples that illustrate how the themes, terms and concepts in this chapter can be implemented in practice.

Notes

1 Earlier in the book I introduced the idea of using warm-up, homogeneous groups as bridges to heterogenous groups to build the confidence of all group members to actively address experiences of sociopolitical power, privilege, and oppression.
2 Circling is a brand of facilitation, training and/or coaching using a communication system based on authenticity, deep empathic listening and meditative presence. The goal of circling is to help people see the world through each other's eyes. See https://circlinginstitute.com.

References

Adler, A. (1927). *Understanding human nature*. Garden City Publisher.

Adler, A., & Fleisher, L. (1988). The child's inner life and a sense of community. *Individual Psychology: The Journal of Adlerian Theory, Research & Practice*, 44(4).

Banegas, D. L., & Glatigny, R. (2021). The ateneo as an effective model of continuing professional development: Findings from southern Argentina. *Pedagogies: An International Journal*. doi:10.1080/1554480X.2021.1897012.

Beauchamp, T. L., & Childress, J. F. (2013). *Principles of biomedical ethics* (7th ed.). Oxford University Press.

Braun, G. (2023). *All that we are: Uncovering the hidden truths behind our behaviour at work*. Piatkus.

Brown, B. (2018). *Dare to lead*. Vermilion.

Brown, J., & Errington, L. (2024). Bowen family systems theory and practice: Illustration and critique revisited. *Australian and New Zealand Journal of Family Therapy*, 45, 135–155. doi:10.1002/anzf.1589.

Byng-Hall, J. (2008). The significance of children fulfilling parental roles: Implications for family therapy. *Journal of Family Therapy*, 30(2), 147–162. doi:10.1111/j.1467-6427.2008.00423.x.

Downey, M. (2024). *Effective modern coaching*. LID Publishing.

Foulkes, S. H. (1986). *Group analytic psychotherapy: Method and principles* (1st edition). Routledge. doi:10.4324/9780429475368.

Furedi, F. (2023). Why is authority always a problem? https://frankfuredi.substack.com/p/why-is-authority-always-a-problem.

Hawkins, P., & McMahon, A. (2020). *Supervision in the helping professions* (5th edition). McGraw-Hill.

Karpman, S. (1968). Fairy tales and script drama analysis. *Transactional Analysis Bulletin*, 7(26), 39–43.

Kochetkova-Korelova, O. V. (2025). Elena Rechkina: "Group therapy is marching across Russia today in search of its rightful place". *Transactional Analysis in Russia*, 5(2), 34–41. doi:10.56478/taruj20255234-41.

Kurtz, A. (2019). *How to run reflective practice support groups: A guide for healthcare professionals*. Routledge. doi:10.4324/9781351112994.

McCalla, D. (2002). A theoretical framework of benign power in school sector decision making: A preface. *Discourse: Studies in the Cultural Politics of Education*, 23 (1), 39–57. doi:10.1080/01596300220123033.

Obholzer, A., Roberts, D. V. Z., & Members of the Tavistock Clinic Consulting to Institutions Workshop (eds). (1994). *The unconscious at work: Individual and organizational stress in the human services* (1st edition). Routledge. doi:10.4324/9780203359860.

Proctor, B. (2008). *Group supervision: A guide to creative practice*. Sage. doi:10.4135/9781446221259.

Proctor, B. (2010). Training for the supervision alliance: Attitude, skills and intention. In J. R. Cutcliffe, K. Hyrkas, & J. Fowler (eds), *Routledge handbook of clinical supervision*. Routledge.

Nitsun, M. (1996). *The anti-group: Destructive forces in the group and their creative potential*. Routledge.

Ringer, M. (1998). Two vital aspects in the facilitation of groups: Connections and containment. *Journal of Outdoor and Environmental Education*, 4, 5–11. doi:10.1007/BF03400704.

Rogers, C. (1951). *Client-centered therapy: Its current practice, implications, and theory*. Houghton Mifflin.

Rogers, C. (1971). Carl Rogers describes his way of facilitating encounter groups. *American Journal of Nursing*, 71(2), 275–279.

Tuckman, B. W. (1965). Developmental sequence in small groups. *Psychological Bulletin*, 63(6), 384–399. doi:10.1037/h0022100.

Tudor, K., & Merry, T. (2002). *Dictionary of person-centred psychology*. Routledge.

Uricchio, W., & Cizek, K. (2022). *Collective wisdom: Co-creating media for equity and justice* (1st edition). MIT Press.

Weber, M. (1978). *Economy and society: An outline of interpretive sociology* (G. Roth & C. Wittich, eds). University of California Press. (Original work published 1921)

Chapter 6

Supportive Leadership

Facilitation in Practice

This chapter is the practical companion to the previous more conceptual chapter on leadership and facilitation. It contains examples that focus on the supportive leadership stance of a group facilitator, what a group facilitator looks like, what they do and how they think about what they do. I regularly refer to the working agreement. When I am facilitating, the agreement shores me up when groups feel unsettled or even chaotic I have included a list of elements you might include in a working agreement as a refresher, even though this appears elsewhere in the book. Because trust is at the heart of supportive leadership, I end the chapter with an illustration of a delicate context where trust is critical. It describes a co-facilitated group and the complex, interconnected threads of trust among and between the leaders and the group members.

Some Elements in a Working Agreement

I call the shared guidelines for communication in the group a working agreement. Another name for a contract or working agreement is a dialogue agreement (Dimitrakopoulou & Theodorou, 2022), which is a similar but briefer version of the working agreement I use.

I share the working agreement out loud with a group in our first meeting so that we can discuss it together. I adapt the specific language I use for each group depending on the context. I have left the components as bullet points so that people can apply their own style of language:

- Confidentiality – extent and limitations.
- Extent and limitations of contact with me and with each other outside of group sessions.
- Respect for difference.
- Commitment to try to attend to intragroup and intergroup social and cultural power dynamics.
- Responsibility for oneself – limits of the group to process members' individual psychological material at depth.

DOI: 10.4324/9781003658924-6

- Identification of individuals' support structures or signposting to support outside of the group.
- Commitment to aim to create as shame-free a space as possible.
- Commitment to try to bring what you haven't done well. The learning potential of mistakes.
- Maintenance of the time boundary – we will start and end on time.
- Communication and metacommunication about the group process – how we will manage turn taking, fairness of speaking time, creating space for those who need help to build their confidence to speak, permission for the facilitator to interrupt in the interest of fairness, we talk about the talking.

Example 1: Micro Level

The Frame Is Challenged

A facilitator has to earn the trust of the group. Once the group trusts them it gives the facilitator permission to occupy a position of authority. Power and powerlessness elicit very strong reactions. Dealing with people's strong reactions is seldom straightforward. The following example is of a challenge to the working agreement, and by extension, a challenge to the facilitator who is tasked with maintaining the agreement. It is not an overt attack. It probably isn't a conscious challenge to the facilitator's authority. But the facilitator is still left with a series of decisions to make. The facilitator has to take charge of the situation authoritatively.

> *You are coming to the end of a session with a group. This is the group's third session. The group's working agreement includes an agreement about timing and the importance of time boundaries. You have agreed with the group that there will be 10 minutes at the end of the session for a cool down and check out. 11 minutes before the end of the session a group member called Yulia becomes very distressed and wants time to talk about something new.*

You've got to do something, whether the meeting is in person or online. However, if the meeting is online there are fewer natural connecting features as there are in-person, such as physical proximity. Online it can be quite disorientating if the facilitator does nothing. What do you do in this situation?

This was not what you may have been expecting. You will probably feel pulled to react compassionately and agree to the stretching of the time boundary. This may be someone who has summoned up the courage to speak. But do you ignore everyone else's needs? Some people may be sitting waiting to use those last 10 minutes as you had all previously agreed. How do you contain this?

Possible Responses

The tension between structure and freedom is exemplified in this situation. You may feel you have to hold on to the agreed structure of the external frame and stop the group member from saying any more.

Alternatively, you may want to use the flexibility of the internal frame, by talking with the group about the dilemma. If you normally have 10 minutes allocated for a check out at the end of the session you may decide to renegotiate this with the group. Even so, as the facilitator you still need to keep your eye on the time so that you don't exceed the final timing of the group (the external frame).

Neither of the two example reactions represents a satisfactory balance between the external and internal frames. If you make the choice to hold rigidly on to the structure, some people may feel you are prioritising structure over compassion. They may try to resist what they see as an imposition of authority. If you ask the group members to choose what to do, some people may feel emotionally pressurised into choosing to relinquish the checkout because of one person's distress. They may be embarrassed to say that out loud. As a facilitator, you may assuage your conscience by telling yourself that you are being non-directive and you are going with what the group wants. But some group members may be anxious that boundary breaches are going to become the norm in this group. They would have found it more honest if you had used your authority to make the choice rather than giving the responsibility to the group. As a facilitator you can sometimes find yourself between a rock and a hard place. An alternative approach could involve a more reflective response that balances compassion with the safety of the containing frame. There are multiple possibilities. Here is what another facilitator might do. I'll call her Zoe.

> *Zoe meets Yulia's statement with empathy, acknowledging her distress and that it may have taken courage for her to speak up. Zoe is aware that there are other participants who need the time to check out. So, she says that although there isn't time now to pay Yulia and her issue the attention they deserve, the group could start with her issue next time. In this way, there will be enough time to give Yulia's issue appropriate attention. Zoe acknowledges out loud how boundaries can sometimes be problematic for groups for a variety of reasons. Zoe then checks out how Yulia feels about her suggestion.*

As you read this how do you feel about Zoe's response? You may not think it sounds reasonable. You may feel that Yulia is being silenced, or patronised or coerced. And you may be right because there is no prescriptive set of behaviours for a group facilitator. But if the facilitator had allowed themselves to be pulled by compassion towards Yulia, the person in the group who is showing distress, what would have happened to the person in the group who was not *visibly* showing signs of distress, but was just about holding it together until the group ended? They were watching the clock, holding their breath until the group finished on time, as the facilitator had reassured them would happen.

The facilitator may give Yulia the time she needs but what happens to the invisible group member? Is there a hierarchy of expressions of distress in the group? This is why the time frame is so important. It holds these competing needs and acts like an anchor that can be relied on, as we saw in Chapter 4.

Facilitator's Reflection

We left the scenario with Yulia at the point where she was being asked how she felt about the suggestion made by Zoe, the facilitator. (It might help to go back and re-read the scenario.)

> *Zoe reflects that she was trying to treat Yulia with respect and compassion in the moment, while bearing the rest of the group in mind, reassuring them about the session ending. She reflects about why she mentioned the boundary. Just noticing the tension around the time boundary was enough. No more needed to be said, she thought. By referring back to the frame and the working agreement, Zoe reminded the group of the container for the group. Zoe's aim was to catch the dynamic of the boundary pushing, using the structure (external frame), and at the same time trying to act with compassion (using the flexibility of the internal frame, which was enacted though Zoe's metacommunication about the boundaries). She reflects that she was trying to achieve some balance between structure and freedom. Zoe hopes the stance of supportive leadership she was trying to adopt will help the group to feel contained enough in this situation.*

Micro Power

What has this example got to do with micro power within the system? The frame serves as an enabler but it is also a constraint. If you feel threatened by anything that looks like a constraint you may be tempted to challenge it. Challenges to the frame are an attempt to exercise power *over* it (Weber, 1978). In the case of micro power, challenges are an attempt to exert power over small, informal structures, such as guidelines, or boundaries, or agreements. Almost always, the challenges to the frame and the facilitator are around the time – someone tries to initiate or extend an activity. This is one reason why time boundaries are so helpful. They help you to catch what is going on, the dynamics and challenges, at the micro level within the system. Although the above example focused on one person's distress, the group member's strong request for extra time created a challenge (intentionally or not) to the authority of the facilitator and the frame they had been tasked with managing by the group.

Example 2: Micro Level

Limits

This brief example illustrates a challenge to the limits of the frame. It takes place in a reflective practice support group for workers at a refuge for women who have experienced domestic abuse.

> *I have been facilitating this group, which meets regularly, for 6 months. It seems to be working well. We are halfway through the session and we start to hear from the second sharer for this session, called Meera. Meera begins by saying that she wants to talk about something a bit different. She says that she is having a hard time at the moment with her teenage daughter. She starts to get into detail about her daughter's relationship with her sister. I can see this is very important for Meera but I begin to wonder if we are straying from our agreed task as a group.*

What do you think about this situation. What might you do?

What do you think about the following possible response?

What might you do differently? Why? What are the possible risks?

One Possible Response

I am tempted to let Meera continue as she clearly needs to talk about this. But we had all agreed on the purpose of this group – to help group members reflect on their practice as workers in this refuge. There may of course be areas of overlap between what Meera is experiencing in her personal life and what she is experiencing at work. I think about how to manage the balance between professional and personal life.

> *I reflect on this silently, in the moment and I decide to wait until Meera has finished. Meera finishes telling her story tearfully. I then aim to connect with her. I say that I can see how hard the situation is and how much pain it is causing her. I thank her for sharing her personal story. I also say that there is a limit to how much we may be able to help her with that. I then say that there may be aspects of her personal experience that connect with what she is experiencing at work. If Meera feels there is a connection that she would like to explore now, we would continue with the reflective practice group process. If not, I would gently ask Meera if she had support elsewhere (as we have agreed in the working agreement) and if not, I would signpost her to other support services. And, if a connection emerges later with work issues, we can return to this.*

Example 3: Micro/Macro Level

Focus

Sometimes group members want to share information. In the following example someone wants to promote one of their own activities which takes place outside the group frame. What should I do?

> *In the check-in phase of a session of a group that has recently formed, Hamida says she would like to tell everyone about her social media activity. She says that it would really help her if everyone in the group joined up to it. She puts the details about it in the chat and encourages everyone to click and join now.*
>
> *I notice that some people are looking uncomfortable. I am feeling uncomfortable. This doesn't fit with the task and the terms we had all agreed to. I am tempted to ignore it and move on but it occurs to me that some people may be feeling pressurised to join up. Do I have a responsibility towards them?*
>
> *I decide I do. I need to say something. But I also don't want to shame Hamida.*
>
> *I say to Hamida that I understand her wish to be supportive and to share information. But I want to say a couple of things about this as far as the group is concerned. I say to Hamida that it may be that some people feel a bit uncomfortable and might feel pressured to join, even though that may not be her intention. I'm therefore going to say that there is no expectation that anyone will have to join the promoted group. I add that, as a group, we have never come across this situation before, so it is an opportunity for us all to agree on how we deal with this in the future.*

This may seem like quite a firm position to take on a minor issue but it is an example of maintaining the frame when the frame is being pushed and stretched across boundaries. A group member might think that they will be sidelined in the group if they don't join. Is that the facilitator's business? One of the group facilitator's responsibilities is to optimise the chances of the group's survival. Without maintenance the frame can become fragile under pressure and the group can feel unsafe, particularly in its early stages.

As the group facilitator I might then add:

> *Of course, information anyone wants to share can be really useful for some people here. So, could I ask that if anyone would like to promote something in future, can you please mention the existence of the activity, but ask people to contact you directly if they are interested in further information rather than putting the details in the chat?*

My rationale and intention with this response is to respect the autonomy of the group members, protect anyone who might (if the group is quite new) feel coerced by group pressure, remind about the group purpose, acknowledge that the information offered might be useful and so provide an appropriate channel for it to be shared, not to shame the person who wanted to promote a service, and finally, to reassure those who need it that I am holding the group frame.

What do you think about this response and the rationale I gave?

What might you have done differently? Why?

Example 4: Micro/Macro Level

Intersectional Dynamics

We have multiple identities which intersect with each other. Looking at the following experience through the lens of intersectionality reveals the different aspects of privilege or otherness these identities carry, and the influence this has on our interactions with others.

> *Sameera is a member of a reflective group you are facilitating. Sameera is originally from Pakistan. She shares about the client group she currently works with. She is aware of how marginalised they are. She says she relates to that feeling of marginalisation as she often feels like an outsider in this group. The rest of the group is composed of white people. Group members are generally supportive and offer Sameera reassurance. Other members of the group talk about their experiences of feeling excluded. A Polish member of the group, Anya, talks about not feeling welcome and accepted in a local book club. Maggie, who is transgender, says they also often feel excluded but they feel ok in this group. You feel pulled in various directions. Important issues of systemic and intersectional dynamics of oppression, discrimination and power are being raised. You are concerned that Sameera's experience of exclusion may be excluded again, buried under other people's experiences. That might replicate macro, sociocultural systemic experiences of power and of the experience of having one's racialised experiences ignored in groups. You are wondering where to start and what you should do.*

A Possible Response

Addressing issues of intersectionality in groups is tricky. It is often mishandled or avoided. If I were the facilitator in the situation of the example, I would be feeling nervous about "doing the right thing". Sameera may be alluding to an experience of feeling excluded because she is the only brown person in the group. Or she may be referring to something else. I don't want to avoid the issue of racism but I don't want to make assumptions either. I am aware of the possibility of being disappointing, and more, if I am clumsy.

So, what would I do? Here is one possible version of what I might have done. What do you think? What might you do differently?

I follow the structure I use which is to respond empathically to the sharer, in this case Sameera, immediately she has shared. I acknowledge the courage it can take to talk about feeling excluded and I wonder out loud if this is an experience that is familiar to Sameera from other groups. I don't enter into a dialogue with Sameera at this stage, but I ask her if she wants to hear from other members of the group. Does she want to hear about other people's similar experiences, for example? Is there anything she really wants to hear or anything she doesn't want to hear? I attempt to respect Sameera's vulnerability, having just shared, but I don't want to remove her agency by making decisions for her. After Sameera states what she does or doesn't want to hear, we hear from some group participants. Listening to the sharing of others' experiences of exclusion I think about exclusion and otherness, power and privilege. After people have spoken I thank them for making a connection by sharing their own painful and difficult experiences. I return to Sameera, reflecting that other people have talked about experiences of exclusion and their sense of difference. I wonder how that felt for Sameera and I ask Sameera if I could add something about difference in this group that might or might not be relevant for her. If Sameera agrees I say that there are many ways to feel different and excluded in groups. In this group, we have heard different stories about feeling like an outsider. We haven't heard about racial exclusion though, because almost all the participants and the facilitator (me) are white. I wonder if that is significant here or not. I would then, as we always do, hand over to the sharer, Sameera, for the last word, to respond to what she has heard or been asked, as she chooses (including not at all). As this is a reflective practice group and Sameera started by talking about practice issues, I would also ask if there is anything she wants to take away from the experience of sharing that relates to the practice issue she began with.

I would also note for myself that in our next review I need to ensure that there is space, if people want to use it, to comment on my facilitation of sensitive issues like this. I feel like I have taken a risk by naming something that was unspoken in the group. I welcome feedback about how that was experienced.

Reviews

One of the ways in which I try to attend to micro and macro level power issues in a group is by incorporating reviews. In the reviews we may attend to the macro power issues of those from minoritised groups who have not traditionally had a voice. By macro power I mean systemic power embedded in systems such as socio-political systems, public services or other organisations that offer advantages to some. Advantages embedded into systemic structures are not always consciously intended or articulated. But the effect is that systemic power creates in-groups and out-groups. The role of the continuous review process helps to hold oneself to account as the facilitator. I make sure there are regular reviews – not just once – so that we can reflect on the process, and unconscious power enactments in the group, as they develop. This could include questions like: Who is being heard, who isn't and how can that be improved by us all? Are we all colluding in avoiding something? Do you feel able to give me negative feedback if it is needed? We talk about how we are talking to each other. We attend to metacommunication about the process of the group.

Some Other Reflective Questions

The following reflective questions may help to think about if/how these issues can be addressed in reflective practice groups (some of the questions are adapted versions of questions taken from Pandya and Lasley, 2025, p. 8). These initial questions relate to personal experience:

- Where do *you* feel pulled in situations like the one in Example 4? What identities are activated?
- What's your own history with difference, exclusion, or privilege?

The following questions are about professional practice:

- Do you walk away from some groups and say: "It's not for me to run this sort of group?" Is there a screening process for the facilitator (are you the best person to run this group?) as there may be for participants as we observe in Chapter 9? Do you look for opportunities to widen your experience, and deepen your commitment to run groups that may challenge you?
- Do you apologise if you don't notice sociocultural dynamics and become consumed by guilt? (An example of this type of response is given by Sophie in Chapter 8.)
- Do you ignore the dynamics?
- How do you offer compassion for all group members while addressing privilege and systemic dynamics?
- What strategies can you use to respond to one group member's experience without alienating others in the group?
- How do you avoid shaming group members in your potential offerings and challenges?
- How do you honour group resistance to exploring racial, cultural or intersectional dynamics, and simultaneously offer the space to explore the resistance?

- Your reflections and choices about a potential intervention depend on the type of group you are facilitating, its purpose, the relationship between group members, its stage, and your own level of experience as a group facilitator. What would you do if you were the facilitator in Example 4?

There is, of course, no one simple answer to any of these questions. Reflective practice grounded in relational ethics is complex and it can be messy. As a supportive leader you would probably be aiming to respond with integrity, humility, and awareness of the dynamics at both the *micro* (individual/group) and *macro* (systemic/social) levels. You would probably want to hold the frame and provide support and containment so that people could stay with the discomfort and find new responses that have depth and staying power. By staying power I mean responses that do not arise from shame and result only in compliance. Your own supervision would be invaluable in this work.

Here are two responses and phrases that might be useful starting points for talking about intersectional dynamics. Although they do not specifically address the example in this section, they offer a template which can be adapted to suit a specific context. (Other go-to phrases, for a variety of contexts, can be found in the Appendix.)

i Name and Acknowledge Difficult Situations

Noticing and naming difficulties slows things down and validates people's experiences of finding things difficult.

> *"I notice there's a bit of hesitation or discomfort as we talk about difference. That makes sense – these are difficult topics. That's why people don't get much practice to talk about them. Can we try to practise talking about them here?"*

ii Start with "Why", Not with "What"

It is tempting to start with stating the problem or finding a solution. Sometimes, a more useful starting point is to begin with the reason *why* talking about this is important, before getting into the content. It puts values first. They are why it is worth making this effort. Transparency is crucial too: acknowledging your own limits without abdicating responsibility.

> *I'm learning how to hold these conversations. I may not always get it right, but I want to try even if it's difficult. And the reason I want to make this effort is that although these conversations may be difficult, they are vitally important. How does that sound to people? How do you feel about what I just said?*

After group members have responded to those questions I might follow up with a question like this, if it seemed appropriate: "Can we try and help each other out in our attempts, here?"

Example 5: Macro Level

Long-Term Group

This example is of a warm-up reflective practice support group which I ran for a relatively homogenous group of multilingual therapists for several years.

> *The reflective practice support group for multilingual therapists was set up to explore the neglected issue of multilingualism in therapy. It ran for four years. It was initiated by multilingual therapists who felt the issue had been ignored in their original training despite multilingualism being all around us and intersecting with race and culture. In fact, many of the therapists had been discouraged from offering therapy in any language besides English. They were all speakers of first languages which held less prestige than English politically and professionally. This affected their confidence, sense of competence, and self-perception in professional or therapeutic roles. They felt judged and discriminated against. They felt misunderstood. They felt that they missed out on professional opportunities.*

As well as a space for reflection about these issues, the multilingual reflective practice support group offered an opportunity for group members to search for the words to describe their experiences among peers. They felt free of judgement which gave them the freedom to stumble, make mistakes and refine what they wanted to say. The opportunity served to build the confidence of participants to move beyond conversations with their peers. It enabled them to speak about their experiences and the experiences of their multilingual clients with colleagues who were not multilingual. It created a bridge from the homogenous community of multilingual therapists to the wider society (the macro level). It was a bridge that became durable. It materialised in the form of outcomes and products.

This was exemplified during the duration of the group, by some group members taking up teaching posts in universities, and by the whole group producing an anthology of creative writing about multilingualism in therapy and a practice guide on working with multilingualism in psychological therapies.

My leadership role, as a facilitator with this group, changed over the four years. I was very active to begin with. I knew that trust would be an issue for this group and that I had to earn it. I began by targeting people with a particular professional profile who might be interested in joining the group. I set the frame and attended closely to the boundaries. It was a group of people, who at the beginning of the four years, were looking for a professional place to belong. The group members were all from multilingual backgrounds. I initially held the boundary for them, between them and the outside world, by not accepting new group members into the group. However, by the end of the four-year period I behaved much more like a non-directive facilitator. The group was open to new experiences, actively engaging with people from outside of its community with confidence.

Why have I included this example? Because I wanted to show how a group, and the role played by the facilitator, can change over the group's life cycle.

Example 6

Getting Out of the Way (and When to Step in)

As noted earlier, in a reflective group the resource is the group rather than the facilitator. When a facilitator gets caught up in the discussions and enthusiasm of the group, it can be hard to remember to get out of the way. Sometimes, as a supportive leader, a facilitator needs to step in, but if things are going well, it is probably the time to step back.

> *I try to remember the primacy of the group as the resource in my practice as a facilitator. After a sharer has presented their case, dilemma, or question I aim initially to make an empathic connection. This is so that the sharer can connect back in with the group after the isolating position of sharing. After I have made an empathic connection, I stop. I don't give my response to the sharer's dilemma or question before others have responded. Sometimes I don't give a response at all after the other participants have spoken, when it is not necessary.*

And sometimes, it is the moment to step back in.

> *I will give my response if I think there is an ethical issue which has been left in a potentially unsafe way. An example of this might be if a group member continues to propose, after several group members have suggested this may not be a good idea, that they are going to keep calling a client until they give them a reason for why they left counselling or supervision suddenly. Acting on the ethical principle of respect for our clients' autonomy to make their own decisions, I would offer the group member other options. Unless the sharer has sufficient cause for concern about their client's safety, I would suggest other options for a different course of action and share my thinking about that. I would also check that the group member was going to take this issue to their own managerial and clinical supervision as soon as possible.*

My aim is to facilitate as a supportive leader, with benign authority. By that I mean to facilitate a group authoritatively with lightness and flexibility, but with safety.

It is good to remind ourselves too that authority is *lent* to the facilitator for the duration of the group only. The group lends it, and the group can take it back if it is not exercised benignly by the facilitator. In reflective practice support groups attendance should never be mandated, although it can certainly be encouraged. This is so that the power remains with the group members to choose whether or not to lend the facilitator that authority. The group members have the power because, ultimately, they can use their freedom and choose to stop coming to the group meetings.

Example 7

Co-facilitation: Trust in the Group

I want to finish with an example that illustrates what I mentioned at the beginning of this chapter, and in Chapter 3, about trust in the group process. It is also an example of what motivates me to facilitate groups. The example is of a group I co-facilitated online with a colleague, Steve Page.

Steve is an experienced therapist, supervisor, group facilitator and trainer, author of two books (Page, 1999; Page & Wosket, 2015) and various articles, including a co-authored article about training pastoral staff in educational settings to give and receive supervision to colleagues (Holmes & Page, 2020).

We co-facilitated the online group during the COVID-19 pandemic in 2020. It was a group for psychosocial workers who were working for a refugee support organisation in the Middle East. They were all from refugee backgrounds themselves, mainly from sub-Saharan Africa. We had already been collaborating with the organisation for several years via a project called Colleagues Across Borders (www.pasaloproject.org/colleagues-across-borders.html).

> *Steve and I met regularly before and after the sessions to prepare and to think about what the group needed from us in terms of facilitation. We built on an already trusting relationship with each other. This helped us to manage our anxiety about working in such a fragile and unfamiliar context. We provided the group with a structure around timings, confidentiality and communication processes.*
>
> *It was a bad internet connection. During the sessions we would frequently sit in silence, wondering if everyone had left the call until the internet suddenly reconnected and we could continue. We tried not to get in the way and fill the gaps with our own anxiety. Despite all the difficulties – sporadic internet connectivity, people's own health worries, different time zones, demanding workloads – people felt able to share their vulnerabilities, to talk about their own fears and isolation and to be honest about their range of frustrations, which were sometimes with their clients. We all agreed that not only anxiety and COVID but feeling inadequate is contagious.*

> *I don't think I could have run the group on my own. The pressures on the external frame (the internet, COVID etc.) were too great for me to hold. But with my colleague Steve, we were able to provide a container for a little while for a group of resilient, if temporarily fragile workers, trying to support others at a time when it felt that there was little safety in the world.*

The group was one of the most extraordinary experiences of my professional life as a group facilitator. I wasn't convinced to begin with that it would be effective but I was determined to give it a try. Because of the trust we all had in each other and in the group process, it worked. The participants were appreciative of the support and made every effort, in very harsh circumstances, to attend the sessions. There were very few absences.

I share it as an illustration of the centrality of trust. Trust is like the oil that makes the machinery run smoothly. As I say at the beginning of this chapter, members of a group, through their trust in you, allow you to lead them.

Different groups need different types of leaders. The appropriate leader will be the right fit for the context, the task, purpose and duration of a group. In the next chapter we look at some more of the challenges. Some of these involve tensions between group members. Some of these involve tensions between group member(s) and the facilitator. You may be asking yourself why you would want to put yourself in this role, with the responsibility of dealing with a group's anxiety and tensions. It's a good question and each individual needs to have an answer that convinces them about the potential creative power and joy of working with groups.

The role of a facilitator is demanding. It is not for everyone. Motivation to do this work needs to be high because we will need to remember why we signed up for the role when we are being challenged and when we are found wanting. The next chapter is called "Being Disappointing".

Summary of Supportive Leadership Practice

Principle	*Practice*
Courage	Stay in the room. Acknowledge discomfort. Name dynamics.
Integrity	Be clear about the values underpinning reflective practice.
Compassion	Respect all identities.
Accountability	Notice and take responsibility for your position and power.
Humility	Acknowledge your limits. Validate the interdependence and collegiate nature of the group as a source of learning from each other. Use supervision.

References

Dimitrakopoulou, D., & Theodorou, P. (2022). Affective facilitation: A framework for surfacing lived experiences and harnessing creativity in focus group research. *International Journal of Qualitative Methods*, 21, 1–13. doi:10.1177/16094069221133225.

Holmes, J., & Page, S. (2020). How pastoral workers in further education are benefiting from supervision. *BACP University and College Counselling*, 9(3), 23–28.

Page, S. (1999). *The shadow and the counsellor: Working with darker aspects of the person, role and profession*. Routledge.

Page, S., & Wosket, V. (2015). *Supervising the counsellor and psychotherapist: A cyclical model* (3rd edition). Routledge.

Pandya, A., & Lasley, M. (2025). *Facilitating authentic communication groups: Integrating process work, DEI, NVC, & IFS*. Discover Press.

Weber, M. (1978). *Economy and society: An outline of interpretive sociology* (G. Roth & C. Wittich, eds). University of California Press. (Original work published 1921).

Chapter 7

Being Disappointing

Introduction

At the end of any training initiative, conference presentation or workshop I deliver, there is almost always a feedback form. Sometimes participants leave positive and uplifting comments. But sometimes I receive a piece of feedback that begins with the dreaded four words: "I was rather disappointed ...". It doesn't matter if the feedback is not necessarily accurate – it might be based on something that didn't actually happen, or it might be about another person, or from someone who was upset about something else – it always hurts a bit. Who likes to be considered disappointing? In this chapter we think about the experiences of being disappointing and being disappointed. What insights, if any, can these experiences offer?

Example 1

Clara is an interpreter in a reflective practice group I have been facilitating for 6 months. She shares about her experience as an interpreter in a social support setting. She has been interpreting for a client called Chantelle whose situation is very difficult. Clara says, "Chantelle wants help to sort out her accommodation and immigration status and she is quite desperate. She is feeling useless and hopeless. I offer to take Chantelle to a housing appointment. I rearrange my appointments so that I can be available. I go to meet Chantelle at the agreed time and place, but Chantelle doesn't turn up. I am annoyed and I start to feel useless and helpless."

Clara tells the group how helpless she still feels and how angry she is. Listening to Clara I feel pulled in. I do something I do not usually do. I start to offer lots of suggestions to Clara. Normally, I would wait until other group participants had connected with Clara. It is unlikely that I would have offered any advice or suggestions. But I ignore my norms and offer suggestions. Clara rejects them all. I start to feel useless and angry. Clara says she is feeling rather disappointed. I ask myself, "What is going on?"

This may be a type of situation you recognise. You may already have formed some explanatory hypotheses about what is happening. In this chapter we

DOI: 10.4324/9781003658924-7

look at some psychological theories and concepts that may shed light on these dynamics. We'll return to this example later.

In a reflective group, there will almost always be times when the group or individual group members find you (the facilitator), or other group members, disappointing. Very occasionally a group may be harmonious, offer little challenge, and be consistently able to function well with minimal support. In my experience, that can happen, but it's rare. When it does happen, I'm likely to sigh with relief that we are going to have a harmonious experience and relax too much. I metaphorically put on my slippers and turn down the lights. I'm then not prepared when conflict occurs. And it generally does occur. That's the nature of groups.

I don't. however, adhere to the view developed in the 1960s (Tuckman, 1965) that groups go through stages that almost always include a *storming* phase. Attacks and rage can create chaos in some groups. They may serve a purpose in other settings. Contexts change. Tastes and cultures change. Storming is not an inevitability in an effective group. However disagreement and dissent may be very productive.

There are many reasons for individuals and groups to experience disappointment and many ways to show it. For example, if the disappointment is about *you*, some group members may not want to let you know they are disappointed because they don't want to hurt you. Others may want to let you know because (often unconsciously) they *do* want to hurt you. Sometimes, some of the group may find you disappointing while the rest of the group members are satisfied and don't have any complaints.

The task of this chapter is to deconstruct the complexities of managing expectations in reflective group settings and the inevitability of the facilitator sometimes disappointing group members. Being labelled disappointing can elicit powerful responses. It can lead to you feeling disappointed in yourself. It can lead to you employing strategies to avoid becoming a disappointing facilitator. You might find yourself adopting saviour behaviour. You might inadvertently make yourself a scapegoat for the group.

In this chapter we also explore and offer some exercises to illustrate how self-awareness can be of use to facilitators. Self-awareness helps facilitators to understand their own responses to disappointment and inadequacy so that they can move away from feeling potentially overwhelmed. They can then reflect, try to understand and help the group to understand the group processes. This leads to richer group dynamics and personal growth for all involved. As we are thinking principally about reflective practice support groups, the amount of time spent focusing on group dynamics with groups may be brief. The aim is to notice and note them rather than work with them extensively, as you would in a personal growth or psychotherapy group. I will say more about this in Chapter 8.

Psychological Theories

Psychological theories about ourselves and others are a series of concepts that can help us understand human behaviour and act as a guide for our decisions and our behaviour with others. I mentioned the potential limitations of theories in the introductory chapter. Theories can, of course be very helpful though, not least for holding us accountable for our actions. But they can also get in the way of presence, authenticity and spontaneity. It is a delicate balance. I offer a caution and example as well, at the end of this section, about how theory can be misused. The compromise I have chosen in this chapter is to offer a selection of theoretical concepts, aligned with practical examples and related to psychanalytic theory and supervision, that have served me well in thinking about disappointment when I facilitate reflective practice groups. We begin with a compendium of working definitions and descriptions of themes, terms and concepts.

Compendium of Themes, Terms, and Concepts

1 Transference and Countertransference

Transference is the process by which we project past feelings onto other people. Maybe a person reminds us of someone with whom we had a significant relationship or with whom we have unfinished business. Countertransference refers to our emotional reaction and response to a person's projection on to us. These processes occur between individuals. They also occur in groups, between group members, between the group and the facilitator and across other relationships in the group. They often cause discomfort between and amongst participants. Feelings from past experiences of abusive or negligent caregivers and teachers, or of bullying/being bullied, can be activated by projections which criss-cross the group. One of the impacts of minority-majority power dynamics in groups is for those dynamics, for example of race and ethnicity, to intensify these processes, especially in multiracial/cultural groups. If anxiety is heightened, it may lead to greater resistance and disappointment which can put the working alliance under strain. Again, as with difficulties in life more generally, this challenge can also provide opportunities for repair given sensitive attention (White, 1994).

2 Projection and Projective Identification

Projection generally occurs when we have feelings or thoughts which cause us anxiety or distress. We try to get rid of them by giving them to someone else.

Projective identification is the response that projections can elicit in us when we are in receipt of someone else's projection of unwanted feelings and thoughts. We respond to a person, often unconsciously, as if their feelings really were our own. A closed communication cycle of entangled projection and projective identification can continue to repeat itself. Projective identification is quite a dense concept. I include an example a little later in the chapter which hopefully makes the concept less opaque. Despite its opacity, projective identification is a crucial process to understand due to the powerful, magnetic pull it exerts on relationships and interactions.

3 Parallel Process

Parallel process is a phenomenon which is referred to in clinical supervision as well as in other contexts. It occurs when supervisees unconsciously mirror the presentation of their clients with their supervisor. A supervisee effectively shows (albeit unconsciously) the behaviour of the client to their supervisor. The supervisor may start to feel and act towards the supervisee in similar ways as the supervisee behaves with their client. It is another form of repetition. The dynamics in the supervisee – client relationship, get repeated in the supervisor – supervisee relationship. Some theorists (Mendelsohn, 2012) believe that there is considerable overlap between the processes of projective identification and parallel process.

Patrick Casement, a retired psychoanalyst and fellow of the British Psychoanalytical Society has been influential in thinking about processes such as transference, countertransference and projective identification in therapy and supervision (although he also cautions against the overuse of concepts like projections and transference as explanatory models). Casement (1985) regards these processes as attempts to communicate and express difficult feelings and experiences. If we think of a projection as communication, rather than as a personal attack, it can help us, as facilitators of reflective groups, to understand what someone is trying to express.

Any of these theories could help to explain what happened between Clara and the facilitator in the example at the start of the chapter. Let's look at how the example might have played out had I (the facilitator) resisted the urge to enact the parallel process or introject the projection.

Example 2

Clara is an interpreter in a reflective practice group I have been facilitating for 6 months. She has just shared about her experience as an interpreter in a social support setting. She has been interpreting for a called Chantelle whose situation is very difficult. Chantelle wants help to sort out her accommodation and immigration status and she is quite desperate. Chantelle is feeling useless and hopeless. Clara offered to take Chantelle to a housing appointment. Clara rearranged her appointments so that she could be available. She went to meet Chantelle at the agreed time and place but Chantelle didn't turn up. Clara was annoyed and she started to feel useless and helpless. Clara tells the group how helpless she still feels and how angry she is. After making an empathic connection with Clara, the facilitator (with Clara's permission) invites the other group participants to respond. The group participants offer lots of suggestions to Clara but Clara rejects them all. The group participants start to feel useless and angry ...

In this example, it is not necessarily the facilitator who gets caught up in the repetition. It's the group. In offering so many helpful suggestions the group parallels Clara's need to be actively helpful with her client. So, what type of intervention is needed here to stop the chain of reactions, projections and pattern of repetitions, and to start some reflective thinking? One suggestion is for the facilitator to be transparent about what they observe. I have identified, in earlier chapters, a strategy of naming and noticing out loud. It could be very useful in the situation with Clara to notice out loud that there may be a dynamic that is being repeated. I wouldn't recommend though, necessarily naming the specific psychological construct e.g. parallel process or projective identification or countertransference. (I explain why not, after this example). It is a good idea to offer this intervention before the repetition has become entrenched. It can feel less shaming and more containing if the naming happens early on. Participants, including Clara, can then be invited to take a step back and disentangle themselves so that they can reflect on the process themselves. This may help Clara to make sense of the strength of the pulls and pushes she has experienced with her client.

The caution I offer about relying on theoretical concepts is that theory can sometimes seduce us into believing that all human behaviour can be categorised and understood. I have been in groups where I've heard a facilitator or group members gleefully identify a behaviour, they think they have identified: "Oh that's the parallel process happening." "I think someone is being scapegoated." "That's transference!" It can feel satisfying to have put a recognisable name to a phenomenon you observe. But then what? What has happened to authentic relating and spontaneity during this intellectual exercise? What happens to differences that don't fit into existing theoretical constructs? As I said in the introduction to this book, I try to use theoretical ideas to support my practice. I want to be careful though, not to lose connection with the experience of being present with the group.

4 Being Disappointing

There are a range of reasons why individuals or a group may find you disappointing. You may have made a mistake by, for example, being clumsy or ill-informed. You may not have taken enough care with the setting up of the group, and communicated poorly. It's not an excuse but the reality is that we are not perfect. Mistakes can happen and people have a right to feel disappointed because of them.

There may however, not be a tangible or straightforward reason for the disappointment. Human beings struggle with the tension between wanting to belong, wanting to be cared for, and wanting independence and freedom. For some group members and groups, it can be very tempting to regard the group facilitator as responsible for their disappointment – that they can't achieve the right balance between belonging and freedom.

As a facilitator, like it or not, for many people you represent an authority figure. Earlier I described the impact of projective identification, as a powerful magnetic pull. Similarly, a facilitator can themselves become a magnet, attracting the many and varied disappointments people have had with previous experiences of authority figures. Is it possible, then, to avoid being disappointing?

As facilitators, our own personal histories impact on us too. People will have disappointed us in our lives and one response is to feel that we never want to be disappointing for others. People may have behaved badly towards us, but we vow to be different. The role of Rescuer or Saviour has a great deal of allure. You may find the group colludes with you and they put you on a pedestal. That's fine while it lasts. But it doesn't last. You can't cling on to a pedestal for ever. Eventually you have to come down and face the reality of your own (just like everyone's) capacity to be disappointing. You can, of course, use other techniques to try to swerve that sobering realisation. You can use humour to make excuses for yourself, or you can exploit your own vulnerability so that the group has to rescue *you.*

5 Impact on the Facilitator

Just like group members, our own personal vulnerabilities and responses, and our memories of early family dynamics get stimulated. This can lead us to a state of collapse. The group and its needs become overwhelming. We may attempt to avoid the pain of our own disappointment by constantly apologising or blaming ourselves. That could result in the facilitator being perceived as the scapegoat for the group: the facilitator draws all the anger/disappointment of the group towards them before the group does.

Or a facilitator might become angry with the group or the group member who expresses disappointment. This anger can be enacted very subtly. For example, by ignoring a disappointed group member's request to share, or by abstaining from giving positive feedback. Conversely, a facilitator might (drawn like a magnet) try to compensate by pouring all their attention on to the individual who expressed disappointment. The danger here is that the facilitator loses the rest of the group.

However, if there is a genuine reason for the group to be disappointed in you, an apology is important. Saying sorry on its own though, isn't sufficient. Saying sorry can let you off the hook. But if the apology is genuine, I think a facilitator needs to commit to changing their behaviour and to being held accountable to the group for delivering on this commitment, maybe at the regular reviews. Again, there is a balance needed. This shouldn't be a masochistic activity. This is an exercise of repair not of punishment. A situation where the group is regularly upbraiding the facilitator isn't helpful for anyone. It is almost impossible to be rebuked and to hold safeguarding responsibility at the same time.

6 "Disappointing Enough"

Our original family, our position in the family, birth order, number of siblings, parents and grandparents all contribute to our relationships with individuals and within groups (Adler, 1927; Adler & Fleisher, 1988). We will return to family patterns in groups in the next chapter, but before we leave families, a word about parenting and being parented. Donald Winnicott (1986) used the phrase *good enough* to describe a satisfactory experience of being parented. The phrase paradoxically involves parents being disappointing too, so that children learn how to enjoy life's ups and recover from life's downs. Winnicott refers to this as *enough frustration*. Kohut (1977) calls this *necessary frustration*. It is also sometimes referred to as *optimal frustration*. It is frustration that helps people to tolerate manageable disappointments and develop self-agency. In this chapter I use the phrase *disappointing enough* to mean frustrating enough. I don't mean that we should intentionally try to be frustrating for the groups we facilitate. I mean that we need to operate with some compassionate acceptance, not just of our good enough sides, but of our disappointing sides too.

7 Self-Awareness and Supervision

Many people will have had experiences that were too disappointing and which fractured their trust in those around them. If that is the case for any of us who want to facilitate groups, it's important to focus on developing our self-knowledge, so that we ourselves can tolerate being optimally frustrating (Kohut, 1977).

The compendium entries, in this chapter, contain descriptions of various strong, unconscious interpersonal processes. Self-awareness can help us to recognise them and bring them into consciousness. However, it can be difficult to untie the knotty processes on our own. This is why reflecting about our work as a facilitator with someone else (with a supervisor, for example), helps to ensure our facilitation is as effective and as ethical as possible.

8 Compassionate and Connected Inadequacy

Winnicott's idea of being "good enough" has helped many people let go of perfectionism. Yet in the twenty-first century, even "good enough" can feel unattainable. Many professionals experience moral injury: they are unable to act in line with their values because of institutional pressures. They disappoint themselves. They feel inadequate. As if that weren't bad enough, they often believe that others are coping much better than they are (Festinger, 1954). Social comparison has been dramatically amplified in the twenty-first century by social media, and by constant exposure to global crises that make individual efforts feel insignificant and pointless. Feeling inadequate is making many people psychologically ill.

However, rather than rejecting inadequacy, it may be time to rethink it. Inadequacy does not mean nothing; it means not enough on one's own. It is more than nothing. In fact, when viewed collectively, individual inadequacies can combine into sufficiency. Isn't that more than enough reason to form groups? *Compassionate inadequacy* is a realistic yet hopeful stance: doing what we can, accepting our limits, and marvelling at the collective mosaic of our combined contributions. It is an antidote to disappointment.

For reflective group facilitators, this means acknowledging our own and others' disappointment, and the feelings they evoke without defensiveness or minimisation. We need to stay engaged and compassionate with ourselves as well as with others. We don't need to make excuses or hide behind defensive humour. Or minimise the potential impact of a mistake. This is important. It is not an excuse for poor practice, but a recognition that despite our best intentions, we will sometimes fall short. In interdependent groups, participants alternate between giving and receiving support, and the collective becomes greater than the sum of its parts.

Let's consider, in the next section, how disappointment with a reflective group facilitator can manifest itself, and the impact of this manifestation in practice. You may want to consider how compassionate and connected inadequacy shows up in facilitation practice. You may find that some of the theoretical concepts we have reviewed connect with your responses to the following section, which combines reflective questions, real-world illustrations, and tips from practice that illustrate ways of developing a facilitator's self-awareness and use of supervision.

The examples in this section rest on four key values: compassion, integrity, a commitment to understanding, and ethical courage. In practice this involves acknowledging pain, acting with transparency, inviting dialogue and addressing your own and others fears, staying in the mess even when it is uncomfortable.

Example 3

You are hosting an introductory talk for people who share an interest in reflective groups for people who work in addiction recovery services. You have sent an email to them all including a link to the event which will be held online. You have asked them not to share the link with anyone outside of the mailing list.

At the event it is clear that there is someone in attendance who is not on your list. He calls himself Bakim and he begins to write judgemental comments about one of the event participants called Hafina in the chat. You manage to evict Bakim quickly from the call.

Reflective Questions 1

How do you react/feel/behave if you make a mistake? What is your default coping response?

How do you feel? How do you think others' feel? What do you instinctively want to do?

> *Hafina and the other group participants express their appreciation of your quick response. Even so, you begin to question whether you could have done more to avoid this happening. You start to imagine that the group feels this way too.*

Reflective Questions 2

What can you do productively with this sense of being disappointing to others and to yourself?

One of the functions of supervision for reflective group facilitators is to reflect on what difficult situations elicit in us, and to stabilise ourselves so that we can think carefully about what we need to do and how we accept what we cannot change. In other words, can we find the disappointing enough position?

Example 4

> *You are attending an online training session which you have been looking forward to. You have planned your working week carefully so that you have two full hours clear. You want to give the session your full attention. 10 minutes into the session, the facilitator says she made a mistake with the information she sent out. The session is one hour long and not two hours. She briefly apologises for her mistake and moves on.*

Reflective Questions 1

How would you have felt if the facilitator had said something like this after the brief apology? (Please bear in mind that this scenario is about a training session and not a reflective group.)

How do you feel when others disappoint you? What do you tend to want to do? What do you actually do? Do you ever feel differently in a scenario like this? Do you ever do anything different?

> *I appreciate that this will be very disappointing for some of you, especially if you had made plans according to the information I gave you. Some of you may feel annoyed or angry and you are fully justified in feeling like that. As we only have an hour, I wonder if it is possible to put those feelings to one side for the hour. However, please feel free to email me after the event if you would like to discuss this further.*

Reflective Questions 2

Might you say something similar? Do you think this is an example of a facilitator using metacommunication? Why/why not?

In what way is this/is this not an example of a facilitator's stance of compassionate inadequacy?

What might you have done differently if you were the facilitator? Why?

From my own experience, I have sometimes been disappointed with group facilitators when they have not adhered to agreed terms and expectations. Sometimes the facilitators responded with honesty and empathy. Sometimes the disappointment was dismissed and interpreted as my transference. In my opinion, this is an inappropriate use of psychotherapeutic explanatory models. Experiences like these have led me to reflect on the importance of honesty and transparency for a group facilitator. Honesty and transparency offer containment. They don't erase a mistake, but they help to frame the experience so that it can be disappointing enough and it can be looked at, thought about and learned from.

In this section of the chapter, we have considered the vital role of honest self-awareness. This approach allows a facilitator to evaluate the extent to which an accusation of disappointment stems from their own mistake or poor practice, and how much of it is an expression of something else. Being disappointing enough may seem like a strange asset. But there are benefits to being disappointing as a facilitator of a group. It gives groups an opportunity to engage with spontaneity, creativity and dynamism that come from responding to mistakes. Ruptures can be repaired, situations can be transformed. Avoiding disappointment and conflict creates an artificial dynamic. "There is no creativity without mess". This statement is attributed to Pablo Picasso.

Example 5

Let's consider a situation where the whole group may be disappointed with you. They might be justified. Maybe you were careless and forgot something significant for the group. Or maybe not. It could be a case of the group pushing the boundary, testing you to see if you can hold the frame. It may be an attack. They may be trying to take the power away from you. How can you tell?

> *This is your fifth meeting with a reflective practice support group you facilitate. You are due to start at 5 p.m. You have an agreement that you will start punctually at 5 p.m. and in the four meetings so far, this has happened. Today though, at 5.05 p.m. only some of the group members are present. Some people start to arrive, apologising for their lateness – traffic, work, computers are all culpable. You decide to ignore the late start this time, but you make a mental note to attend to it if it happens next time. It*

does. Next time, no one arrives on time. The group starts late. You want to try to understand what is going on. You decide to be transparent. You mention it to the group with sensitivity. The response of the group takes you back. They are all defensive and say they experience you as judgemental. They are disappointed!

Reflective Questions

How do you feel? What do you instinctively want to do? What do you do, in the moment? What do you think would be an unsatisfactory way of responding to the group's disappointment? What do you think would be a constructive way of responding to the group's disappointment? What do you think of the following possible response from the facilitator?

A Possible Initial Response

> *I can hear and see that some of you are angry with me, others are disappointed, others may be both. Have I got that right?*

The first step the facilitator takes is to check her understanding of what is happening with the group. She doesn't justify herself but tries to keep the space open for multiple explanations. Depending on what she hears back from the group, she'll decide what to do next. Here are some possible responses from the group.

The group members might share that the facilitator has done something of which she is unaware. Or they might try to deny that they are disappointed or angry. Or they might find some relief from having their feelings acknowledged by the facilitator, and that might free up some space to think about what the group might be experiencing and about the facilitator's perspective.

You can ignore the feelings that come up for you when a group finds you disappointing. Or you can be overwhelmed by the feelings. Either stance distances you from the group. I recommend staying connected. Everything that happens in the group gives you data. It's all information. You don't have to react. You can pause and reflect on what you want to do with the information.

What Else Might Facilitators Do?

The following are examples of, and rationales for, actions facilitators might take when they are perceived as being disappointing.

- Notice out loud that what is happening in the group is difficult for everyone, including (for you) the facilitator. Connect with the whole group. Try to avoid isolating yourself from the group.

- If the disappointment is about you holding the ground rules/working agreement, remind everyone gently that this is an agreed set of ground rules that the group has effectively asked you to hold.
- If opinions about the working agreement have changed, suggest a review.
- Be honest at the review. If people suggest rules that you don't feel you can work with, be sincere and say you don't feel confident to run a group with that kind of frame.

Example 6

In a trial one-hour reflective practice support group session some people express disappointment that this is not a regular reflective practice support group. You never promoted the session as a regular reflective practice support group. You wonder what happened for different expectations to have arisen and the ensuing disappointment to have been created.

Reflective Questions

What might a response. that engages the facilitator's compassionate inadequacy, look like?

What do you think of the following response?

Possible Response

I can see you are disappointed that we aren't tackling real cases today. We ask people to join a trial session and then if they are interested, we hope they will join the series of sessions when we look at real cases if enough people want to join. Can I ask everyone to please send me an email if you are interested in the continuing sessions? And also, please feel free to let me know by email if we could make the trial aspect of this group clearer in the promotional material in future.

The Rationale

This type of response includes an acknowledgement of the disappointment while not opening this up for further exploration given the short time available and the task of the group. The group may feel this is inadequate but if the facilitator adds her compassion to this response, she gives an indication of her commitment to open-mindedness and learning. She can also acknowledge that later the misunderstandings can be explored and rectified if needed. *Compassionate and connected inadequacy* doesn't shut things down. It keeps the potential open for new responses to emerge.

Example 7

Jo, a member of a group you run. emails you about an administrative issue. In the email Jo also makes it clear that they would like to have a special relationship with you outside of the group. You know you will have to let Jo down. You think carefully about how to do this. For a moment you question if you really need to discourage this because (a) you really like Jo or (b) it's too embarrassing to deal with or (c) it's only one person – surely everyone will understand?

But that only lasts a moment. You remember your frame, your commitment to the ethical framework of your professional organisation and your understanding of boundaries. You don't want to respond by acting on anxiety or fear of what this might result in. You want to respond with compassion but absolute clarity about the boundaries and the significance of the boundary.

Reflective Questions

How do you feel about holding the boundary if someone's feelings may be hurt as a result?

What do you do in situations like this?

Possible response

Thank you for wanting to connect with me in that way. As you probably expect anyway, having been in a group with me for a while now, I am going to disappoint you by saying that a further connection isn't possible. We all agreed at the beginning of the group that we wouldn't have contact beyond the group setting. That may not be of much comfort at the moment. You may even feel angry as well as disappointed. You may want to make a decision about what you want to do next, but can I please suggest that you take some time – maybe a few days before you let me know how you want to proceed? You are very welcome in the group as I hope you know. Is it ok if I don't make any assumptions about what you want to do and wait for you to let me know?

Rationale

This response acknowledges Jo's desire for further connection and reminds them of the agreed frame as non-judgementally and as compassionately as possible. As the facilitator, you emphasise your relationship with them as part of the group by reiterating how welcome they are to be part of the group. You further acknowledge their possible disappointment in your response. You invite Jo to take some time to think about how they want to proceed so that they know they have the power to choose what position they want to take. Jo may still be disappointed in you. They may find you wanting. This may be an experience they have had before, maybe several times. But by responding with compassion and acknowledging that the response may feel inadequate for them there is a chance that Jo may be able to hear the care in the response, when previously they may have been met with anxiety.

We finish this section with a final reflective question, case example, and possible response.

Example 8

Reflective Questions

How would you proceed with a group if it becomes clear that some of the group members are disappointed with you and some aren't? Notice your reactions to this situation.

> *After you have named the split you have observed, and if the group agrees with this observation, you ask people to identify for themselves which part of the group they are in (disappointed or not disappointed). If some people feel neither way, invite them to choose a position for the following exercise. Invite all the group members to take two minutes in silence and imagine this: "During these two minutes try to imagine you are in the* **other** group. Why aren't you disappointed or why are you?"

Rationale

If I was the facilitator in this situation, I would want to attend to the group process by creating some ways for us to communicate about the split in opinions, safely and dynamically. The initial approach involves everyone in doing the exercise, whichever side of the split they occupy (or don't). This keeps the group together for the moment. The exercise gives an opportunity for the process of perspective-taking and relational empathy. My intention is to attend to the process first not the problem.

At the end of the two minutes, I would ask people: "What emerged from doing that exercise that was of value for you?" or "What did you discover, if anything, that was of value?" We start by talking about the process. We start with the outline or frame of the process itself, and then we move into the detail of the content. It often feels safer and less emotionally heightened to have the conversation about the issue after a slow approach rather than by starting with a head-on approach.

As with all the suggested approaches I would take, there are alternatives. One alternative to working with split groups might be to apply Yvonne Agazarian's theory of systems-centred groups (Agazarian, 1994). This theory offers insights into developmental stages of groups, and groups which split and sub-divide.

You may find it useful to re-read the previous examples while considering these questions. What do you like about the responses? What don't you like? How might you respond? Can you give a rationale for your response?

Summary

How can we be compassionate with others' disappointment if we have no acceptance for our own? It is so easy for a facilitator to lose their footing when they are challenged. A very helpful idea in non-violent communication practice is that "empathising with someone's 'no' protects us from taking it personally" (Rosenberg & Chopra, 2015, p. 121). Some of the examples in this chapter attempt to illustrate how that could be implemented in facilitation practice.

We have looked at disappointment from the points of view of both group members and facilitators. Being deemed disappointing is very powerful. It can demolish a person's sense of confidence. Sometimes it is deserved. But it can be used as an offensive weapon with intent to harm, although it is frequently used without conscious desire. Whether or not the intention is conscious, the effect is that it normally hurts. It's not surprising that we try to find ways to avoid the hurt. However, in an attempt to avoid the dynamics of disappointment we may end up with a negative outcome. We may create an inauthentic connection based on fear, and an impulse to avoid Picasso's "mess".

If we can dare to be *disappointing enough*, we can provide the opportunity for real, deep connection and for transformative experiences to emerge. I use the word dare because it takes courage not to collapse, not to blame and to punish. Negotiating group dynamics that are potentially destructive takes courage. It can be worth it though. When facilitators dare to behave with *compassionate inadequacy*, they become powerful role models for growth, self-awareness, and relational courage. They model what happens when you admit your mistakes and you commit to learn from them. They model reflective practice in action.

Facilitating groups in the process of transformation from destructive group dynamics to a creative group energy is one of a facilitator's greatest joys. In the next chapter we address the task of working constructively with power and group dynamics.

References

Adler, A. (1927). *Understanding human nature*. Greenberg.

Adler, A., & Fleisher, L. (1988). The child's inner life and a sense of community. *Individual Psychology: The Journal of Adlerian Theory, Research & Practice*, 44(4), 431–441.

Agazarian, Y. M. (1994). The phases of group development and the systems-centered group. In V. Schermer & M. Pines (eds), *Ring of fire: Containing primitive emotional states* (pp. 36–85). Routledge.

Casement, P. (1985). *On learning from the patient* (1st edition). Routledge. doi:10.4324/9780203714829.

Festinger, L. (1954). A theory of social comparison processes. *Human Relations*, 7(2), 117–140. doi:10.1177/001872675400700202.

Kohut, H. (1977). *The restoration of the self.* University of Chicago Press.
Mendelsohn, R. (2012). Parallel process and projective identification in psychoanalytic supervision. *Psychoanalytic Review,* 99(3), 297–314. doi:10.1521/prev.2012.99.3.297.
Rosenberg, M. B., & Chopra, D. (2015). *Nonviolent communication: A language of life: Life-changing tools for healthy relationships.* PuddleDancer Press.
Tuckman, B. W. (1965). Developmental sequence in small groups. *Psychological Bulletin,* 63(6), 384–399. doi:10.1037/h0022100.
White, J. C. (1994). The impact of race and ethnicity on transference and countertransference in combined individual/group therapy. *Group,* 18, 89–99. doi:10.1007/BF01457420.
Winnicott, D. W. (1986). The theory of the parent–infant relationship. In P. Buckley (ed.), *Essential papers on object relations* (pp. 233–253). New York University Press.

Chapter 8

Power and Group Dynamics

Example 1

In a reflective practice support group for refugee support health workers, the sharer called Sameera shares an experience of witnessing a health professional act discriminatively towards her client. The health professional accuses the client, who is from a refugee background, of wasting public money because, "He hasn't bothered to learn English". Sameera feels bad because she didn't challenge the health professional. The health professional occupies a position of high status and Sameera says she felt intimidated by his knowledge and experience. Lots of group members want to respond to what Sameera says. One of them, a young man called Femi becomes quite upset. He starts to confront Sameera about not taking action.

Reflective Questions

If you were the facilitator of this group, how would you be feeling now?

What would you want to do? Why?

What would you *not* do? Why not?

We will return to a discussion of this case example and others later in the chapter.

Introduction

I train people in group facilitation skills, a lot. I get asked this question: "When are we going to cover group dynamics?" a lot. And every time the question surprises me. Or rather, it used to. Because I thought we were covering group dynamics constantly throughout the training. Group and power dynamics are what we are thinking about in every session. I have come to understand though, from the regularity of the question, that it can be useful for many people to bracket off group dynamics as a phenomenon and examine it closely before integrating it into practice. That is what this chapter attempts to do.

As a term, group dynamics is used in policy, practice and personal contexts. According to the American Psychological Association's *Dictionary of Psychology* group dynamics are:

DOI: 10.4324/9781003658924-8

> the processes, operations, and changes that occur within social groups, which affect patterns of affiliation, communication, conflict, conformity, decision making, influence, leadership, norm formation, and power. The term, as used by Kurt Lewin (1947), emphasises the power of the fluid, ever-changing forces that characterize interpersonal groups.
>
> (American Psychological Association, 2025)

Group and power dynamics can be positive or negative. In a study (Knight et al., 2010) that explored the personal and professional impact of reflective practice groups for qualified clinical psychologists, the quality of the facilitator's management of dynamics was a significant factor in predicting levels of perceived value and safety of the groups. One recommendation from the study was for reflective practice support group facilitators to have sufficient training in group processes. The types of interpersonal feelings, interactions, attitudes and behaviours that result from negative group dynamics can be very challenging for group facilitators. It's the challenging dynamics that trainee facilitators frequently ask about. That is why we will focus more on negative than positive dynamics in this chapter. I have selected examples from my direct experience of facilitating groups. I realise it's not a comprehensive selection. I've chosen examples that I think are relevant to reflective group facilitation.

Some group dynamics test the frame of a group. It can be tempting, in these moments, to rely heavily on set rules and procedures – the external frame. Unfortunately, clinging to the external frame, often obstructs creative responses that the more sensitive and flexible internal frame offers. A group facilitator may find that the frame (external and/or internal) slips out of their hands, often just momentarily, in the anxiety that challenging dynamics provoke. This can be a particularly difficult moment for groups in their early stages of formation. If the group picks up on the absence of a steady pair of hands, anxiety starts to unravel the frame for everyone. We will see in this chapter that concepts and processes introduced in earlier chapters, such as *containment, working agreement, psychological safety*, and *continuous review process*, help the group to address even some of the most challenging tests that are presented. They also help the facilitator to hold the frame.

We have already looked at the position of the facilitator in groups and what that position represents for others, and for themselves, in terms of power and authority. At the macro level of interpersonal group dynamics, facilitators may want to consider how their own position in society comes with them into the group. If you are a facilitator, people might already know about you from your public profile. They may be aware of your social class, your education, your skin colour, your occupational prestige. They may not know about, for example, your sexuality or sexual preferences, your religion, your age, your linguistic repertoire, your financial circumstances, whether you are a person with a health condition or a disability, whether you have caring responsibilities.

You may tell the group. You may not. People will still use their imaginations about you whether you do or you don't. The same of course is true for all the group members. How do real and imagined societal positions impact on group power?

We are now going to look at varied ways in which power and powerlessness are manifested in group dynamics.

Theory and Practice about Group Dynamics

Theory provides information, but to turn theory into knowledge that you can use, you also need skills and experience. Wisdom combines knowledge and experience. When you apply knowledge and experience thoughtfully, in situations as they unfold in front of you, that creates wisdom.

Theoretical ideas are useful, up to a point, with the types of reflective groups I run. I try to illustrate up to what point, later in the chapter. Unsurprisingly there are many theories about group dynamics. Dynamics change throughout the life and stages of a group. Group stages, systems and family therapy models, person-centred and psychodrama models have been mentioned in previous chapters. The following compendium of eight themes draws from varied theories. Some psychoanalytical ideas about groups and group processes have already been introduced in Chapters 3–5.

Compendium of Themes, Terms, and Concepts

1 Group-as-a-Whole

The *group-as-a-whole* is an entity with an identity, that is more than and different from a composite of the identities of the individual group members (Bion, 1961). This has significant implications for facilitators in terms of their communication. It can be easy to get drawn into protracted conversations with an individual in a group as if you were engaging in a one-to-one discussion. What happens to the rest of the group when that occurs? One of the ways that I try to avoid that is by agreeing communication patterns of turn-taking, and thinking in advance about how we will deal with questions and answers as a group. This is an example of the metacommunication about process or *talking about the talking* (Costa, 2020). I also try to put Bion's theory of the *group-as-a-whole* into practice by communicating in a way that involves *shifting focus.*

2 Shifting Focus

In filmmaking, racking or *shifting focus* refer to times when the focus shifts, or racks, from one subject to another. In groups, I use the idea of shifting focus to refer to a dynamic form of communicating with the group. When I respond to an individual, I try to keep my direct response to the person as concise as possible. I then quickly bring the *group -as- a-whole* into my subsequent response. I aim to keep the group engaged and to resist the pull for a series of individual conversations to take place between myself and a group member, or between group members.

I have included examples of shifting focus throughout the book. For example, in Chapter 6 a case is presented in which a group member tries to promote, and encourage other group members to join, an activity. The response from the facilitator is:

> *I understand your wish to be supportive and to share information. But I want to say a couple of things about this as far as this group is concerned…, as a group, we have never come across this situation before, so it is an opportunity for us all to agree on how we deal with this in the future.*

In two sentences the facilitator moves from directly addressing the individual to quickly widening out the audience for whom their response is intended. It is a simple method that attempts to include everyone, neither isolating nor allowing someone to dominate the talking. The method helps to avoid the group meeting being taken over by a conversation between two individuals. By avoiding a pattern of individual conversations, the commitment of a shared responsibility to the group-as-a-whole is reinforced.

It does though, often feel simpler to engage empathically with people individually. The pull to engage intensely with an individual is even stronger if you feel that a group member(s) is (are) pushing the frame in some way. We saw this with the case of the split group in Chapter 7. I regularly use the one-minute silent reflection exercise to bring the focus back to the whole group.

3 Psychodrama Role Theory

Psychodrama role theory (Moreno, 1987) attempts to explain our interactions with ourselves and with each other. People interact from different personal, somatic and sociocultural roles throughout their lives. We may be familiar with some of those roles in our repertoire and less familiar with others. Role reversal involves exchanging roles with another person/idea/object etc. It gives someone a perspective other than their own. They can get a glimpse of how their own behaviour is perceived by others. Role reversal is a form of deep empathy. In non-violent communication this compassionate empathy is considered a commitment to "sense others' needs no matter what they are saying" (Rosenberg & Chopra, 2015, p. 68).

An example of the technique of role reversal is included in the Chapter 7. Some of the group members were disappointed with the facilitator and some were not. In silence the two groups were invited to imagine they were in the *other* group. They were asked to consider why they were or why they weren't disappointed. Role reversal can also be applied to some of the examples about interpersonal and intergroup dynamics in this chapter.

4 Family and Systemic Therapy

Groups are formed of individuals with unique experiences who have and may continue to hold specific roles and positions (micro level) in their families. Individuals are also socially influenced and hold roles and positions at the social (macro) level.

In popular culture there are plenty of terms about group dynamics and the positions people occupy in groups such as, scapegoat, golden (or favourite) child, saviour. These frequently relate to positions people have taken in their family systems as they were growing up. The terms are often used as a way of explaining people's behaviour in groups. Of course, even group-focused frameworks such as systemic theory, have limitations when they are applied in practice. It would be easy, for example, to identify a scapegoat and scapegoating behaviour in the example later in this chapter of Sameera and Femi. But going for an easy option, such as relying on unexamined intuition, or applying theory indiscriminately, can signal a red flag. The more difficult and complex issues are being missed. Theory is used wisely and creatively when people pay attention to the red flags.

Let's consider three theoretical ideas we might apply from family and systemic therapy. They are *family dynamics, triangulation* and *parentification.*

5 Family Dynamics, Triangulation, and Parentification

In the 1970s the family therapist and theorist Murray Bowen created a model for understanding families and *family dynamics* (Bowen, 1978). It has been critiqued and updated (Brown & Errington, 2024) and is still currently used. Bowen proposes that family members are inextricably interconnected. They impact on each other's present and future relationships, their emotional development and emotional expression. Group members, like family members, are part of an emotional system. They are interlinked and impact on each other. Sometimes they may need help to disentangle their feelings from their thoughts to bring out the best in themselves and to get the best out of the experience of their system.

Salvador Minuchin developed the concept of *triangulation* (Minuchin, 1974), also recently critiqued (McCauley et al., 2021). Triangulation is the strategy that children may adopt in a family to placate or to divert attention from their parents' conflict with each other. This can occur in a group when someone creates a problem that needs to be resolved urgently because they are anxious to divert attention from potential conflict in the group, if the facilitator appears to have lost their authority.

Parentification is a concept proposed by Gregory Jurkovic (1997). Parentification occurs in families when a child takes on adult roles and responsibilities, often because of the parents' inability or incapacity to parent. So, in a group you may find someone who regularly takes on a placatory role. It seems to me that if a facilitator discounts their power for any reason (e.g., they may get distracted or caught up in their own preoccupations, or they may start to fear the group) a group participant(s) emerges, who challenges the facilitator's authority in some way.

Although other practice examples follow the compendium entries, I include one brief example here to illustrate how as a facilitator I use ideas from systemic therapy.

Compendium Example

> *Half-way through a session I become aware that I have been rather inattentive, as I have been distracted. I manage to bring myself back to the facilitator role and, to my horror, I observe a process occurring in the group. A group member seems to be trying to manage the group by e.g. pointing out that some people haven't spoken, that a group member looks upset, reminding us of the time frame etc. This gives me a very useful hint that I have stepped out of my role as the facilitator. The group member is stepping up because I (unconsciously) stepped down. It looks like the process of "parentification "is occurring.*
>
> *Having stepped back up, I then notice out loud with the group, that it seems to me that we are getting a bit off-kilter. I acknowledge that I have been distracted. I apologise. I thank the group member for stepping up and reassure them that I am now fully present and that I intend to remain present. I remind the group to feel free to let me know if they have any cause to believe I am not present in the future. I suggest we take 1 minute to think about how we are doing with our principal task.*

I am feeling rather ashamed of myself for allowing myself to be distracted. The group deserved my attention. I try not to make things worse by getting caught up in my own shame. I offer an effectively ad hoc review. I am asking the group if we can get back to the group as a work group (Bion, 1961). Do they still trust me to lead them in that task? Noticing the parentification alerts me to the fact that the frame needs some attention. The external frame has become loose. My inattention had caused the frame to slacken. We aren't going to examine people's personal psychological motivations in depth, but I need to check if the group still trusts me to hold the frame.

Reflective Questions

How did you feel when you read the example? What might you have done in this situation, and why? Would you use any other explanatory models to help you understand what is happening here?

6 Shame

Let's take some time to consider the topic of shame. It is easy to ignore. Shame is tricky. It is shaming to talk about shame. But if we hide it away, it refuses to disappear and may even grow bigger. I find this definition of shame useful. "Shame is generally defined as strong negative emotions characterised by perceptions of the global devaluation of oneself" (Budiarto & Helmi, 2021, p. 131).

A person who is shamed can feel that they have been isolated and that all connections with them have been severed. They can feel like they no longer exist or that they do not deserve to exist. Shame is an extremely powerful form of social control. It is made more powerful by the fact that shame is so difficult to acknowledge or talk about without a person's feelings of shame being exacerbated. And yet we need to talk about shame if we are to find out anything new about ourselves and the way we operate in the world. If we are to be reflective.

And because shame is experienced within groups, and by a facilitator of groups, as we saw in the above example, it is particularly pertinent to our discussion of group dynamics.

Shame can occur at the micro level between group members. For example, some group members' observations and offerings in a reflective group can be regularly dismissed or given less attention. The facilitator may focus their attention on other group members' interventions. Or a group member can be sidelined or rebuked by another group member for mispronouncing someone's name, for example (perhaps because the rebuker wants to gain prestige in the group by signalling their own cultural awareness).

7 Cultural Shame

At the macro level *cultural shaming* can be experienced by everyone in any groupings in society. Cultural inferiority and cultural shame are not personal, individual experiences. They are collective ones. The group context is often a fertile setting for them to emerge. Experiences of cultural shame link us, for example, with a colonial history of oppression which affects everyone (Fernando, 2010; McKenzie-Mavinga, 2026). The feelings that emerge from the personal histories and relationships with this oppression can feel unbearable and unsafe to discuss. A facilitator may reinforce cultural shame in very subtle ways. I include, in later examples, how this may show up in reflective groups in practice. For those who would appreciate additional consideration of other issues relating to culture, race and discrimination, I include some suggestions for reading, after the References section. I include my own experience, here.

The pervasive, slippery nature of shame becomes even more elusive when we think about it at the sociopolitical level of cultural shame. Cultural shame is freighted with a history of normalising oppression so that it becomes almost impossible to discern. My own cultural background is that I am half Greek Cypriot. My father was born in Cyprus when it was still a British colony. He left Cyprus to find his fortune in England. Or so he thought. He didn't make his fortune but the move to the UK opened doors for his family. I received a free education up to graduate level. I felt very grateful for this opportunity. I knew how hard my dad had worked for us to have these opportunities. But I always had a vague sense that these opportunities weren't rightfully mine. I was proud of my achievements but ashamed that I felt I had to keep showing my gratitude for the goodwill of the UK. I didn't express these views and feelings to anyone. To be honest they felt a bit weird. No one was overtly telling me to feel grateful. It was only much later that I discovered that mine was not an unusual experience for people who grew up in a context of emigration from the ex-colonies. For marginalised communities, this dynamic often gets repeated and played out. It is an experience which can result in an ensuing feeling of having no agency to act independently, as an individual. It is an experience of shaming at a collective level. At the professional level, it can manifest in supervisory and reflective practice group settings.

8 Liberatory Supervision: Addressing Cultural Shame in Practice

The model of liberatory supervision practice is a useful frame through which to address cultural shame in supervision and reflective practice groups. Inspired by Paolo Freire's work in Brazil in the 1960s and 1970s, liberatory supervision practice (Freire et al., 2018) focuses on creating a relationship based on equality, care, compassion, and collaboration (Kortegast et al., 2024). A liberatory supervision approach is equally appropriate for reflective practice groupwork. It addresses oppressive systems and promotes empowerment, agency, and social justice. You may be wondering what culturally responsive reflective practice, grounded in care, compassion, and collaboration, might look like in practice. I offer Mothertongue (first introduced in the introductory chapter of this book) as an example.

Mothertongue was an organisation I set up in 2000 to offer free counselling to people from the local community in their preferred languages. All who worked and volunteered for Mothertongue were first- or second-generation immigrants to the UK. Many of us were born in or had parents who were born in countries that had been colonised by Britain. Coming together under the umbrella of Mothertongue was important for us all. It validated our experiences, often of cultural shame and oppression. Sharing that experience empowered us, strengthened our confidence, and expanded our sense of agency beyond the boundary of Mothertongue. We began as a homogeneous, cohesive group. It was the right starting point for us. We felt we had somewhere we belonged, where we didn't need to feel ashamed of our backgrounds. It provided a buffer which offered some protection from the outside world. Over nearly 20 years, our shared experiences, challenges, and learning transformed us, enabling us to challenge dominant but ineffective structures through care, compassion, and collaboration. We expanded our outlook, confident not just to let others in, but to go beyond the group and engage with the outside world. Mothertongue is, of course, not a strict example of a reflective practice support group. However, it followed the pattern of a group of marginalised people moving from a cohesive group experience to a group position of coherency.

A reflective practice group is different. In a reflective group, other decisions about participants' experience of cultural shame/shaming need to be taken. How, for example, do you balance the needs of participants who come from a mixture of majority and minoritised backgrounds? How do you attend to the ethics (Pérez & Molpeceres, 2018) of the rights of minoritised people within a group (Nancheva, 2016)? This is a major challenge for facilitators who want to be fair and to be anti-oppressive practitioners. Sometimes it is more appropriate to start with a homogenous group of participants. We will look at some examples of practice that illustrate this later in the chapter.

How Theory Does and Doesn't Help a Facilitator

The eight themes in the compendium are not a complete overview of the theory of group dynamics. I've been selective. As a reflective group facilitator, you aren't given permission to occupy the position of a psychotherapist. You aren't invited, in the way that is the case for a group psychotherapist, to offer interpretations, challenge defences and dysfunctional behaviour, and explore previous relational patterns in a group member's life experience, at any depth. A reflective practice support group is not a therapy group although it may prove therapeutic for some people. People are advised to find appropriate help outside of the group if they wish to explore their own personal issues further. It is true though, that exploring people's personal responses to casework can shed light on troubling dynamics in cases brought for exploration. Ideas from theories can help a facilitator and the group to untangle themselves from a dynamic, and fully occupy their role and commitment to the group task. Theoretical models can also help a facilitator to make fair assessments about people's toleration and capacity to be challenged, without becoming overwhelmed by shame.

There is another reason why my selection of theoretical concepts from group psychotherapy is selective and doesn't need to be comprehensive. I think that when people ask me the question "When are we going to cover group dynamics?" what they also mean is – "Can we discuss what we would *do* in the moment when things get a bit tricky in a group?" I wanted to leave space for practice examples too.

The next section contains two examples of interpersonal group dynamics and two examples of intergroup dynamics. You will see from the examples though, that this division is not always clearcut. In the following example the division between interpersonal and intergroup dynamics is blurred. This example fits under both categories and could be approached in different ways. I include it as an example of the complexity of group dynamics. Group dynamics do not fit neatly into micro and macro levels. The title of the award-winning 2022 film expresses so well the plurality of group dynamic experiences: *Everything Everywhere All at Once.*

Interpersonal Dynamics

Recall Example 1 from the beginning of the chapter:

> *In a reflective practice support group for refugee support health workers, the Sharer called Sameera shares an experience of witnessing a health professional act discriminatively towards her client. The health professional accuses the client, who is from a refugee background, of wasting public money because, "He hasn't bothered to learn English". Sameera feels bad because she didn't challenge the health professional. The health professional occupies a position of high status and Sameera says she felt intimidated by his knowledge and experience. Lots of group members want to respond to what Sameera says. One of them, a young man called Femi becomes quite upset. He starts to confront Sameera about not taking action.*

Reflective Questions 1

What do you do if you are the facilitator?

How are you feeling right now? If this has stirred you up emotionally, what is going to help you get back into the role of facilitator so that you can continue to serve the group from this role?

What might you be thinking?

Response

This is an example of what a facilitator might do. Let's call the facilitator Errol.

> *Errol tries to meet Femi's anger with an empathic statement quickly. He then says: "Before we go any further, I have a suggestion. It seems Femi, you have something urgent that you need to communicate to us about this experience. Can I suggest though, that you take a moment to think about how you want to communicate this with us that optimises the chances of us understanding and connecting with you? If I come back to you after two other people have spoken would that be ok with you?" Whatever Femi's*

response, Errol quickly checks with Sameera to see if she is ok, and to reassure her that she isn't going to be ignored.

Rationale

Here's a brief explanation of what I think may have informed Errol's course of action. You will see that it includes ideas from theory as well as here-and-now responses.

Errol quickly noted with himself his own instinct also to be angry about the situation. He found that he was also drawn towards blaming Sameera for not acting. Errol realised they could quickly get into a situation of scapegoating and shaming Sameera. Sameera could become a lightning rod for everyone's anger and frustration with the health professional.

Errol found a way to calm himself, get back into his role as the facilitator, and offer that insight subtly in his intervention with Femi, making sure that Femi realised Errol connected with him empathically. He made no further statement as he wanted to make sure he left space for others to comment, and he left space for Femi to comment a little later as well. He chose to step in quickly though, so that the situation could be cooled rather than enflamed by the anger and blame swirling around. He also made sure that Sameera was included in the process. He could have referred to the working agreement about not judging other members of the group. But in an effort not to shame Sameera, he felt he could end up shaming Femi.

Reflective Questions 2

What do you think of Errol's response? What would you do differently? Why? What theories do you think are most helpful for you in this example?

Example 2

In a reflective practice support group that has been running for 5 weeks it has become increasingly obvious that a group member called Elena regularly reminds the facilitator called Shu-jun that some people haven't spoken much in the group. She also reminds Shu-jun about things Shu-jun may have forgotten to do in her role as the group facilitator.

Reflective Questions 1

What do you think about this situation? What would you do in Shu-jun's position?

Response

Initially Shu-jun feels that she should act on all of Elena's observations. But when she starts to reflect on this, she realises that she does not want to single out anyone who has not spoken much in the group. Some people don't want to say much but Shu-jun wants them to know that there is still a place for them in the group. Shu-jun finds that she is beginning to feel annoyed about the pressure she is feeling from Elena. Some theoretical ideas occur to her. Is her authority under attack? Is Elena trying to occupy the golden child role in the group? Is Elena testing her to see if she can trust her?

Shu-jun decides to share with the group that she has noticed that sometimes, when she seems to have forgotten or ignored something in the group, it is helpful to have a reminder. She tells the group that they may notice, though, that she doesn't act on some reminders immediately. They may want to ask her about her decision-making process in the regular reviews they have together.

Rationale

Why did Shu-jun choose to say this? Here are some possible reasons.

Firstly, she didn't want to shame anyone in the group by seeming to tell them off. The interventions may have been motivated by purely good intentions and Shu-jun wanted to acknowledge that. She also wanted to gently assert her authority by clarifying that she would still make a decision about what actions to take or not take. But in the spirit of transparency she is open to being questioned about her thinking. Shu-jun reminded everyone that they had already set up a review process for this to happen. But she didn't invite people to question her in the moment. If, on reflection, people in the group felt they needed some answers, the review process would be available for them to ask questions. She notes to herself, that she may have opened herself up to being questioned about every decision she makes. This isn't necessarily going to be helpful in terms of the group fulfilling their agreed task so she needs to be mindful about this. To sum up, Shu-jun didn't focus in any depth on Elena's behaviour but used the theory to think about the kind of intervention that would be most helpful for a reflective practice group.

Reflective Questions 2

What do you think about Shu-jun's response. Would you do anything differently? What other theories might you draw from?

Intergroup Dynamics

Example 3

Sophie is the facilitator of a reflective practice support group for case workers who work with people who have experienced gender-based violence. She shares

> *the dates for the next group meetings. Two group members called Hamsa and Shruti are from Muslim and Hindu faith backgrounds. They point out that all the breaks coincide with the Christian calendar of festivals. Sophie is horrified that she missed this. She offers her profound apologies. She is so full of guilt and shame about this that she keeps checking every aspect of practical arrangements with them, ignoring everyone else in the group. Hamsa and Shruti aren't comfortable with this. They didn't want to be foregrounded for everything. They had hoped that by mentioning this, Sophie would contain her own shame and think with the group about the best way forward. They had expected her to take a reflective rather than a reactive approach.*

Hamsa and Shruti tried to reclaim some agency by pointing out the focus and bias of the date-setting. However, Sophie's response paradoxically puts them into a more dependent, enmeshed position. Sophie is feeling terrible about what she has done. Hamsa and Shruti are uncomfortable that they have upset the facilitator. They may even think they have to play a placatory role to make things alright for her by reassuring her they are ok. They wish they hadn't said anything. They are back to feeling they have no agency. It is so easy to slip into this circular and ever-repeating dynamic.

Reflective Questions and Comments

Could the facilitator have created an opportunity for something more creative to have occurred?

Reading this account, how do you feel? What might you do differently? Would ideas about parallel processes, cultural shame, in group/outgroup, scapegoating etc. be of any help to you?

Does spending time reflecting on your own assumptions, cultural prestige or lack of prestige, help you to maintain a reflective rather than a reactive position? Apologising profusely is what many of us might want to do in this kind of a situation. It's intuitive. However, a reflective facilitator questions their intuition. Is their intuition based on assumptions and biases? Is their intuitive response going to make matters worse?

Possible response

What do you think of this as a more reflective response from Sophie?

> *Sophie apologises and acknowledges that this was an oversight on her part. She thanks Hamsa and Shruit for pointing out the error. She says she will review the dates and she asks people to send her any other significant dates for cultural holidays. She says she will then send out new dates that more equally reflect cultural holidays. Sophie says that she will be taking this*

into consideration when setting new dates in the future and she asks the group (not individuals) how they feel about pointing out when she may have missed something important.

Reflective questions

Which of the eight compendium terms, included in this chapter, does/do Sophie's possible response connect with?

What might you do differently? Why?

Example 4

Hannah runs a reflective practice support group for multilingual therapists. It has been meeting regularly for six sessions. The therapists had all been looking for a place where they could feel less marginalised, more validated and where they could share experiences where they felt they would be understood. They say they feel relieved to have found such a group. It is a cohesive group. They feel they belong.

However, Hannah is starting to feel uncomfortable with a kind of groupthink that seems to be developing. It is difficult to imagine anything but a consensus view being acceptable in this group. It seems that the professional world outside the group is viewed as hostile, whereas the group is safe.

Hannah is concerned not to collude in maintaining this view, but she reminds herself that this is still the early stages for the group. They may only be ready, at the moment, for a single dimensional version of safety. Her job is to help them to find a place from which they feel able to view themselves as well as others with a critical (in the creative sense of the word) eye.

Hannah reminds herself of her job to hold the frame. She needs to hold the external frame for this group so that they have some protected time and space together. She thinks about jelly. You pour loose jelly into a mould. Until a jelly has set, it cannot hold a shape without the jelly mould. Once it is set, it doesn't need the container to surround it. It can tolerate some pressure from outside without disintegrating. At the moment, Hannah thinks, this group still feels tender and a little loose. It is not the time yet for the outside world to take up a position in the group. The group needs time to set.

Reflective Questions

What do you think about how Hannah thinks about the group?

How might Hannah's own anxiety contribute to how she misses the needs of the group to take time to repair from their experiences of marginalisation and of being misunderstood?

What do you think about challenging group conformity or groupthink (Janis, 1971) in this kind of situation? If you decide not to challenge, how do you manage not to collude with "us and them" thinking?

Concluding Thoughts

In this chapter we have thought about the preoccupying issue of group dynamics for facilitators of groups. Trainee facilitators often express their concern about group dynamics by asking for help to deal with difficult conversations and difficult people. Facilitating difficult conversations seems to transform in people's minds into the management of difficult people. The conversations remain difficult if they aren't facilitated well. I hope this chapter has shown a more complex side to group dynamics. It's not just about a group of difficult, separate individuals. A group is a dynamic system of interconnected members. I have tried to demystify some of the concepts that have sprung up since the term group dynamics was first used. They may help to explain what is going on in the system of the group. I also offer a caution about relying too heavily on theoretical conceptualisations and hypotheses.

There are however connections between people's behaviour in groups and their early experiences of family contexts. Shame and addressing shame in groups presents particular challenges. This includes individual shame, collective shame and cultural shame. We have viewed shame from both group members' and facilitators' perspectives and thought about how difficult it is to unveil shame in a way that does not embed shame more deeply into the fabric of the group.

The practical examples in the chapter illustrate both interpersonal and intergroup dynamics, and possible responses from facilitators. There are clearly many different ways of responding. I have tried to keep the purpose of a reflective group clearly in mind, aiming not to wander into the territory of a facilitator of a therapeutic or clinical supervision group.

Theory should serve our practice, not the other way round. Theory can be useful in helping us to unravel ourselves from the projections and pushes and pulls that occur in groups. It can be tempting, though, to lean on the theory and rely on it for support, like a prop. That is understandable when we are starting out. But at some stage we will need to be brave enough to remove the prop, trust in our own footsteps and leave our own footprint. We will need to make ethical decisions that require ethical maturity. This is what we focus on in the next chapter. But first, a couple of reflective, meta questions.

Meta-questions

How are you finding the structure of the chapters so far? They are generally following a pattern: introducing the topic, looking at the topic in depth, concluding with a summary of the main points. Do you like it as a structure? Is it boring and repetitive? I am trying to model the structure of reflective practice groups. How do you react to that structure? Why do you think that is? Is there anything interesting or useful that emerges for you from considering the answers to these questions?

References

American Psychological Association. (2025). Group dynamics. Retrieved from https://dictionary.apa.org/group-dynamics (accessed 29 May 2025).

Bion, W. R. (1961). *Experiences in groups and other papers.* Tavistock Publications.

Bowen, M. (1978). *Family therapy in clinical practice.* Jason Aronson.

Budiarto, Y., & Helmi, A. F. (2021). Shame and self-esteem: A meta-analysis. *Europe's Journal of Psychology,* 17(2), 131–145. doi:10.5964/ejop.2115.

Brown, J. & Errington, L. (2024). Bowen family systems theory and practice: Illustration and critique revisited. *Australian and New Zealand Journal of Family Therapy,* 45, 135–155. doi:10.1002/anzf.1589.

Costa, B. (2020). *Other tongues: Psychological therapies in a multilingual world.* PCCS Books.

Fernando, S. (2010). *Mental health, race and culture* (3rd edition). Bloomsbury Academic.

Freire, P., Ramos, M. B., Macedo, D. P. 1., & Shor, I. (2018). *Pedagogy of the oppressed* (50th anniversary edition). Bloomsbury Academic.

Janis, I. L. (1971). Groupthink. *Psychology Today,* 5(6), 43–46, 74–76.

Jurkovic, G. J. (1997). *The plight of the parentified child.* Brunner/Mazel.

Knight, K., Sperlinger, D., & Maltby, M. (2010). Exploring the personal and professional impact of reflective practice groups: a survey of 18 cohorts from a UK clinical psychology training course. *Clinical Psychology & Psychotherapy,* 17(5), 427–437. doi:10.1002/cpp.660.

Kortegast, C., Teso, L., & Jaekel, K. (2024). Supervision as a liberatory practice: Supporting early-career residence life professionals. *The Journal of College and University Student Housing,* 50(3), 84–97. doi:10.71348/ 001c.133731.

Lewin, K. (1947). Frontiers in group dynamics: Concept, method and reality in social science; social equilibria and social change. *Human Relations,* 1(1), 5–41. doi:10.1177/001872674700100103.

McCauley, D. M., Sloan, C. J., Xia, M., & Fosco, G. M. (2021). Same family, divergent realities: How triangulation preserves parents' illusory harmony while adolescents navigate interparental conflicts. *Journal of Family Psychology,* 35(2), 128–137. doi:10.1037/fam0000785.

McKenzie-Mavinga, I. (2026). *A Black empathic approach to psychotherapy: Growing from rage to compassion* (1st ed.). Routledge. doi:10.4324/9781003479994.

Minuchin, S. (1974). *Families and family therapy.* Harvard University Press.

Moreno, Z. T. (1987). Psychodrama, role theory and the concept of the social atom. In J. Zeig (ed.), *The evolution of psychotherapy* (pp. 341–358). Brunner/Mazel. www.psychodrama.org.uk/wp-content/uploads/2021/01/Psychodrama-Role-Theory-The-Social-Atom-.pdf.

Nancheva, N. (2016). Power and minority rights. In A. Farazmand (ed.), *Global encyclopedia of public administration, public policy, and governance.* Springer. doi:10.1007/978-3-319-31816-5_1401-1.

Pérez, J. A. & Molpeceres, M. A. (2018). The new moral power of minorities. *International Review of Social Psychology,* 31(1), 5. doi:10.5334/irsp.18.

Rosenberg, M. B., & Chopra, D. (2015). *Nonviolent communication: A language of life: Life-changing tools for healthy relationships.* PuddleDancer Press.

Suggested Further Reading on Culture, Race, Oppression, and Discrimination in Relational Work

Ahmad, M. (2026). *A new introduction to counselling and psychotherapy: Embedding context, diversity, and equity into practice* (1st edition). Routledge. doi:10.4324/9781003497592.

Ellis, E. (2024). *Transforming race conversations: A healing guide for us all.* W. W. Norton & Company.

Khan, M. (2023). *Working within diversity: A reflective guide to anti-oppressive practice in counselling and therapy.* Jessica Kingsley Publishers.

Ryde, J. (2019). *White privilege unmasked: How to be part of the solution.* Jessica Kingsley Publishers.

Turner, D. (2025). *Decolonising counselling and psychotherapy: Depoliticised pathways towards intersectional practice.* Routledge.

Chapter 9

Making Difficult Decisions

Introduction

Case Example

I am facilitating a reflective practice support group which has been starting to meet regularly. This is the third session. The Sharer, called Ayesha has just finished sharing her dilemma and I make an empathic connection with her. Next, I check that she wants to hear from the rest of the group. Ayesha is happy to hear from the other group members. There is nothing she particularly wants or doesn't want to hear back from people. I open up the floor to the rest of the group. A group member, called Mo is keen to respond and begins by asking a question. Ayesha replies to the question. Mo and Ayesha quickly get into a conversation. Before long, I notice that the rest of the group is beginning to disengage.

Reflective Questions

What would you do? Does the situation in the example cause you any anxiety? Why? What are the stakes involved with any intervention you might make? We look at this case, in detail, later in the chapter.

It can be tempting to avoid making difficult decisions. They are, by definition, uncomfortable. Why can't someone else make them? Yet facilitators of reflective groups must make decisions continually, often minute by minute. The question is not whether decisions will be required, but how they can be made with ethical maturity.

Drawing on the work of Michael Carroll and Elisabeth Shaw (Carroll & Shaw, 2013), I understand *ethical maturity* as the ability to recognise and apply ethical principles thoughtfully and consistently, with courage and humility, particularly in situations where there may be conflicting values.

Making difficult decisions ethically, relationally and contextually is an inherent feature of challenging conversations. Throughout this book – and especially in this chapter – I offer numerous examples of facilitators grappling with ethical dilemmas and making complex decisions grounded in ethical maturity. In this

DOI: 10.4324/9781003658924-9

chapter, we consider the ethical frameworks that inform such decision-making. What supports reflective group facilitators to act with ethical maturity?

The Purpose of Ethics

One of the principal purposes of ethics in the supportive professions is to protect those who hold less power and agency within a relationship. "First, do no harm" captures this intent. It is a principle which has frequently been associated with the Hippocratic Oath – an oath of ethics taken traditionally by medical doctors. Ethical codes establish non-negotiable boundaries – core principles that define responsible and safe practice.

In practice, however, reflective group facilitators frequently experience tension between ethical guidance and their own drive to act on empathic or compassionate impulses. You may feel drawn to offer more than the guidelines permit. The phrase "I was only being human" is often, however, invoked to discourage scrutiny and justify actions that stretch or challenge policies and codes. While policies may at times warrant review, such challenges are generally most productive when explored reflectively, through dialogue and open discussion.

I certainly understand how powerful the pull of compassion can be. It can be hard to give a considered rationale for the pull which leads to our actions. Developing such a rationale requires careful examination of our own needs, our impulses to rescue, and the potential unintended consequences of undermining another person's autonomy and agency. Invoking "humanity" can be an expedient explanation for difficult decisions, It is, of course, true that at times a response grounded in human instinct may indeed be appropriate. However, we cannot know this unless we are willing to scrutinise our motivations with honesty and care. The "easy (or instinctual) option" may not be wrong, but it should signal a red flag for reflection.

The purpose of an ethical framework is not solely to protect clients; it is also to protect practitioners. Limitless generosity carries a cost. Over time, it can lead to exhaustion and collapse – like a balloon slowly losing its air. Thomas Skovholt offers an alternative to this model in his concept of *Boundaried Generosity*, which he describes as "this paradoxical style of giving and protecting at the same time" (Skovholt, 2012, p. 139). Boundaried Generosity supports resilience and sustainability in relationship-intensive professions. How facilitators attend to their own care and limits is therefore not separate from ethics; it is a clear expression of ethical maturity and professional sustainability.

Relational and Contextual Ethics, Ethical Maturity, and Ethical Practice

Relational ethics and ethical frameworks help us think about how to behave in relationship with others and with the world around us (Gabriel & Reeves,

2024). Contextual ethics are integral to relational ethics (Ahmad, 2025). They guide us in considering our own and others' contexts, identities, worldviews, and social status when we are making ethical decisions.

Ethical maturity (Carroll & Shaw, 2013) and effective reflective group facilitation share many common characteristics. Ethical maturity is demonstrated in the reflective capacity to discern right from wrong and to accept that there may not be such clearcut and absolute divisions between them. Ethical maturity also requires the courage to act and to remain relationally accountable, as well as the humility and the acceptance and willingness to learn from mistakes. It requires a commitment to continuous learning. It's about internalising ethical principles and making decisions based on them, even when there are no official guidance or prohibitions. Ethical maturity can be regarded as a form of *practical wisdom*: "a worldly understanding born of reflection and experience." (Luxmoore, 2022, p. 139).

A study by Argyris and Schön (1978) revealed that people were surprised to find that they didn't actually practise their *espoused theories* (what they said they believed) but they practised according to other guiding principles, their *theories-in-use* (the actual theories that guided their behaviour). Or in other words: "What people say, what people do, and what they say they do are entirely different things" (attributed to the anthropologist Margaret Mead).

Doing what we say we do is a good definition of ethical maturity in practice. It is ethical integrity. But there are contextual pressures that may make this common sense position difficult to maintain.

The concept of moral injury was presented in the introductory chapter. Moral injury helps to explain the distress people can experience when the system around them prohibits them from acting on their values. Sometimes, this differential between what we say and what we do comes about because of a clash between our professional ethical guidelines and the practices of the institutions for which we work. We may experience pressure to stretch or ignore guidelines. However, faced with so many demands, how can we know if we are stretching the framework because of our own needs?

The Role of Reflection

Ethical integrity ties together our knowledge, experience, openness to failing, learning, and our courage to act. Ethical integrity and ethical maturity are difficult to achieve in isolation. This is why supervision, or reflecting with others, plays such a crucial role. Supervision implements reflection-*in-action* (Schön, 1983). Reflection-in-action involves us thinking and drawing from ourselves, as well as from theory about practice, in the moment. It helps facilitators to review potential entanglements and anxieties that get in the way of putting into practice their espoused theory. Facilitators don't just rely on the ethical code to make their decisions. Ethical practice is performative

(Phelan et al., 2019). In fact, it involves people in continually reflecting and making choices or, as Marilyn Silverman puts it, engaging with everyday ethics (Silverman, 2003).

Existing Guidelines for Reflective Practice Support Group Facilitation

Ethical codes help to steady a facilitator's external frame. In a reflective group the wise application of the ethical code, and the maintenance of the external frame, enable the internal frame to function.

There are some published guidelines available for facilitators. For example, the Association of Facilitators UK has its own code of practice.[1] The Association for Specialists in Group Work (ASGW),[2] a division of the American Counseling Association, offers guidance to equip helping professionals with essential knowledge and skills to foster ethical and socially just group work practices. The guidelines include observations about values and value-based beliefs such as:

- Fidelity to diversity, equity, and inclusion.
- Conviction that group work has specific, distinct, and unique benefits.
- Belief that group work holds great potential to facilitate human growth, development, and healing in the robust interpersonal environment.
- Research-informed practice.
- Excellence through ongoing professional development that includes continuing education, supervision, and ongoing examination and adoption of culturally competent practices.

These are all useful principles. They may not, though, help practitioners with difficult decisions in the moment. Existing ethical frameworks for related professions such as the British Association for Counselling and Psychotherapy Ethical Framework (BACP, 2018) offer guidance on ethical behaviour for counsellors and psychotherapists. The BACP and other frameworks may help you to develop your own guidelines. Here are ten of my ethical practice guidelines for reflective group facilitation which, together with the tips in the Appendix, may help you in difficult moments.

These guidelines attend to ethical tensions I have experienced in groups as a participant, and which I aim to apply in the groups I facilitate. Some of these ethical practice guidelines have already been introduced earlier in the book. In order to illustrate how they apply in practice, relevant case examples are included below.

Ten Ethical Practice Guidelines for Reflective Group Facilitation

1 Be clear about the psychological level of the group. A reflective practice support group is not a therapy group. You can be informed by psychological models but do you have permission to act as a psychotherapist for group members? (The answer is *no!*).
2 Know your group. Before you begin, ask yourself a selection of screening questions e.g., Am I the right person to facilitate this group? Do I need a screening process for potential group members? Is this a group that is ready for challenge? Keep context in mind. Don't force a cohesive group into coherency if it is not ready. Does it need to warm up before it can tolerate difference? (The example of Mothertongue in Chapter 8 illustrates this.) Am I aware of potential intergroup power dynamics?
3 Have a working agreement.
4 Put in regular reviews so that participants have a chance to react, respond to, and influence the group process as it develops. It is better not to assume that everyone is ok and in agreement with your proposals and interventions.
5 Make it clear to the group that you won't talk about the group process (this doesn't include administration issues) with any group member outside of the group. This is in the interest of fairness for all.
6 Keep in mind the group-as-a whole as well as the individual group members. Try not to isolate an individual or yourself from the group. Avoid focusing on one member of the group and losing the rest of the group. Avoid two group members engaging in a conversation between them that excludes the rest of the group.
7 Conduct yourself with transparency and accountability and work on your relationship with your own authority. Notice as the group develops and position yourself as the facilitator correspondingly. Talk about the process of the group with the group (*talk about the talking*).
8 Strive to own, without condemnation, your inadequacy and your capacity for being disappointing, and learn from those experiences.
9 A commitment to self-awareness goes with the role of facilitator. You have a responsibility to your group members for your continuous personal development.
10 You need your own supervisory resource for this work.

The following six practice examples relate to the ethical practice guidelines on this list. It is often the case that examples about ethical dilemmas present situations where things have gone wrong. I sometimes receive feedback about training materials I have developed from people who want to see what it looks like when things go well. So, as well as the unfortunate examples, I also provide some ideas for what I think might have worked better. In Example 4

I show how specific ethical practice guidelines influence my thinking and actions. They are just suggestions, though. I invite you to reflect on my suggestions. What might you have done differently? Why?

Example 1

(Corresponds to numbers 1 and 4 of the ten ethical practice guidelines above.)

> *I start to facilitate a new reflective practice support group for six cultural mediators [3] who work in a health service. I begin by sharing a suggestion for a working agreement with them. I say that it may not seem very democratic, but I would like to start with a suggested agreement rather than co-creating the working agreement with them from scratch. I make it clear though, that we can discuss the recommended principles and we can add or remove some, except for those principles which I need in order to hold the group effectively.*

Rationale

In theory it may seem ideal to construct a working agreement from scratch with a group. This models democratic principles of negotiation, collaboration and compromise. In practice though, this may be hard to achieve without sacrificing elements that contribute to establishing and building trust at the early stage of a group. Here are some thoughts about why that might be the case.

Firstly, a co-designed working agreement takes a lot of time. Although that is not a bad thing (in fact setting up the working agreement needs not to be rushed), you could spend the whole of the first session on establishing and getting consensus and compromise for an agreement. There is then no time for any of the principal task of the group to be broached (e.g. reflective practice in refugee case work, interpreters' approach to self-care etc.). Group members, who do not have prior experience of this type of group, could be forgiven for feeling frustrated and for querying the point of a reflective practice support group.

Additionally, trust at this early stage in the group is fragile and it is easy to shatter. If members of a group decide they want something in the agreement that, for example, I as a facilitator don't feel I can deliver with ethical integrity, I have effectively created a difficult situation on day one.

Let us imagine a group that agrees on a communication style in which any member may speak for as long as they wish, without interruption. At first glance, this may seem a reasonable and inclusive approach. But in my experience, both as a facilitator and as a group member, such agreements often result in one or two voices dominating the conversation, frequently without challenge. This can be very frustrating for other members of the group who may leave the group as a consequence. Members from under-represented backgrounds may encounter difficulty in finding a space in a group for their voice to be heard above the clamour of louder voices. However, it isn't only more traditionally confident group members who take the floor. Some group members, shaped by their own past experiences of disempowerment, may assert a strong right to be heard, unintentionally limiting space for others who feel less able to speak. This is a difficult dynamic to manage with care and compassion, without reinforcing inequality.

For these reasons, a request that group members be allowed to speak for as long as they wish without challenge conflicts with my values and ethical principles regarding good practice in groups. I do not suggest that my values are objectively right or wrong; others may hold different beliefs. However, I could not facilitate a group in which extended, uninterrupted speeches were an accepted feature of the group culture. If this were a core requirement, the group would need a different facilitator.

It is important to me to be honest and transparent about my position, including the power I hold in the facilitator role. This power is not owned by me but lent by the group for the duration of the work and in service of the group's purpose. Used responsibly, it is a vital element of containment and safeguarding – responsibilities I take seriously.

Even at this early stage in the life of the group, some members may feel alienated by not being invited to co-design the agreement. But thinking carefully with the group from the beginning about our impact on each other, means that difficult feelings and comments can be acknowledged and the group can talk and think about them productively. Incidentally, this also gives an opportunity to model "talking about the talking", early on in the life of the group.

So, one of the principles in the working agreement I offer is for participants to be mindful about how they are speaking and to aim to be concise so that they allow space for others to contribute. Because the working agreement lends the facilitator the role and the authority to maintain agreed principles, this means that as the facilitator I have been authorised by the group to remind people if they forget. It is very easy to forget to be concise when you are enthusiastic. But, by using the working agreement, I can refer back to the agreement with respect and without shaming an enthusiastic participant. I have found that some people, including those who are neurodivergent or who have never had support to think about their communication before, welcome the gentle explanation of the rationale and some guidance.

Example 2

(Corresponds to numbers 3, 4, and 7 of the ten ethical practice guidelines above.)

> *I start to run a reflective practice group for therapists, some of whom have recently finished their training. This is the first session after the trial group session. There seems to still be some confusion about the nature of the group. Some of the group members are familiar with personal development groups where participants are encouraged to express and explore their feelings. In the personal development groups they have attended they have often sat for long periods in silence and discomfort, until something emerges, with minimal intervention from the facilitator. They are expecting something similar from the reflective practice support group I am facilitating and they express their frustration with me. I am an experienced psychotherapist as well as a reflective practice group facilitator and I feel I can offer the type of group they are talking about. I am tempted to do so but I decide not to.*

Reflective Questions

How might you have felt as the facilitator in this situation? What do you think about the decision I make? Might you have decided to do something different? Why?

This is what was going through my mind when I was deciding what to do.

Response

I could see the group members' perspective and I could understand that they would feel disappointed if this was not the type of group experience they were expecting. I also felt that perhaps I needed to prove myself. Maybe they thought I had chosen this type of a group structure because I didn't feel able to run a loosely structured group. Fortunately, I managed to catch myself quickly. That was my ego talking.

I quickly reminded myself about the level of the group and the working agreement we had all signed up to. I didn't have the permission of all the group members to run a group at the psychological level, as some of the group members were hoping. I reminded myself to trust in my confidence to facilitate reflective practice groups. But I didn't want to respond from a sense of pique. I wanted to respond with ethical maturity and integrity. Here is what I said. I offer my rationale for what I said afterwards.

> *I think some of you may have had recent experience of a type of personal development group that is often used in psychotherapy training courses. Is that right?*
>
> *The answer was "yes" so I continued.*
>
> *A reflective practice group is a bit different from a personal development group. My understanding of the difference is that a personal development group foregrounds people's personal growth, sometimes related to practice,*

> *sometimes purely for the development of the self. A reflective practice group aims to increase self-awareness, but always foregrounding practice. In a reflective practice group, participants also think about methods, critical thinking, the consideration of what went well or not so well, and collaboratively they dare to imagine new responses to new situations.*
>
> *It may be that you decide that this group is not for you, but are you ok for us to continue for the three sessions we have organised? That way it gives the group a chance to get going, and you can experience it more fully before making a decision. In the third session we have a review planned and we can talk some more about the experience then if you like. How does that sound?*

At that stage some of the group members might still have decided that they wanted to leave there and then. As it happens, they all agreed to give the three sessions a try and by the review they all said they were satisfied enough to continue.

Rationale

In my response I try to recognise people's feelings and prior experiences. I try not to act defensively. I don't apologise for the group format but I acknowledge some people may not like the format. I want people to have the opportunity to give the group a chance. From my experience, I can see that there is a good chance that these group members will find some benefit from it. But I also want to respect the ethical principle of client autonomy (BACP, 2018). The group members can still leave right away if they want to but my response aims to slow down the decision-making on all our parts, so that we can arrive at a more considered conclusion.

Example 3

(Corresponds to numbers 2, 4, 7, and 8 of the ten ethical practice guidelines above.)

We return to the example which first appeared at the start of this chapter.

> *I am facilitating a reflective practice support group which has been starting to meet regularly. This is the third session. The Sharer, called Ayesha has just finished sharing her dilemma and I make an empathic connection with Ayesha. Next, I check that she wants to hear from the rest of the group. Ayesha is happy to hear from the other group members. There is nothing she particularly wants or doesn't want to hear back from people. I open up the floor to the rest of the group. A group member, called Mo is keen to respond and begins by asking a question. Ayesha replies to the question. Mo and Ayesha quickly get into a conversation. Before long, I notice that the rest of the group is beginning to disengage.*

Response

I was feeling under pressure and I considered saying this: "Can we all please remember what we agreed about asking questions in the working agreement?"

I didn't say that though. I realised I had made a mistake and I wanted to be honest and at the same time not make it all about me! This is what I said.

> *Ayesha and Mo, excuse me, but can I just pause this conversation for a moment? It is my mistake and I should have intervened earlier. If you remember in our agreement, we said we would refrain from asking the Sharer questions and getting into a two-way conversation at this point. We also agreed that if we forgot and a question was asked, the Sharer wouldn't answer in the moment but would have a chance to answer any questions they wanted to, at the end when we come back to them for the last word. It was my responsibility to manage that and I am afraid I got carried away with listening to the conversation. I apologise and I am asking now if we can revert back to the process we had agreed on. Ayesha, you will get a chance to answer anything you want to at the end and I will make sure I manage the time so you get that opportunity. Is that ok with everyone?*

Rationale

In the first response, the facilitator would be adhering to the principles that have been established, and which constitute the external frame.

In the response I actually give, I try to attend also to the internal frame. I talk about the process. I want to take into account my own position, my relationship with Ayesha and Mo and with the rest of the group. I try to respond with sensitivity so that Ayesha and Mo don't feel blamed. I accept responsibility for the deviation from the agreement and the frame. I renew my commitment to hold the frame in terms of the time boundary. I am aiming to adhere to the principles of ethical thinking, while responding to the specific situation in front of me and making an ethical decision (Gabriel & Reeves, 2024). As in the previous example, I check with the group members to see what they think about my proposal. I don't want to assume the group is with me. If they don't agree, we'll talk about it. It's how I try to remain accountable, and how I perform or enact ethical integrity in practice. What I have offered isn't the definitive way of managing a situation like this. It is *one* way of trying to act with ethical maturity.

Usually, in a working agreement with a reflective practice support group I include a section about the communication processes in the group. In the interests of transparency, I prioritise talking about the talking, or meta-communication. We think about what we are saying, the words we are using to say it, and how many words and how much of the allotted time we are taking to say it. We think about our potential impact on each other. We think about when and why questions may be a good idea and when not. We also talk about situations where two people can end up having a long conversation while the rest of the group watches on. In a group that is time-limited it is important to think about how we make the best use of the time, and we give the fairest opportunities for everyone to be heard. This aligns with the ethical principles of fairness and inclusion (BACP, 2018; see also www.asgw.org).

Reflective Questions

What do you think about my response to Ayesha and Mo?

Does it seem to be an example of performative ethical practice, and/or of acting with ethical maturity? Why or why not?

What might you do differently?

Example 4

(Corresponds to numbers 1, 2, 4, 6, 7, and 10 of the ten ethical practice guidelines above.)

> *Yana has been running a group for caseworkers who support bereaved parents who have recently lost a child. Although the group members come from different organisations, the group seems to have gelled and people seem comfortable with each other. At the fourth session, one of the group members, Nidia, shares that she has been supporting parents whose child died by suicide. It is a very difficult and painful story to hear. When Nidia has finished, another group member, Sachin, wants to respond. Sachin is visibly very upset and he starts to talk about a family he knows, whose child killed herself. He says the other children in the family have never emotionally recovered from the experience, (and probably never will). Sachin continues to say that he thinks parents whose children die by suicide should take responsibility for having messed up their child's life so much that the only option a child feels they have, is to die. The room goes silent. Some group members are looking very uncomfortable.*
>
> *Yana isn't sure what to do. She suggests that as it is near the end of the session, the group can finish early and have a review next time.*

Reflective Questions

What are your thoughts about this?

What do you think about the facilitator ending the group early and offering a review for next time?

I have some concerns about this.

My concern is that by ending the group early, people including Nidia, are left feeling uncontained. They may be wondering if the facilitator feels out of her depth. They might be left wondering what to do with their anxiety. Some group members, including Sachin, may feel judged. They might start to worry about the review. Although regular reviews are generally a good principle, applying that principle without reflection is not. An ethical principle is not a panacea. Ethical maturity means that we assess constantly what, how and if a principle should be enacted. This is a justification in itself of reflective practice. When Donald Schön talked about *reflection-in-action* (Schön, 1983) he said that we first need to gain experience of reflecting *on* action in spaces away from the action. To think back about what we have done. With space, and without the pressure in the moment, we can transform our experiences into knowledge. Knowledge is flexible. It can be applied to future situations. A reflective practice support group provides this type of space. With the opportunity this space provides, we can reflect on our actions, build our confidence to *reflect-in-action* and make difficult decisions in response to situations, as and when they arise.

A Suggested Response and Rationale

Hopefully as a facilitator Yana has supervision (as recommended in ethical practice guideline 10) so she has the opportunity to reflect on a situation like this. There are competing needs and tensions in this example. I am not going to pretend to have an ideal solution for this situation but I would probably not have finished early. I like to think that I would have connected briefly with the group member, Sachin, who responded to Nidia, with empathy. This links with the idea we have already seen of *empathising with the "no"* (Rosenberg & Chopra, 2015). I would be aiming not to isolate or scapegoat Sachin, neither endorsing nor silencing him. This also links to ethical practice guideline 6, which emphasises keeping in mind the group-as-a whole and avoiding isolating individuals. For the same reason, I would connect only briefly with Sachin and then connect quickly with Nidia, the Sharer. I am not aiming to isolate her either. I would also have said out loud, with transparency, that we all seemed to be strongly affected by what we had heard. Some people might feel a connection with Nidia or Sachin, with both of them, or with neither of them. This links to ethical practice guideline 7, which recommends transparency and the facilitator's use of their own authority with accountability and awareness.

One aim of my response would be to ensure that people knew they had permission to feel however they wanted, without taking things any further for the moment. I might even suggest we do a one-minute silent reflection to connect with how we feel. This would be a small break with a clear purpose. It might give us all some breathing and cooling space so that we could come back to a reflective mode and start to think together about what we would do next. Can we be a group that acts with coherency as well as cohesion? I would try to optimise our chances of remaining a group even if we have different opinions and feelings.

Example 5

(Corresponds to numbers 2, 5, and 6 of the ten ethical practice guidelines above.)

> *I am setting up a new reflective practice support group which I am planning to facilitate. It is for a group of experienced caseworkers and nurses working in a voluntary sector (NGO) clinic called RR, which specialises in reproductive rights. I know that I need a minimum of four group members for the group to be viable. Three people have signed up and are very keen for this to go ahead. They say they are beginning to feel burned out from the work and they feel they need some support. I am also very keen to get this initiative going. I know how useful reflective practice support groups have been for other workers in similar contexts. But it is looking unlikely that the group will be viable as we only have three members so far. I am about to communicate this to the three interested people when I receive an enquiry from a different organisation, called CARA. They want to know if I have space for one of their workers, Caroline, who is keen to join a reflective practice support group. I say yes! Now the group will be viable.*

Reflective Question

What, if any, do you think are the ethical issues in this example?

Ethical Issues before a Group Begins

Facilitators must be clear about a group's nature, purpose, and membership before it begins. You might ask yourself questions (as recommended in ethical practice guideline 2). Is this going to be a group for people who share the same professional values? Is it going to be a cross-disciplinary group? Is it for people with different levels of experience? What is its purpose? Is it a group that is ready for challenge? What is the context? Is there a likelihood of intergroup power dynamics? These are all questions for the facilitator before the group begins.

In this case, the group was designed for professionals sharing similar values and experiences within a sensitive field. Admitting someone from outside that context – without ethical reflection – risks destabilising the group, especially when members are already fatigued and vulnerable. Decisions driven by practicality rather than by ethics can compromise safety and trust. A premature or poorly matched addition could create conflict and harm group cohesion.

Possible Alternative Response from a Facilitator

Before agreeing, I could speak with Caroline to explore her goals and to discuss the group's focus and context (without identifying potential group members). Together, we could explore whether this group was a good fit. Let's imagine that during this conversation it emerges that Caroline holds strong anti-abortion views and her intention in joining this group is to promote her views. I would probably decline her participation. This decision is not because I believe Caroline does not have the right to hold, or to promote her views. Given the fragility and level of need in this potential group though, my view, is that it is the wrong time to invite someone in, with a clear agenda that they wish to promote. I don't think the group will be able to hold itself, in the face of robust challenge at this stage. My decision is informed by ethical guidance which prioritises protection. Though a disappointing decision for Carolne, this is about the group's safety and purpose.

It may feel risky to have a conversation like this. It can be riskier not to.

Let's imagine the recommended conversation never occurs. This is what happens instead.

> *The group member joins the group and makes her anti-abortion views clear. The other group members are very upset. This long-awaited group ends abruptly. There are no further meetings and the already fatigued three workers (and possibly Caroline as well) feel battered by this experience.*

Broader Reflection

Ethical facilitation requires courage and relational accountability. Difficult decisions need to be made regularly in order to preserve the integrity of the group. Screening is not foolproof, but early attention to suitability can prevent harm. In rare cases, a facilitator may need to ask a member to leave if their participation undermines the group's function. The following example is based on a combination of my own experiences with different people.

> *A new member, who I will call Jenna, joins a long-standing group and quickly begins to dominate the sessions. Jenna finds turn-taking almost impossible and she leaves very little room for anyone else. There are several other behaviours that make it clear that she can't really tolerate being a member of a group. Some of the other group members are beginning to show signs that they can't really tolerate* ***her*** *being in the group.*

Some people can function well in communication on a one-to-one basis but they find a group overwhelms them and produces such levels of anxiety that they start to fragment. They may collapse, or they may flail about like Jenna.

When Jenna originally joined, I had thought that her challenge to the frame could be an opportunity for the group. However, it had begun to look like the group might not survive. I needed some help to think through my responsibility to Jenna and my responsibility to protect the integrity and purpose of the group. After careful consideration with my supervisor, and knowing Jenna had other therapeutic support in place (as we had already agreed at the contracting stage for this group), I decided to offer Jenna a meeting outside of the group to share my concerns about her and my dilemma about the suitability of the group. (I know that in the working agreement I make it clear that I don't talk to individuals about the group process outside of the group, but this meeting was about Jenna).

> *On a one-to-one basis we communicate well. Jenna listens closely to what I have to say. Then she responds. She says that she agrees. She thanks me for the opportunity to join the group. She says the opportunity has helped her to see she isn't ready for this kind of groupwork yet. She is already beginning to address this in her own therapy. Before she leaves our conversation, she says that she very much appreciates my honesty with her. She says that the clarity will help her to make something productive from the experience.*

It had been a difficult situation but I didn't view Jenna as a difficult person. I felt very optimistic about her. I truly believed she would transform this experience into something better.

Example 6

(Corresponds to numbers 9 and 10 of the ten ethical practice guidelines above.)

> *You have been facilitating a reflective practice support group for six months with a group that is very engaged and committed, The sharer has just finished telling the group about the case they want some help to think about. Listening to their story has touched you deeply. You want to be empathic and you think that disclosing a similar experience you had would be a good idea. You start to share a little bit and you realise suddenly that 15 minutes have gone by and that you are feeling very emotional.*

Reflective Questions

What do you think about this situation? Are there any ethical issues involved in the decision to self-disclose in this example?

I think there are.

Rationale

A facilitator could justify their decision by saying that this was a human response. I have already noted that it can be difficult to challenge someone who says, *"I was only being human"*. It is a phrase that may be used to justify behaviour and actions. Of course, engaging with our humanity is crucial in this work. But the phrase rationalises a reaction. It does not invite exploration and reflection. Supervision of our own work helps us to do that.

In the example, I lost track of time while I was self-disclosing. It is the facilitator's responsibility to hold the time boundary. What happens to the group if the facilitator unconsciously lets go of the responsibility the group has entrusted them with?

Once, in a discussion about whether to self-disclose, especially in groups, I was advised by a supervisor to "Only self-disclose if you *don't* need to". I have found this advice to be very useful. It helps me to notice whose needs are being met in the moment. If I *need* to share, then this is about *me*. If I don't need to share, then I can take a reflective position about whether or not this will be useful. This stance is both boundaried and generous.

Maintenance of trust is a long-term, rather than a short-term activity. Empathic connections can be quick to make and they are satisfying in the moment. They satisfy our short-term needs to be kind, and also to be appreciated. Both of which are fine in the short-term. But *long-term empathy* requires us to ethically consider the longer-term impact. Long-term empathy involves a commitment to maintain our empathic engagement over a sustained period of time. This takes work and it can be tiring. But the impact of having someone walk alongside you with boundaried generosity (Skovholt, 2012), someone who may be fallible yet reliable, cannot be overstated. Engaging fully with our humanity requires long-term empathy. I try to make difficult decisions as a group facilitator, thinking about the long-term implications as well as the short-term need.

Summary

Making decisions, difficult or otherwise, go with the job of holding the frame. Supervision can help us recognise when we are convincing ourselves that something is right even though we are aware it's a bit "iffy". Supervision, to paraphrase Maragaret Mead, helps us to recognise what we say, what we do, and what we say we do … so that we can *remind ourselves to do what we say we do*!

Ethical maturity is not something that can be learned from a manual. However, we all need to begin somewhere and I think it can be useful to have examples, even possible scripts when we are beginning, that act as props and prompts. Often trainers and supervisors frown on this idea. They encourage trainees to find the answers from within. Perhaps they forget what it is like to be a beginner. Being exhorted to draw repeatedly from a vacuum can be demotivating. Having a scaffold can help you to build your own structure and frame. When you are ready, you can take the scaffold down and go it alone. We will look at training in detail in Chapter 11.

I offered ten ethical practice guidelines for reflective group facilitation in the chapter. However, having recourse to ethical codes and guidelines is not sufficient. If we are to make our decisions with ethical maturity, then we need to reflect on them and act with courage according to our values and beliefs. That is not as easy as it sounds. It can take us many steps, repetitions of mistakes, resistance to change and many chapters of our story.

In her poem "Autobiography in Five Chapters", Portia Nelson (1993) tells a story. Each of the five chapters describes how she repeatedly falls into a hole in the sidewalk of a street she regularly uses. This happens four times. The fifth time, something changes. As she explains, "I walk down a different street."

Notes

1 See https://associationoffacilitators.co.uk/code-of-practice.
2 See www.asgw.org.
3 Cultural mediators facilitate communication between practitioners and clients in health and social care and other contexts by interpreting not just language but also cultural context.

References

Ahmad, M. (2025). *A new introduction to counselling and psychotherapy: Embedding context, diversity, and equity into practice* (1st edition). Routledge. doi:10.4324/9781003497592.

Argyris, C., & Schön, D. (1978). *Organizational learning: A theory of action perspective*. Addison-Wesley.

BACP. (2018). Ethical framework for the counselling professions. Retrieved from www.bacp.co.uk/events-and-resources/ethics-and-standards/ethical-framework-for-the-counselling-professions.

Carroll, M., & Shaw, E. (2013). *Ethical maturity in the helping professions: Making difficult life and work decisions*. Jessica Kingsley Publishers.

Gabriel, L., & Reeves, A. (2024). *Navigating relational ethics in day-to-day practice: Working ethically in the counselling professions* (1st edition). Routledge. doi:10.4324/9781003354970.

Luxmoore, N. (2022). *Supporting young people through everyday chaos: Counselling when things fall apart*. Jessica Kingsley Publishers.

Nelson, P. (1993). Autobiography in five chapters. In P. Nelson, *There's a hole in my sidewalk: The romance of self-discovery*. Beyond Words Publishing.

Phelan, M., Rudvin, M., Skaaden, H., & Kermit, P. (2019). *Ethics in public service interpreting* (1st ed.). Routledge. doi:10.4324/9781315715056.

Rosenberg, M. B., & Chopra, D. (2015). *Nonviolent communication: A language of life: Life-changing tools for healthy relationships*. PuddleDancer Press.

Schön, D. A. (1983). *The reflective practitioner: How professionals think in action*. Temple Smith.
Silverman, M. (2003). A personal journey in rural Ireland, 1980–2001. In P. Caplan (ed.), *The ethics of anthropology: Debates and dilemmas* (pp. 115–132). Routledge.
Skovholt, T. M. (2012). The counselor's resilient self. *Turkish Journal of Counseling and Guidance*, 4, 137–146.

Chapter 10

The Support–Challenge Continuum

Safety Revisited

In Chapter 4 I introduced the notion of dynamic safety as support plus challenge. In this chapter, I begin by thinking about specific mechanisms that contribute to dynamic safety. In a reflective practice group, the facilitator offers a working agreement and works with the group to create a safe enough space for everyone to feel free to reflect on their work and the impact their work has on them and on others. The working agreement represents a shared understanding and expectations of how everyone will behave, collaborate and communicate with each other so that sessions run fairly, sessions are effective, and the task the group has set itself is achieved. The safe enough space should provide enough support to help group members to improve their practice for the benefit of themselves, the people *they* support, and for their own work satisfaction. The working agreement comprises the frame for this safe enough space. The responsibility for holding the frame lies with the facilitator, particularly in the early days in the lifespan of a group. If the facilitator holds the frame too rigidly, the group has to adapt itself to fit the frame. If the frame is too loose, the frame cannot be trusted to hold. An effective frame allows for growth and change. It supports people to feel safe enough to trust and to be trusted, so that all the group members and the facilitator can dare to take risks together. Dynamic safety in a reflective group means safe enough, disappointing enough and confident enough to trust that if you make a mistake, together, with the other group members, you will all try your hardest to make sense of it and find a better response next time.

The Support–Challenge Continuum

How safe do people need to feel to be able to bring examples of incidents at work they are not proud of (as well as those they are)? There needs to be a balance between support and challenge. If there is only support, then even poor practice won't be challenged. If there is only challenge then people may

DOI: 10.4324/9781003658924-10

feel reticent to bring their mistakes. They think they will be automatically judged.

The support–challenge continuum comprises single and two-dimensional safety. Single-dimensional safety offers the dimension of support. Two-dimensional safety allows for an additional dimension. This dimension is challenge. A reflective practice group facilitator helps a group to navigate the continuum with sensitivity and also an awareness of the context.

Kurtz (2019) refers to the beliefs, behaviours and strategies in modern high-risk industries for managing organisational errors (Edmondson & Verdin, 2018). The thinking is that if workers are encouraged to be reflective and to feel that they can share mistakes within a non-blaming culture, then the organisation can learn from mistakes and improve itself. By modelling a compassionate attitude towards mistakes and valuing their learning, facilitators can help participants access the courage to share and learn from them, thus occupying the challenge end of the continuum. Obviously, there are different levels of errors. If you can catch a small error early, you can avoid and prevent a bigger one being made later on.

The context matters. The small mistakes that concern us in reflective and clinical practice, are often not at the technical level of practice. They involve entanglements in dynamics, getting caught up in any of the triangles – the drama triangle (Karpman, 1968), triangulated relationships (Minuchin, 1974), the triangle of power (Hawkins & McMahon, 2020). Feeling safe enough to trust that you can bring examples of those kinds of errors without fear of judgement means that taking a considered risk, and possibly failing, becomes a valued activity because of the potential for learning.

Of course, bigger errors of judgement that raise safeguarding concerns, require an appropriate response, balancing challenge with support. In the working agreements I use, I make it clear that if I have a safeguarding concern I may need to take action, or let an appropriate person know of my concern outside of the group. Safeguarding is philosophically challenging in all areas of life where we want to offer a safe, judgement-free, supportive and confidential space. Safeguarding imposes limits on that space. For reasons of honesty and transparency, those limits need to be made clear at the beginning of the first reflective group session.

How We Learn (and How Change Happens)

When we think about how people learn, and how real change happens, it helps to look at a few well-known learning models and how they're used in reflective groups. Kolb's *learning cycle* (1984) and Gibbs's *reflective cycle* (1988) both show learning as something that grows out of experience, reflection, and feedback. Learning isn't just repetitive practice. *Deliberate practice* (Ericsson, 2008; Husby, 2025) adds another useful perspective. What really makes the difference is the quality of the feedback. Knowing how to give good quality feedback is an important skill for everyone in the group. In reflective groups, that feedback doesn't just come from the facilitator; it also comes from the group itself.

In Kolb's learning cycle the starting point is a concrete experience. The experience is reflected upon. The learning from that reflection is applied to practice. A new experience occurs and the whole cycle is repeated. In Gibbs's reflective cycle the cycle is augmented by the incorporation of feelings and the emotional component of the experience.

The evaluation phases in the cycles help learners to achieve a more critically reflective approach where learning is deepened, dynamised and turned into action. This kind of reflection can open the door to creativity and spontaneity, helping people change how they think and act, and continue learning along the way.

Taken together, these models offer a strong foundation for reflective practice groups. The ongoing cycles of experience, reflection, and feedback help create groups that are both challenging and supportive – places where people feel safe enough to learn, grow, and change.

Bridging

As a reflective group facilitator I put the cycles of learning into action through a three-stage group model I built from practice. The stages are: *repair* (support and connection), *reflexivity* (learning from challenges), and *response* (the application of insights into individual/systemic practice) (Costa, 2024, p. 90).

Lev Vygotsky's (1978) ideas about learning, the zone of proximal development (ZPD) and scaffolding can be helpful for a facilitator. The ZPD represents the gap between what an individual can currently do and how far they can extend themselves with guidance and support. Scaffolding is a light frame that acts as a support, helping individuals bridge the gap and put new ideas into action. Bridging is also a concept in Page and Wosket's cyclical model of supervision (Page & Wosket, 2015). A *bridge*, in both clinical supervision and reflective practice, is an essential component. It is where reflection and action meet. In a reflective group, bridging might occur when the sharer is invited to have the last word. The sharer might summarise what they have heard, ask for any information they need and make a statement about what they are going to take with them from the experience of sharing and receiving responses. Sometimes there might be resistance to taking things forward. But frequently a sharer wants to think about what they will do differently, and imagine, perhaps through a scaffolding technique like trial role-reversing, how this new behaviour or intervention could impact on their clients. A reflective practice support group session might end like that.

We now turn to a closer look at how reflective groups can be structured in practice.

Structuring Reflective Practice Support Groups

The structure consists of three components:

1 The group session.
2 The stage of the group.
3 The sociocultural context.

1 The Group Session

The structure of the group session was referred to in Chapter 4. We look at the group session in more detail in this chapter. There are many ways of structuring a session. Arabella Kurtz's (2019) *intersubjective model*, for example, offers an a seven-step structure for a group session. The model I have developed is called *connect–share–respond.* This has six steps:

- agreement and warm up
- selecting and scheduling cases
- sharing
- connecting and responding
- last word from the sharer
- close.

Agreement and warm up involves agreeing to, or reviewing the working agreement (depending on whether this is the first session for a reflective practice support group or a continuation session). We also spend a few minutes checking in and warming back up to the group. Connecting back with previous sessions may happen at this point but there is no specific phase allocated for this activity.

Selecting and scheduling cases occurs next. In the reflective practice support groups I run, group members are encouraged to have thought of a case or a dilemma they want to bring in advance of the session, so that we can make maximum use of the time we have together. We call whoever brings a case or dilemma the *sharer.* The rest of the group members are called *participants.* We set the schedule for the session. We decide on the order of sharers at this point within the time available.

Sharing is the moment when the Sharer shares what they want to bring.

Connecting and responding is the opportunity for the participants to connect with and respond to the sharer. The responses vary. They may occupy different positions on the support–challenge continuum.

Last word from the sharer. We go back to the sharer for the last word. They may want to answer questions that participants have raised or create a bridge to the outside world in terms of new actions they may take.

Close. We allow at least 5 minutes for the group-as-a-whole to reflect, and for group members to share a closing comment that may link them with what they are going on to do after the group session finishes.

2 The Stage of the Group

In Chapter 5 we discussed stages of groups in different models. One was Tuckman's (1965), another was Proctor's (2008) normative, formative, and restorative (management, learning, and support) model. Different interventions are appropriate for different stages of a group. The support–challenge continuum is a good example of this. At the forming stages of a group, interventions will probably cluster around the support end of the continuum. As the group reaches a stage where it feels more robust and confident, it may need and be able to tolerate interventions at the challenge extreme of the continuum where change and transformation can occur.

3 The Sociocultural Context

The third component to consider when structuring reflective practice support groups encompasses the whole process of a reflective group. The focus is neither on the individual group session nor the developmental stages the group passes through. It is concerned with the way in which a group is put together, how it comes about, what sociocultural and political pressures it is subject to: the system in which it is situated and it functions. In various chapters I have discussed sociocultural pressures on groups and individual group members, and how some groups need to warm up slowly to be able to tolerate challenge. Individuals who come from communities, or who have had individual life experiences, where they have been oppressed, may understandably find it too difficult to occupy the same space as their oppressors. It may be that some people, for example those who feel especially vulnerable, want to be in groups that are cohesive and which remain cohesive, where there is little challenge and little change. This needs to be respected. We referred to this in Chapter 4 when we considered that a support group rather than a reflective group might be more suitable for people who are currently feeling vulnerable.

Other people may want to start in a cohesive group, building their confidence and warming up over the group sessions to an experience of greater coherency, where challenge and debate on different opinions and views is valued. There is no right or wrong way. There is no right or wrong position on the support–challenge continuum. As I have said before, there is no manual. But I offer the following examples from my practice to provide some scaffolding to support you as you engage with the structures and challenges of facilitating reflective groups.

Practice Examples

Example 1

> *I am running a reflective practice support group for a group of interpreters who interpret in psychological therapy consultations. A sharer, called Mara, shares that she recently interpreted for an NHS psychotherapy session. Mara was not at all impressed by the performance of the therapist. Mara says that at the end of the session she could tell that the client was not happy with how the session had gone. Mara says that she told the client that this therapist didn't seem very good and that she had the right to ask for a different therapist. At the response phase participants try to challenge what she did. They refer to their code of ethics. Mara replies that her actions were justified. She feels she had to intervene or she would be doing harm. She says she was only being human.* [1]

Reflective Questions

What do you think about this situation? What would you have done as the facilitator? How might the support–challenge continuum and other structural considerations inform your decisions?

Response

What do I do?

After the participants respond I give a response.

> *I acknowledge how difficult this type of situation can be, how we can be pulled by compassion to act outside of our codes of ethics. I add that as I wasn't there, I can't make an assessment of the therapist. I say that I am careful about expressing my opinion about another professional unless I think the level of jeopardy justifies it. I suggest we think together about tensions with ethical compliance more generally, as it is an issue that affects us all.*

Rationale

I could have said more. I didn't. Why not?

My decision to say what I do is based partly on the stage of the group. This is a fairly new group and I can tell from Mara's defensive comment that she isn't inviting challenge. My decision is based partly on ethical practice. I don't want to collude with what seems to be debatable ethical practice. But as I say, I wasn't there. Mara was. I defer to Mara's assessment of the jeopardy.

My response is also based on the sociocultural nature of this group. Interpreters have very few spaces where their own voices and opinions can be heard. I do not want to immediately shut down a voice that has so little professional agency. I try to find the right balance by widening out the discussion.

Reflective Questions

What do you think of my response? Would you have responded differently if you had been the facilitator? Why? What might you have said?

Example 2

> *I am running a different reflective practice support group for a group of interpreters who are interpreting for people who are seeking asylum. A sharer called Habiba shares that she has lent one of her clients some money. Habiba says she knows she shouldn't have done it and she is scared she will lose her job. She keeps apologising and saying she knows she did wrong.*

Response

Before the other group members respond, I ask Habiba if she can think of any other position she could occupy with regard to her actions besides apologising continuously. She looks confused and doesn't answer.

Reflective Questions

What do you think about this situation? What do you think about my intervention?

Rationale

I ask Habiba that question in that moment, as I am wondering what purpose the continual apologising is serving. It seems to me that it will be difficult for any learning to emerge from this situation at the moment. Although this is a very different response from Mara's in the first example, the repeated apologies are also serving Habiba as a barrier that stops her reflecting on the situation. Mara used the phrase "I was only being human" as a way to avoid reflection. I try to challenge Habiba directly about her repeated apologising. I am thinking that there is not a lot of point for group members to respond if Habiba is not able to truly hear them. But Habiba's response shows me that I have probably got it wrong. She is not ready yet to let go of the protection the apologies are offering her. Yanking away the protection is counterproductive. It would have been more productive to stay at the support end of the continuum for a while longer. I might acknowledge to myself that there may be many reasons for Habiba's response of which I am unaware. Can I be patient enough to wait until/if Habiba is ready to share and explore a bit further? Or maybe I take another approach. I might take things forward, at the same time taking some of the heat off Habiba, by widening out the discussion and suggesting we all (including Habiba) think about the helping continuum and imagine giving different possible responses to Habiba's client from different positions on the continuum.

Example 3

> *I have been running a reflective practice group with a committed group of workers from a domestic violence refuge. This is the sixth session and one of the group members says that the group has become a bit repetitive. She thinks the group should be a bit "edgier".*

Reflective Questions

How might this make you feel? You might feel that you are being called boring. You might feel your authority is being challenged.

How do you use your self-awareness to honestly assess what is being evoked in you and the stance that is required from you as the facilitator?

Response and Rationale

I feel a bit rattled. Then, I scrutinise myself and my reactions carefully. This is *reflection-in-action*. Once I have got my "facilitator shoes" back on, I think again about the group. They are a group of committed, compassionate workers who work with women who have been very badly abused and who are often frightened for their lives. The workers have been showing signs of vicarious trauma. This was why the reflective practice support group had been set up. Although we have met for six sessions, it still feels like quite a new group. People are still quite fragile. My decision to not be so edgy seems right. But I want to take the suggestion seriously and treat the group member who made the "edgy" comment with respect.

So, I suggest we think about this in our next review session. The group member agrees and in the next review session we consider where people are and how they are feeling in the group. I share the support-continuum model. The group agrees to continue at a gentle pace for another three sessions and review the pace again in three sessions' time. The "edgy" group member says she is happy to go with the majority decision. She also says she appreciates that her suggestion was taken seriously even if the group isn't going to act on it for the moment.

Example 4

> *I have been facilitating a reflective practice support group for community organisers and this is the fifth session. We are at the stage in the session when we go back to the Sharer for the last word. The Sharer, called Annie, reflects on a couple of the responses she has received and says this is enough for her. I prompt her to think about something she is taking away with her, something she might do differently etc. Annie doesn't immediately respond. After a while she says that there isn't always something that people might want to do differently after a reflective group session. Sometimes you might want to think about things or just do nothing. I can feel myself getting annoyed about the comment. It is not the first time it has felt that Annie is being dismissive and it is getting to me.*

Reflective Questions

What do you think about Annie's comment? What do you think about my response?

This is what I thought about my response. And this is what I did.

Response and Rationale

> *I feel myself getting annoyed. Annie has a way of getting under my skin. I am about to make a critical comment about Annie's lack of appreciation and how that could feel like a lack of respect for the group and the group process. Then I catch myself. It is true that some of what I am planning to say might be correct. It is also possible that I am experiencing some pushback of my authority from Annie. But my urge to respond isn't based on any of that. I am annoyed and I am about to act on my annoyance.*

At the very last moment, I catch myself. I manage not to act on my annoyance but I am left feeling dissatisfied. I take this to my supervision session.

With my supervisor I am able to reflect. Once I have examined what is going on for me personally, I start to think more clearly. I remember a quote from Maya Angelou along the lines that if you can't change something you don't like, change your attitude. There wasn't some *thing* I could change. But I could change my attitude.

If I moved away from my annoyance and listened to what Annie had said I realised that I had been pushing Annie to make a bridge from the responses she had heard, to the outside world. I wanted her to make a plan and to commit to change something as a result of this session. But she couldn't do that for me. I was troubled to realise that I wanted Annie to make the session a success. And success, on my terms, meant that we would have gone through all the stages of *my* model. She was right though. Life can't be systematised. I needed that reminder. I was troubled because I realised that I had been taking a directive stance of leadership, when I prided myself on serving the group. This is a salutary example for me of how authority can slip from an authoritative to an authoritarian stance when our anxiety takes over.

Example 5

> *A reflective group I facilitated went through a phase of not bringing any material to discuss. Our agreement was that the group wouldn't have an agenda. We had agreed we wouldn't spend time in the group generating ideas. The group had agreed to think before the sessions and to bring material they wanted to reflect on with the group. But they had stopped bringing material. As a result, I had started to bring anonymised cases as back-up material for us to discuss. But then I stopped doing that.*

Reflective Question

Why do you think I stopped?

Rationale

I stopped because I remembered the task of the reflective practice group. This wasn't a teaching group. We had an opportunity to have precious time and space to think about real, live practice with each other. How was that being achieved if I kept rescuing the group and acting as the teacher? So, what do I do?

Response

> *I suggest to the group that we spend 5 minutes in silence reflecting on why it has become so difficult to find material to bring to the group. We then share our thinking. I do this partly, because I think it might give an opportunity for the group members to review what they are getting out of the group. Is this the type of group they want to attend? Do they actually want to be in a training group instead? It also gives me time to reflect rather than to rush in.*
>
> *The discussion after the 5 minutes of reflection time is very useful. It gives us the space to explore issues such as, the ethical responsibility we have as practitioners for ongoing self-care and reflection, the fact that reflecting on our work is not a self-indulgence, the fears group members continued to have about being judged for sharing poor practice. The discussion is very fruitful. It is reflective. It frees something up. The group continues to meet for a year and group members return to regularly bringing issues, cases and dilemmas from their work for us all to reflect on and learn from.*

What I learned from this situation was the importance of not making assumptions, not rushing in to provide a solution, and of using the review process to make sense of difficult experiences.

What Has This Chapter Offered?

In this chapter, I've introduced a model that brings together a sliding scale of support and challenge with different learning cycles. These ideas help us think about how reflective groups, and individual group sessions, can be structured in thoughtful and responsive ways. I've suggested that reflective practice groups can be understood through three key components: the group session itself, the stage the group is at, and the wider sociocultural context.

I've also shared the connect–share–respond model as a way of structuring individual group sessions. Alongside this, I've explored the sociocultural dynamics that can arise between groups who are, or have been, oppressed and those they experience as oppressors. To bring these ideas to life, I ended the chapter with five examples from my own reflective group facilitation practice. These examples illustrate what I've learned about the balance between support and challenge – and how ideas about group stages and structure can be helpful at times, and limiting at others.

We began this chapter thinking about change and the power of groups to gain different perspectives, to offer challenge, and to change minds and actions. Our anxiety can get in the way of change. It hitches itself to familiar ideas and concepts that make us feel better, temporarily, even if they are not what is needed in the longer term. The examples in this chapter show that I, like any facilitator, am still learning, even after many years of practice. I still resist change. I often need to refresh my thinking, my sense of purpose, and my memory about the basics.

In the next chapter, we turn our attention fully to those basics. We'll explore a training programme that focuses on the core skills needed to facilitate reflective groups.

Note

1 Elaine Hsieh, Professor and Chair of the Department of Communication Studies at the University of Minnesota, USA, writes about her early experience as a healthcare interpreter where she was unprepared for the emotional impact on her of the assignments. She talks about weighing up different options for her response, *considering "the impact on the immediate interaction and the long-term consequences of my strategies …"* (Hsieh, 2024, p. 19). It is not an uncommon predicament for interpreters.

References

Costa, B. (2024). Reflective practice support for interpreters: Why, what and how? In A. Nevado Llopis & A. Foulquié Rubio (eds), *Medical interpreting* (pp. 185–200). Peter Lang Verlag. doi:10.3726/b18108.

Edmondson, A. C., & Verdin, P. J. (2018). The strategic imperative of psychological safety and organizational error management. In J. Hagen (ed.), *How could this happen?* (pp. 81–104). Palgrave Macmillan. doi:10.1007/978-3-319-76403-0_5.

Ericsson, A. (2008). Deliberate practice and acquisition of expert performance: A general overview. *Academic Emergency Medicine*, 15, 988–994. doi:10.1111/j.1553-2712.2008.00227.x.

Gibbs, G. (1988). *Learning by doing: A guide to teaching and learning methods.* Oxford Polytechnic, Further Education Unit.

Hawkins, P., & McMahon, A. (2020). *Supervision in the helping professions* (5th edition). McGraw-Hill.

Hsieh, E. (2024). More than words: Communicating for the quality of care. *Narrative Inquiry in Bioethics*, 14(3), 159–161. doi:10.1353/nib.2024.a947852.

Husby, V. M. (2025). Challenge and support: Scaffolding the practicing therapist in DP supervision. *Journal of Clinical Psychology*, 81, 366–378. doi:10.1002/jclp.23774.

Karpman, S. (1968). Fairy tales and script drama analysis. *Transactional Analysis Bulletin*, 7(26), 39–43.

Kolb, D. A. (1984). *Experiential learning: Experience as the source of learning and development*. Prentice-Hall.

Kurtz, A. (2019). *How to run reflective practice groups: A guide for healthcare professionals.* Routledge.

Minuchin, S. (1974). *Families and family therapy.* Harvard University Press.

Page, S., & Wosket, V. (2015). *Supervising the counsellor and psychotherapist: A cyclical model* (3rd edition). Routledge.

Proctor, B. (2008). *Group supervision: A guide to creative practice.* Sage. doi:10.4135/9781446221259.

Tuckman, B. W. (1965). Developmental sequence in small groups. *Psychological Bulletin*, 63(6), 384–399. doi:10.1037/h0022100.

Vygotsky, L. S. (1978). *Mind in society: The development of higher psychological processes.* Harvard University Press.

Chapter 11

Training Facilitators of Reflective Groups

Introduction

Good training passes on knowledge. It builds on what has already been discovered, and it helps to shape those who come next. Elsewhere in this book, I say that knowledge combined with practical experience, ethical decision-making, discernment and reflection, passes on wisdom. Although this chapter is called "Training Facilitators of Reflective Groups", frankly the whole book is about training group facilitators. There are various models of training available. I present the model of training that I have developed and delivered, which focuses on group process. (In the Appendix you can find supporting written and filmed information about the training.)

In earlier chapters we considered the personal attributes and characteristics of a facilitator. In addition to these attributes are specific skills which can be learned. Here is a list of skills participants learn on the course I deliver on foundational reflective group facilitation skills:

- ability to create a psychologically safe space
- ability to set and maintain boundaries for all
- facilitation of conversations about difficult issues
- humility and ability to learn from mistakes and to repair ruptures
- capacity to contain participants' anxiety and fear of mistakes/judgement
- ability to model and encourage intelligent empathy
- appropriate navigation of the "support–challenge continuum"
- pre-empting, identifying and managing (appropriately) possible triggers for participants
- recognising the limits of the role, and signposting as needed
- facilitating the cycle of experiencing/learning/application
- giving and receiving feedback appropriately
- self-awareness and management of your and others' emotions.

Next, we are going to look at evidence for the need for robust training of group facilitators, and the creative apprenticeship method of training

DOI: 10.4324/9781003658924-11

reflective group facilitators. The model of the containing frame is introduced. I also share examples, evaluation responses and resources from the training programme I have delivered, and information about where and to whom I delivered the training and what trainees have gone on to do next.

Critical Participation and Creative Apprenticeship

In almost all of the earlier chapters there are practical examples of group facilitation, followed by a deconstruction of the facilitator's reflection-in-action, or problem-solving in the moment. Taking apart a facilitator's behaviour and motivations is itself reflective practice. The aim of deconstruction is to share an understanding of the process, values and behaviour that have informed someone's practice. Trainees are asked simultaneously to *participate* in reflective practice groups, *observe* the process, and then *critique* the process. This is what I mean by *critical participation*. It isn't easy to combine participation with observing and critiquing. It is a skill that requires practice. It is also a useful and perhaps necessary skill that has applications beyond learning to become a facilitator. It develops critical reflexivity, providing a way of exploring assumptions and taken-for-granted behaviours. This is essential if systemic change is to occur.

In the introductory chapter, I introduced the four-step structure of the training model: *show, deconstruct, reflect, practise*. This method underpins the creative apprenticeship model of training. I call it a creative apprenticeship training model because trainees who attend this training learn on the job. That is how an apprenticeship usually works. The *creative* feature of the apprenticeship is the element of *reconstruction*. The requirement is that trainees don't just observe, they are expected to critically assess what they observe. They then put their critically assessed observations into practice. This involves thinking, questioning and spontaneity. It encourages reconstruction (reflection-*for*-action). Reconstruction encourages trainees to question and challenge the trainer. The trainer is not presented as an infallible expert, but as someone who is also continuing to learn. The training model supports the trainees to take risks, to make a mess and to be creative.

The Containing Frame

Passing on learning about how to provide and make use of support is increasingly important. It is important because we need new group facilitators to emerge across many practice professions. This is so that facilitators can support themselves and each other, at the cross-disciplinary and intra-professional levels. It is not just a matter for individuals. Institutions that support relationship-intense professions have a social responsibility to support and keep practitioners resourced. I propose a containing frame model (Figure 11.1) which illustrates the position occupied by professional institutions in relation to their social responsibility. These institutions may be services, registers, commissioners, regulators or membership organisations that support practitioners such as public service workers involved in health and social care, policing and housing, workers in legal, immigration and casework contexts, journalists, interpreters and arts facilitators.

The containing frame diagram (Figure 11.1) is depicted as a stacked Venn which shows part-to-whole relationships. It is a model of interdependent relationships. Each relationship contributes to the whole. The client[1] is at the ground level and at the centre of all the relationships. The client is grounded in their own autonomy and agency. The frame around the client contains the practitioner. Surrounding the practitioner is support in the form of reflective practice support groups and training for reflective practice support group facilitators to run them. The overarching frame includes, for example:

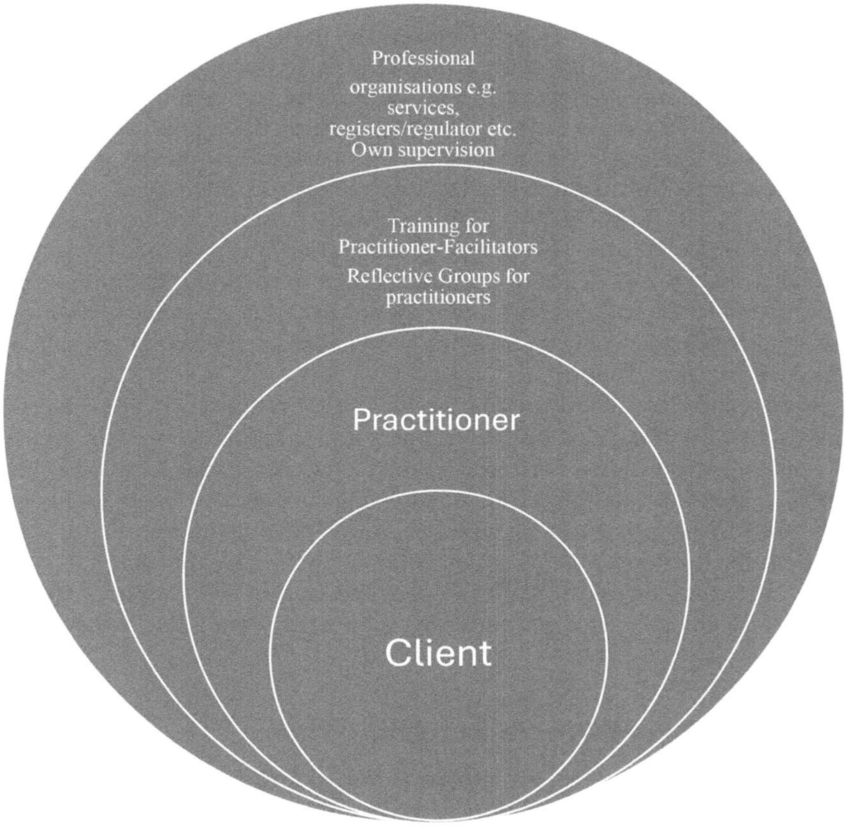

Figure 11.1 The containing frame
Source: adapted from Costa (2026).

regulatory bodies, membership bodies, training organisations, supervision provision for facilitators, and services. The active involvement, support and institutional accountability from those in this external circle in the frame, is what will make systemic change a reality. Reflective practice support group facilitation is a new role for many relational professions. It is the role of *practitioner-facilitator.* I recognise that training new facilitators uses resources and takes energy. But as we will see later, this investment is substantially amplified by the supply of energy it creates in the form of self-sustaining circles of support. (Burgess, et al., 2023).

Evidence and Experience

The need for training reflective group facilitators is endorsed by research. For example, a review of the literature about facilitating reflective practice groups in a mental health inpatient setting, found that one of the barriers to facilitating reflective practice groups included the needs and competencies of the facilitators themselves (Galway et al., 2024). According to Gardner et al. (2021), a key success factor for group supervision among allied health professionals is having a trained facilitator leading the group.

In a study that explored the personal and professional impact of reflective practice groups for qualified clinical psychologists (Knight et al., 2010) just under half of the participating 124 psychologists reported distress *as a result of attending* the groups. The quality of facilitation was a significant factor in the participants' experience of the group's perceived value. The provision of reflective practice groups alone is not a panacea. One recommendation from the study was that only people trained in group facilitation should run reflective practice groups.

In my experience, good training needn't be too arduous. It may indeed be enthusiastically welcomed by practitioners and others who work in relationally intense professions. Over the years I have been struck by how much people appreciate equally receiving and giving support. All the practitioners I have worked with want to maintain their compassionate and highly skilled practice. By training *practitioner-facilitators* to provide this support themselves, at the intra-professional or intra-group level, a self-sustaining circle of support is created. The supporter is supported *within* the profession or activity.

Training Delivery: Where and With Whom

Although facilitating reflective groups is not specifically within some practitioners' skill sets, many practitioners' skills are transferable and their professional skill sets can be developed and expanded (Hewson & Carroll 2016). This is evidenced by initiatives to train interpreters and teachers to facilitate peer-to-peer support and reflective support groups which have already taken place. These include projects in the UK. For instance. The "360 Supervision" Diploma in Supervision trains sign language interpreters in supervision skills.[2] In an initiative for the British Association for Counselling and Psychotherapy, Jo Holmes and Steve Page trained pastoral staff in educational settings to give and receive supervision to colleagues (Holmes & Page, 2021). In the USA, the Interpreting Institute for Reflection-in-Action and Supervision (IIRAS) has its own facilitation training programme for practitioners.[3]

The training model I offer focuses on group rather than individual or paired, peer-to-peer supervision. My experience of training non-psych practitioners to become reflective group facilitators dates from 2019. I piloted a practitioner-facilitator training programme for interpreters in London, UK. From this experience I learned a lot, and the interpreters reported that they did too. The three-day-plus training programme, that I currently offer, emerged from this pilot training programme. The current training programme has now been delivered to a variety of individuals and organisations e.g., for interpreters in the interpreting and translation service of the Grampian Regional Equality Council (GREC) in northeast Scotland;[4] for intercultural mediators who work for the Belgian Healthcare Service in the Intercultural Mediation in Health Care Program organised by the Intercultural Mediation and Diversity Management Unit of the Federal Public Service Health, Food Chain Safety and Environment; for a group of therapists and coaches training with Temenos Education[5] an online counselling and psychotherapy training institute; and for a group of caseworkers in a refugee support agency in the UK.

Introduction to the Foundation Training Programme in Reflective Practice Group Facilitation Skills

Throughout this book I have referred to the challenges and the courage that a facilitator needs to bring to the task of leading authoritatively even if that can make them feel vulnerable. Brené Brown gave a Ted Talk in 2010[6] on vulnerability. From her research, she concluded that vulnerability involves courage, compassion and connection: courage to be imperfect, compassion for ourselves, which leads to connection. The training programme I have developed for reflective group practitioner-facilitators is based on a commitment to act with courage, compassion and connection.

I have tried to address the vulnerability of trainee practitioner-facilitators by providing scaffolding and a structure to support them. This is not to eliminate vulnerability, which would run the risk of eliminating the opportunities vulnerability offers. The structure is offered to optimise the level of vulnerability needed to function. Too much vulnerability and we can collapse, too little and we lose authenticity. Having an appropriate structure and scaffolding that trainees trust, provides the containment necessary for them to dare to begin the formidable process of facilitating groups. The course strives to be an ethically grounded and safe foundational training which gives participants skills that are transferrable to other contexts too. As the participants gain experience, they can step forwards and take risks so that they can eventually dismantle the scaffolding and find their own personal style as a facilitator, which matches their own courage, compassion and connection.

In recognition of the fact that professional practitioners' time is often under pressure, the training programme is brief but intensive, integrating both theoretical insights and hands-on facilitation techniques (Costa, 2023).

The creative apprenticeship/learning-by-doing methodology encourages active learning (Kolb, 1984; Vygotsky, 1978; Collins et al., 1991). It is not a manualised set of instructions but a pedagogical approach. It makes the decision-making process of the facilitator visible. It builds on practitioners' skills and encourages them to put their adapted skills into practice from day one of the training. There are practical homework tasks between sessions and four follow-up, supervised practice sessions after the taught, three-day training programme has been completed. The leadership role of the trainer shrinks in size over time. The trainer's responsibility reduces gradually as the trainees gain in confidence and take responsibility for more of the session and for their own learning themselves. This model of *gradually releasing responsibility* was pioneered by the educationalists Pearson and Gallagher (1983), who developed their ideas, drawing on the work of Vygotsky (1978).

Using a learning-by-doing, deconstruction and reconstruction approach draws out the competencies and skills that a facilitator of a reflective practice group needs to develop. This is achieved by the trainees' participation in reflective group sessions (facilitated initially by the trainer) and post-group session discussions about the process. Participants are encouraged to identify issues, ask questions and share concerns. The trainer is questioned about their rationale for decisions they made when they were facilitating the group sessions.

Here are some examples of the issues addressed and the questions asked by participants during the training:

- What happens if someone in the group acts disrespectfully towards another member of the group?
- What do I do if a member of the group gets triggered by the discussion?
- How do I encourage quiet people to participate?
- Why didn't *you* encourage quiet people to participate?
- How do I manage people who dominate the conversation?
- What is my responsibility for creating a psychologically safe environment?
- How do I stop people giving unwanted advice?
- How do I get people to listen to each other?
- Why are you so strict with us about the time?
- How do I keep control of the time when some people are talking for a long time?

The learning-by-doing approach means that trainees identify their own concerns and issues for which they want support. The trainer has to be prepared to go beyond the theory, draw from and share their own practical experiences. As one trainee said about the training experience: "not everything comes from books".

You could say that trainees set their own agenda to some extent. However, this training approach also requires that, if any essential skills and competencies have not been addressed, the trainer completes the gaps they observe to ensure that all the competencies and skills, needed to facilitate a reflective practice group, are covered. You can find more details of the course structure in the Appendix.

Three Examples from Training Practice

The teaching is underpinned by the reflective approach of deconstruction (reflection on action) to reconstruction (reflection-for-action). One of the key features of the deconstruction methodology is teaching by example, or modelling what you are teaching. The following three examples, taken from different points in the training, give in-depth description and analysis of the methodology implemented in practice.

Because practitioners may not have had experience of participating in pastoral, or reflective practice groups, the training programme is highly immersive. As part of the immersion, all the trainees take part, as active participants, in reflective practice group sessions facilitated by the trainer. After each session, everyone – participants and trainer – disassemble and discuss the process of the group facilitation which the trainer has modelled.

A key feature of reflective groups, that can be new for trainee facilitators, is that they do not have a set agenda. Their effectiveness is driven by the material that members of the group are willing to bring to discuss. People new to reflective practice groups may not know what to bring. I begin by offering an example of an anonymous case to the group for them to think about, before we move on to cases they have brought. The conversations about the cases are guided to demonstrate the repair, reflection and response phases of reflective practice. I have often given a prompt to participants in advance (in the joining email) so that they know the type of issues that are suitable. Here are some example prompts:

- an experience from an assignment/consultation that may have left you with a lot of turbulent feelings/emotions
- a situation where you had to make an ethical decision
- a concern that you may be burning out or becoming vicariously traumatised
- a general question, concern or observation you wish to share and to hear group members' thoughts about

The following is an example of the method (based on an amalgamated and fictionalised situation).

Example 1: Counterintuitive Structures

> *A group of eight caseworkers is attending a three-day training course to learn how to facilitate a reflective practice support group. It is day one of the course and, as an introduction to learning about how to create a psychologically safe space for a group, they take part in a reflective practice support group facilitated by James, the course trainer. Mia offers to be the Sharer. She tells a story about a difficult ethical dilemma she faced.*
>
> *The trainees are active participants in the reflective practice support group. They are all asked to participate in the group and simultaneously to observe the behaviour and decisions made by James. The trainees make notes on James's behaviour, actions and attitudes. When the group session finishes, James invites the trainees to offer feedback to him about the skills and competencies they witnessed, or that they thought were missing, in his performance. What has James done that the trainees have found helpful and what have they found not so helpful? What did James do that contributed to their feeling psychologically safe/unsafe in the group? Do they have any questions for James about the decisions he made during the facilitation of the session?*
>
> *When the trainees have made some general observations, one trainee, Diego, asks James a question about his instruction to the group. After Mia had told her story James asked the group to share their own thoughts and feelings but to try their best not to ask Mia further questions. If they did ask a question James said he would ask Mia not to answer it straight away but to wait until the end when they would go back to the Sharer for the last word. Diego said it felt strange and he also felt a bit annoyed at not being able to ask Mia anything else. He asks James why he instructed them not to ask questions. James replies that he thinks he asked people to refrain from asking questions. But if they did, he would ask Mia to wait until the end to answer them, if she wanted to. James shares part of his rationale for this. One of the reasons, he explains, is to allow the Sharer – in this case, Mia – some space and to release her from the spotlight. The Sharer may feel quite vulnerable and isolated after sharing. Now it is the Sharer's time to receive something back from the group without anything else being required of them. This is an opportunity for the rest of the group to reach out and connect with the Sharer. After everyone in the group, who wanted to, had spoken, Mia had the opportunity to respond to what she had heard. She also had the chance to have the last word. James goes on to explain more of the psychological thinking behind these decisions and their relevance for the concept of a safe psychological space in a group (adapted from* Costa, 2024, pp. 124, 125).

The content from the session that has just been described could have been taught in a lecture format. However, the learning-by-doing and deconstruction approach allows the group to feel the impact of the facilitator's behaviour and to discover for themselves how safety in a group can be created.

We now consider two other examples from the training programme. The next example illustrates a frequent challenge for trainees.

Example 2: Boundaries

After the first day of the training programme, trainees start to facilitate reflective practice support groups within the training group. After each facilitation, we all give feedback about what we liked and suggestions for what could be improved. Giving and receiving feedback provokes strong reactions in many people. However, feedback is an essential element of the learning process. In the training groups we try to employ suggestions about delivering feedback from deliberate practice (Ericsson, 2008), and from supervision (Hawkins & Shohet, 2012, p. 160) – be specific and base your feedback on observable behaviour which the recipient can change.

One aspect of facilitation that trainee facilitators often struggle with is the upholding of boundaries, and in particular, *time* boundaries. Frequently, after a practice reflective practice support group I will remind the facilitator of the importance of the time boundary. Frequently, a trainee (usually supported by the rest of the group) will push back. Although they may have intellectually understood and appreciated the theory about the need for boundaries around time, in practice it becomes another matter. And of course, they are right. Holding the time boundary is difficult. That doesn't mean though that, because some of our values are difficult to implement, we should change our values to accommodate something easier. During these feedback and deconstruction sessions, trainees sometimes ask me for materials or tips to support them in holding the time boundary. We have considered and tried out some of the following:

- Having a prepared list of helpful phrases and reminders.
- Being mindful of your responsibility to guide the group to regard the last ten minutes of the session (or whatever time you have agreed on) as wind-down time.
- Being prepared to interrupt if some people are speaking for a long time, using the working agreement to support you.
- Sharing the responsibility of keeping to time with the group. For example, towards the end of a session I ask everyone speaking to keep their eye on the clock, to make sure they leave time for others who might like to comment, so that we end on time.

We also discuss how you can be flexible with the timing within a session, as long as the group ends on time (for the reasons already discussed and illustrated in earlier chapters).

By the end of the training programme all the people in training groups I have run have developed considerable skills and improved their confidence to hold the boundaries. Learning how to hold the boundaries is, of course, an endeavour which is boundless.

To illustrate that, I will share an example from my own practice as a facilitator, which I attempt to deconstruct as I go along. As you read it, you might notice your feelings, opinions and even judgements. At this stage in the book, you probably don't need a reminder that I regard feelings, opinions and judgements as important information. By reflecting on them, something useful may emerge for you. It does for me, as you will see in this case!

> *I am running a reflective group for university students. I can feel myself getting anxious about whether or not there will be enough time for it to be useful. Unusually, the group is running only for a single session rather than a series of sessions. The group agrees to the working agreement, which includes the time boundary. We then agree to go round the group and see who would like to share. I make it clear that we will divide up the time for each Sharer depending on how many people want to bring something to discuss. We go round the group. Some people want to bring something. Some people don't. When we get to the last person to speak, she says that she is feeling under a lot of pressure and that she won't be able to bring anything if there is a time constraint. However, she says that she could share some information about another group she attends instead.*

What happens to me?

I immediately feel that I am being judged. That I am making things difficult for this group member, putting unnecessary pressure on her because of the time. I think to myself: "I bet the other group she just mentioned is better. I bet that group facilitator doesn't make the members feel pressurised."

What do I do?

I start to explain why the time boundary is important and how, in order to be fair, we try to divide up the time so that there is some equity for all.

What's going on?

Well, that seems a reasonable intervention, doesn't it? Yes. On the surface. But I know myself enough to recognise that I am being defensive. I am trying to justify myself.

> *The group continues and we have quite a lot of time left after we have heard from and responded to the Sharers who wanted to bring an issue. I feel a strong desire to tell the group member, who had expressed concern at being pressurised, that we have all this extra time left over because of her. She has wasted the opportunity in the group.*
>
> *What **on earth** is going on?*
>
> *"You are so wrapped up in your own anxiety that you have lost connection with your empathy." I hear words that my supervisor might say to me, in my head. They act as a wake-up call. I will need to attend to this*

anxiety and the projections it elicited later. I'll probably do that in real life with my supervisor, but for now I am able to turn my attention back to the group and to the group member.

There is longer time than usual to share what people are taking away from the session. With my empathy re-engaged, I don't feel the need to blame the group member, onto whom I had been projecting so much. When she speaks, her sharing is generous, insightful and much appreciated by all of us. I am grateful I heard my supervisor's words in my head. We come to the close of the session. We make our farewells. We end on time.

This may not have been the type of example about time boundaries you were expecting. But pushing the time boundary manifests itself in many ways – for group members, and for the facilitator. My anxiety made me want to hold on tightly to the boundaries and the frame. Simultaneously, there was also a part of me that wanted to ignore the time boundary so that the group member would think I was *nice*. Neither position is ok. Either the boundary is serving a purpose or it isn't. If it isn't, it shouldn't be in the working agreement. I believe it does serve a purpose. As I have said before, the boundary is another provider of information. The push up against it, gives us an opportunity to view things in a sharper focus than usual.

Reflective Questions

Does anything useful emerge for you if you reflect on your feelings, opinions and judgements that arose from reading this account?

Where in your professional experience have you struggled to hold a boundary, even when you knew it was necessary? What did you learn from that experience?

Example 3: Intelligent Empathy and Compassion

This is an example of a feedback session I facilitate as an experiential part of the training programme. I am not happy with my response to something that happens in the session. I try to illustrate in this example how we dismantle my decisions and behaviour around this response, to deepen the learning for us all.

A trainee, who I'll call Lily, has just facilitated a reflective practice support group. We move into the feedback phase. I think Lily has done quite well but she receives some feedback from a member of the training group which is quite harsh. I am surprised by the feedback. I can't see that it matches the facilitation we have just witnessed. I assume that Lily will also feel that the feedback is a bit off. But I am wrong. The feedback hits Lily hard and Lily appears quite distressed. I am still thinking that she won't be especially impacted by the feedback and I ask Lily if she has anything else she would like to say. Lily is too distressed to answer. I then ask her what she would like to do next. Lily asks if she can have a break from the group for a moment.

Deconstruction

Later on, when we have had a chance to address the issue to the satisfaction of Lily, and clear up what was in fact a miscommunication and misunderstanding about the feedback, we turn to my handling of the situation. On the surface it may not look too bad, but I encourage the group to think about two of the principles we have discussed about intelligent empathy and empathic communication.

In the spirit of deconstructing interventions, the group asks me for my rationale for what I said to Lily after the feedback. I explain that I was thinking about intelligent empathy and the cognitive-emotional continuum. Lily then speaks. She says that when I was asking her, at the cognitive level, about what she thought or wanted to do next, she couldn't really hear the questions at that moment as she was overwhelmed by her emotions.

It dawned on me then what had happened to me. Intelligent empathy (introduced in this book in Chapter 4) involves holding the tension between an emotional and rational response and being informed by both responses together. I had been responding from, and trying to pull Lily into, a cognitive response. What I had neglected to do was meet Lily empathically in an emotionally connected way first, to help her to feel seen and to give her time to regain her emotional-cognitive equilibrium. My intentions may have been good, but in that moment, I missed Lily. It was an opportunity for learning for me.

It was also a moment of embarrassment and even shame for me. I had missed something that now seemed so obvious.

I was tempted to move us all on, past my mistake, to shine the flashlight somewhere other than where we were. I managed to resist the temptation. I found some courage, compassion (for myself) and connection (with the group) so I could turn the beam of the flashlight back to where we were. We talked about what had happened. We talked about my mistake. We reflected on it.

After our discussion, the participants said that the dismantling of my behaviour – my intention and its consequence had been a learning opportunity for them too.

Supervision and CPD

Once trainees start to facilitate their own groups they are encouraged to have their own supervision. I currently run an ongoing supervision group for facilitators. I also offer an online development and question and answer session for people who are new to facilitation, or who are thinking about starting. This development group is attended by practitioners from a range of professional backgrounds including therapists, interpreters, journalists and educationalists. Here are some of their opinions about the value and impact of the group.

- Understanding more about the importance of holding the frame for the creation of a psychologically safe space.
- Awareness of how race, religion, language etc. shape our attitudes towards self and others.
- Increased confidence in beginning to facilitate. The facilitator and the other members of the group have provided answers to questions (both mine and others'), and also ways of thinking, that have helped shape my mindset and planned approach in a way that I know is professionally and ethically sound.
- The value of the collective mind.

The following questions and responses from the supervision and development groups represent three frequent themes for new facilitators.

1 Know Your Limits

Question: What do you do if someone is regularly distressed in the group? Do you keep meeting up with them after the session to support them?

Response: In general if someone is upset during a group session, I work on the principle that everyone in the group agreed, in the working agreement that they had support outside of the group, and so if I meet with someone briefly after a session I would be checking out with them where else they could go for support.

If a participant was regularly distressed, I would meet with them to check out how they were feeling. I would then gently remind them that we had agreed there was a limit to how much this group would be able to work with personal issues. I would then ask if there was somewhere they could go to process their feelings more deeply than the group was able to offer. I would resist offering more support myself. We can all go through periods of time where we are feeling particularly vulnerable. If more support was needed, and that is perfectly understandable, I would discuss with the participant if a reflective group format was the most appropriate form of support for them at the moment. Sometimes one-to-one support can be more useful than a group.

2 Starting a Group

Question: Can you give us some tips on starting an independent group?

Response: I would suggest starting with a taster/information session (for which I wouldn't make a charge) and targeting about four potential participants. (I would avoid targeting personal acquaintances.) If you can't think of four people in your professional acquaintance who might be interested in this type of a group then it's probably better to wait until you are able to identify them. With an initial group, it is a good idea to maximise the chances of it being a success, so targeting appropriate group members may help you feel more confident.

I would be clear about the time commitment and any payment which will be involved after the taster session. I tend to start with a request that all participants make an initial commitment to attend 3 sessions and a review. I suggest, that as the facilitator, you choose times that work for you, that you can sustain. By that, I mean a day and time that are consistent and regular. Before you begin, send a joining email with information about timings, venue or online platforms, policy about late arrivals at sessions, payment processes (if payment is involved) and any other requests you may have.

At the first meeting, I recommend you spend time and avoid rushing the negotiation and agreement of the working agreement, which needs to be maintained with care and consistency.

Later on, when you are opening up the group (i.e. inviting other potential participants), I would suggest adding some kind of a screening process (for example, an initial conversation with a potential participant so that you can both see if the offering fits with what they are looking for and what you can offer).

3 Mixed or Single Professional Groups?

I run both single and mixed professional supervision and question and answer groups. They are both useful. Which type of group you set up depends on your context. This is what one participant in a mixed group said about her experience:

> Even though I come from a different professional background to many others in the group, I found many of the questions and subsequent discussions applicable to various contexts and I'm grateful to have a space where difficult questions are thought through and discussed with such care, clarity and openness. I've found the group sessions a hugely useful resource.

Evaluation of the Training Programmes

I mentioned that I piloted brief interventions to train interpreter-facilitators between 2019 and 2022, drawing on a creative apprenticeship approach. Twelve qualified and experienced interpreters who participated in the training gave feedback through an anonymous online questionnaire. The two most important outcomes people identified from the training were: learning about psychological safety; learning how to listen and allow space for others to comment. Eight participants rated the course as highly effective in building their confidence to become a facilitator of reflective practice groups. The other four participants felt that they wanted some further training before going on to run groups independently themselves. Several of the participants from these early cohorts have since drawn on their training to provide intra-professional support for interpreters, including those who work with some of the most vulnerable people in our communities.

In 2024, I delivered the expanded model of training described in this chapter to a mixture of therapists, educators and coaches. The overall satisfaction rating with the training was 95%. A deeper awareness about learning about what it takes to hold and contain a group was mentioned as a significant outcome. The following outcomes were also regarded as significant: learning how to hold the frame, how to use the working agreement, and understanding one's own relationship with authority. The experiential nature of the course was highlighted.

In 2025, I asked trainee facilitators what they thought were the important considerations for the delivery of group facilitator training. The four top considerations were that the training should focus on the fundamentals of group facilitation skills, be time efficient – e.g., a three-day course, have low financial cost, and be experiential.

The following piece was written by one of the twelve interpreters who completed the original training in 2019. It was written for the Bilingual Forum online event on 7 July 2022. The theme of the Bilingual Forum was "The aftermath for interpreters in highly demanding emotional situations". The piece is now published on the Pásalo website.[7] Chartered linguist, interpreter and translator Zora Jackman, who wrote the piece, has given permission for an excerpt to be included here:

> Thanks to having training and ongoing support I am now aware that as a facilitator I have many responsibilities. First on the list is always setting the ground rules, something I would have never thought of when meeting with a colleague and chatting about difficult cases over a cup of coffee: setting firm boundaries, providing a safe environment, knowing how to keep everyone informed about what is happening without interfering too much, encouraging non-judgemental conversation, and last but not least, managing time, so everyone feels included and is given fair time to talk –

this is perhaps the most important skill for me personally as a facilitator. I also had to learn to listen and not to bring my own issues into the conversation, always keeping in mind that I am there to facilitate, to provide a safe space for others and to manage their expectations, so all participants can feel the benefits of such reflective practice.

It is not an easy job, and I am sometimes confronted with my own dilemmas or emotions as a result of facilitating reflective practice support groups. Therefore, it is vital to also have my own supervision. My colleague facilitators and myself attend a regular "supervision of supervision of interpreters" group. This is a great opportunity to share experiences with my colleagues as well as to continue learning about reflective practice and developing my relatively new skills.

I have asked members of our Welsh group that I facilitate for their feedback, and I would like to share one piece of feedback with everyone who may not be sure about the benefits of reflective practice support groups.

Group member:

> Having somebody facilitating the sessions makes them more productive and focused, as there is a structure and clear aims, and everybody is given a chance to participate, without anybody dominating the conversation or getting off-topic. As a consequence, I personally feel that my experiences and views are acknowledged and valued, and I feel I'm in a safe space.

What participants do next as a result of this training depends partly on their starting point and experience. Some people who have had experience in leading groups feel confident to set up their own reflective practice support groups. Others with less experience may wish to develop their skills by facilitating a group together with a more experienced colleague. Some people may want to participate in more practice and training opportunities before they feel confident to facilitate a group.

Already mentioned are the results from the post-training evaluations which indicate a significant improvement in confidence. This level of confidence is evident in the practical outputs from the pilot training interventions. A number of new groups, facilitated by the newly trained practitioner-facilitators have been established. Here are five examples.

1 Two interpreting organisations set up reflective practice support groups for new and inexperienced interpreters who had been recruited quickly, with little time for induction, as a result of the large numbers of refugees from the conflict in Ukraine, and elsewhere, settling in the UK. The sudden events of war and other catastrophes can mean that interpreters

have to be recruited and trained very quickly. These reflective practice support groups have been facilitated by three of the "graduates" from the (practitioner) interpreter-facilitator training programmes.

2 Two interpreter-facilitators are running reflective practice support groups for a local authority which provides language support for individuals and families.
3 A successful funding bid has enabled a practitioner-facilitator (a "graduate" from a training cohort) to be employed to run a reflective practice support group for interpreters who work with people held in immigration detention centres and with victims of trafficking.
4 The Intercultural Mediation and Diversity Management Unit within the Belgian Healthcare Service has trained intercultural mediators who now facilitate ongoing reflective practice support groups for all the intercultural mediators within the Intercultural Mediation in Health Care Program.
5 The Chartered Institute of Linguists[8] in the UK is providing reflective practice groups, as a pilot project, in 2026. These are facilitated by a trained interpreter-facilitator.

What about the future? One goal is for a foundational training course for practitioner-facilitators in reflective practice skills to be offered and accredited by universities and other official institutions. A foundational practitioner-facilitator training course is proposed for delivery as a *microcredencial* jointly by the universities of Murcia and Alicante, Spain.

Summary

Here's how the case examples and questions address the facilitator skills and competencies outlined above.

The case examples on counterintuitive structures and boundaries illustrate examples of the facilitator's ability to offer a psychologically safe enough space.

The case example on intelligent empathy illustrates how intelligent empathy can be used and misused.

The questions section "*Know your limits*" *shows* how the facilitator can make use of signposting as needed and manage possible triggers for participants.

All the examples that demonstrate *deconstruction* illustrate facilitator humility, being *disappointing enough*, and finding ways to repair ruptures.

The cumulative nature of emotional demands takes its toll on practitioners who work in relationship-intense contexts. Their need for appropriate support has been well documented elsewhere and commented upon in this book. Facilitated support can breathe life back into a deflated worker. Facilitators from within a profession understand and know their own contexts. By training them to provide this support themselves, at the intra-professional level, a self-sustaining circle of support and solidarity is created: colleague to colleague(s). When institutions live up to their espoused commitments to social responsibility for their members (i.e. they do what they say they do), this circle of support is further strengthened. The container is contained (Bion, 1961).

Notes

1 The term client refers to the service-user and their context, which can include other service providers, family members, etc.
2 See https://360supervision.co.uk.
3 See www.iirasinternational.com/about-us.
4 See https://grec.co.uk.
5 See www.temenos.education.
6 See www.ted.com/talks/brene_brown_the_power_of_vulnerability?language=en#t-546090.
7 See www.pasaloproject.org/bilingual-forum.html.
8 See www.ciol.org.uk.

References

Bion, W. R. (1961). *Experiences in groups*. Tavistock/Routledge.

Burgess, M., Costa, B., Jackman, Z., & Norton, I. (2023). The circle of support. *The Linguist*, 62(1).

Collins, A., Brown, J. S., & Holum, A. (1991). Cognitive apprenticeship: Making thinking visible. *American Educator*, 15(3), 6–11, 38–39.

Costa, B. (2023). Supporting the supporters. *Therapy Today*, 34(1), 42–45.

Costa, B. (2024). Reflective practice support for interpreters: Why, what and how? In A. Nevado Llopis & A. Foulquié Rubio (eds), *Medical interpreting* (pp. 185–200). Peter Lang. doi:10.3726/b18108.

Costa, B. (2026). Setting up a mental health spoken language interpreting service. In R. Tribe, K. Thompson, & H. Raval (eds), *Working with interpreters in mental health* (2nd ed., in press). Routledge.

Ericsson, A. (2008). Deliberate practice and acquisition of expert performance: A general overview. *Academic Emergency Medicine*, 15, 988–994. doi:10.1111/j.1553-2712.2008.00227.x.

Galway, R., Wilkinson, D., Mistry, D., Beryl, R., Mackay, K. L., Gaynor, B., & White, J. P. (2024). Rapid review of facilitating reflective practice groups with staff in adult inpatient mental health settings. *Reflective Practice*, 26(2), 277–291. doi:10.1080/14623943.2024.2426281.

Gardner, M., McKinstry, C., & Perrin, B. (2021). Group clinical supervision for allied health professionals. *The Australian Journal of Rural Health*, 29(4), 538–548. doi:10.1111/ajr.12775.

Hawkins, P., & Shohet, R. (2012). *Supervision in the helping professions* (4th edition). Open University Press.

Hewson, D., & Carroll. (2016). *Reflective practice in supervision*. MoshPit.

Holmes, J., & Page, S. (2021). How pastoral workers in further education and sixth form colleges are benefiting from supervision. *BACP University and College Counselling*, 9(3), 24–28.
Kolb, D. A. (1984). *Experiential learning: Experience as the source of learning and development*. Prentice Hall.
Knight, K., Sperlinger, D., & Maltby, M. (2010). Exploring the personal and professional impact of reflective practice groups: A survey of 18 cohorts from a UK clinical psychology training course. *Clinical Psychology & Psychotherapy*, 17(5), 427–437. doi:10.1002/cpp.660.
Pearson, P. D., & Gallagher, M. C. (1983). The instruction of reading comprehension. *Contemporary Educational Psychology*, 8(3), 317–344.
Vygotsky, L. S. (1978). *Mind in society: The development of higher psychological processes*. Harvard University Press.

Chapter 12

What Was the Point?

When you come to the end of a book (reading it, or writing it) it's probably not a bad idea, if a bit late, to ask, "Well, what was the point of that?" So rather than "Conclusion", I have called this chapter "What Was the Point?".

Throughout the book I have shared some ideas about what I believe being in a small, supportive, reflective group with others can offer individuals. I've set out some of the answers I have come up with to the questions: Do groups need facilitation? What's the point of a facilitator? What does a facilitator do?

Some answers and corresponding themes have made an appearance more than once. Many of the themes sit on a continuum of reciprocity. Here's a list of a few of them: internal and external spaces; authoritarian and authoritative stances; vulnerability and courage; safety and risk; limits and creativity; status quo and transformation; theory and practice; instinct and accountability; inclusion and exclusion; connection and dissent.

When I facilitate reflective practice groups, at the end of a session I often invite group members to think about something that will stay with them from the session. At the end of the book, I invite you to do the same.

For myself, I have been thinking not only about what I am taking away, but also about what I hope I have shared. I have summarised what I hope I have conveyed in six key messages.

1 Conversational Dissent and Perspective Taking

When I first thought about writing this book, I imagined it would be a book about facilitating reflective practice groups. And it is. But I also came to realise that the book needs to have a broader remit. It is situated, after all, in a broader context. One of the reviewers of my original book proposal hinted at that. It just took me until I started to write the first version of the final chapter to really understand what she was getting at. The book you are currently reading has had several re-writes.

I still firmly believe that reflective practice groups can help us improve our practice in relationship-intense professions. These groups are for

DOI: 10.4324/9781003658924-12

practitioners who work with people in need. I also think that the model of reflective groups, of holding the frame, can help us with our urgent and contemporary societal need for conversational dissent and perspective taking. Difficult conversations.

Chantal Mouffe, the controversial political theorist I mentioned in the introductory chapter, warns that consensus can be dangerous: "Too much emphasis on consensus, together with aversion towards confrontations, leads to apathy and to a disaffection with political participation." (Mouffe, 2013, p. 7).

We are in danger, in our reflective groups, of leaning into this apathy if we suppress confrontation. Confrontation, though, can easily turn into destructive attacks and defensive postures. In turn, fear of confrontation leads groups to return to safe, well-rehearsed ideas and routine ways of thinking which become like habits, unconducive to innovation and reflection.

If a facilitator can find the courage to guide a group on a journey through confrontation, to perspective taking and perspective widening, maybe reflective groups have something to offer the wider world.

A transdisciplinary team at the University of Technology Sydney, Australia researches global social challenges. The team makes several observations that are relevant here. They note that there is a growing appetite for discussions that aren't always easy. People are searching for ways to talk to each other so that the potential chaos that can ensue from difficult conversations, is recast into constructive, dynamic solutions. They observe that people are "looking for practical ways to support constructive discussion of global social challenges (which are) essential to make progress on the vexed, conflictual issues" (Paredes et al., 2025, p. 2).

The research team suggests a conceptual framework for constructive discussion and beneficial decision-making across personal, conversational, institutional and cultural spheres. Isn't that what reflective groups try to do?

As far as I can tell, although theorists encourage us to embrace dissent and have constructive discussions in groups with each other, there is little if any guidance on how to implement and facilitate constructive discussions. And yet, constructive discussions are unlikely to happen and to be sustained without effective facilitation. Without effective facilitation, a difficult conversation remains a difficult conversation.

Some books about group facilitation offer important examples of exercises to raise self-awareness (Pandya & Lasley, 2025). Some emphasise the need to implement Freire's conscientização (Freire Institute, 2025) if constructive discussion and change are to happen.

Additionally, I have attempted to show that this process often needs to be slowed down. Confronting people early on and challenging them to recognise their unconscious bias may lead to compliance which comes from shame, but it is unlikely to lead to long-lasting, deep-rooted positive behaviour. What I have attempted to show in this book is a type of facilitation that recognises that people sometimes need time to warm-up to being challenged. It is a developmental process. Challenge is important, but if it is offered too early, a facilitator runs the risk of shaming someone, increasing their misunderstanding and unintentionally decreasing their awareness.

2 Confidence to Slow Down as Facilitators

Slow food, slow fashion, slow cities and now slow facilitation. For deep reflection to occur we need the slow pace. That's what a protected space for thinking can give us. Slow behaviour is an antidote to frenzied activity produced by fear and anxiety. Nick Luxmoore was a highly regarded school counsellor and psychotherapist. He wrote several books, including his last book before he died in 2019, the poignantly titled *Supporting Young People through Everyday Chaos: Counselling When Things Fall Apart* (published posthumously in 2022). I heard him say once that probably the most important thing he did in school was to move around the buildings slowly. He never rushed, even if he was in a hurry. He said that rushing around intensified anxiety. It stirred up the chaos. It inhibited thinking.

It is good advice for facilitators of reflective groups too. At the micro level, within a group session it is important to take time to set up and allow discussion of the working agreement. It's the facilitator who has to make sure that the time doesn't just run out at the end of the session, with the ensuing panic that can cause. It is important that enough time is allowed for reflection. It is important to ensure that group members aren't casually joining late or leaving early. The space and timing for this work are protected for a reason. Slowly we create spaces for deep reflection.

Going slowly, as we have seen in other chapters, is an important principle when we think across group sessions, to the life cycle of a group and beyond, to the macro context of sociocultural influences. The warm-up process can help with that. It slows us down before we even begin. At the micro level before a group session, I warm up by thinking about what I need to do to arrive at the session so that I don't end up rushing to join. I think in advance about what I need to do to prepare for the session. I think about what I need to do, and I aim to have completed all my preparation at least 10 minutes before the session is due to start. Warming up is a process that applies at the macro level for groups too. Some group members will feel more vulnerable than others when it comes to speaking up in a group. I have suggested in this book that groups can be set up consciously, bearing in mind the differentials in sociocultural dynamics. Some groups need to stay at the cohesive, non-confrontational level for a while. This gives a space for people to heal slowly, to gain confidence in mutual support, to try out talking about what is important for them, and experience being listened to. With this slow build in the confidence of group members in cohesive groups, vulnerability can draw on courage. Group members dare to try listening and responding to messages that may be in conflict with their own messages. Slowly they may find that they are able to bear to hear these conflicting messages without feeling diminished and demolished by them. New people, maybe from other disciplines, cultures, or with different beliefs, join the group. Transdisciplinary groups begin to be appreciated. People feel they can let go of some safety structures and risk entertaining new ideas. The group now operates on the principles of cohesion *and* coherency.

3 Transformation and the Power of Multiplicity: Reflective Groups and Social Change

In the face of simultaneous and multiple global crises and systemic embedded unfairness, individual action and small group initiatives often feel inadequate. That can also lead to apathy. No one wants to feel inadequate. This might be a disheartening thought for some people. It isn't for me. I talked about compassionate inadequacy in another chapter. The compassionate part of the phrase refers both to the compassion for ourselves and our limitations, and the compassionate act of connecting with others in their inadequacy. Inadequate can become adequate when we add a variety of inadequacies together.

The often-quoted words attributed to the anthologist Margaret Mead are about the power of small groups: "Never doubt that a small group of thoughtful, committed citizens can change the world; indeed, it's the only thing that ever has."

The combined power of small groups is even more powerful. I have frequently heard people refer to small initiatives as inadequate, calling them sticking plaster solutions. It's true. But I also know that a sticking plaster can help to prevent infection. It is not enough. But multiple *not enoughs* can make a difference. As a minimum, they help us maintain our hope and our realistic optimism. Optimism attracts people. It is a magnet for good. Here's an example:

> *Colleagues Across Borders*[1] *is a project within Pásalo, UK. It was set up in 2013, and it offers reciprocal, collegiate support to humanitarian workers who are themselves refugees. Each pair of colleagues consists of a UK based practitioner, matched with a refugee-worker from a partner organisation, principally in countries such as Egypt and Bosnia. The humanitarian workers have supportive roles, such as psychologists, psychosocial workers, doctors and interpreters, offering support to fellow refugees in the countries where they are currently settled. Colleagues Across Borders is a small group. There are about ten members of the UK group – all volunteers, all counsellors, supervisors, psychotherapists or interpreters. Over 13 years it has worked discreetly, making hundreds of quiet connections, like a magnet.*

Rutger Bregman, the Dutch philosopher, suggests in his book called *Moral Ambition* (2025), that networks of people can achieve durable change. I want to be clear though, that I am not talking about small groups combining to make one big group. The kind of facilitation and the skills to facilitate that I have been describing in this book are principally related to small groups of between four to ten people. Any smaller, and they are fragile and susceptible to collapse, if one or two people become unavailable. They are also only able to offer a small number of perspectives. Any bigger, and you lose connectedness and the intimacy that is necessary for genuine trust to emerge. But multiple, individual small groups can connect, share their stories, be friendly, help each other out. That's something that multi-group conglomerates don't do so well.

4 Facilitation with Kindness and With Courage

The support that a group can offer its members cannot be underestimated. Some groups can hold their frame without any need for a facilitator. But sometimes, group members feel fragile, overlooked, anxious, or just plain tired. That's when a facilitator, who can hold the group and offer space for repair and refreshment, is appreciated. With the support of a facilitator, group members have more energy to give to each other.

That is very important because, once people feel reenergised and they begin to gain in confidence, they may be ready to engage with challenge as well as support. A clinical supervisor, who was talking about my psychotherapy practice, once told me that my clients would only be able to go as far as I had been prepared to go myself. The same is true of groups. This is why facilitators need courage. They need to dig deep and do the kind of self-development work that involves them in feeling vulnerable, daring to take risks and daring to encounter the personal, social and cultural sides of themselves they would rather turn away from. A facilitator has to be prepared, not only to confront those parts in their self, but (even harder) to develop a compassionate relationship with those parts. It is our own *conscientização* (Freire Institute, 2025), or consciousness raising, as facilitators that will give us the integrity to be able to support people to stay with the more scary and unpleasant experiences of being in divergent groups. These are groups that are founded on a commitment to coherency as well as cohesion. In other words, you can't support and challenge others to go where you weren't prepared to go yourself.

I think facilitators need *kind courage*. It has become acceptable to engage in behaviour known as "calling someone out", to decry someone for their bad behaviour. In fact, it's not just acceptable, it is often regarded as commendable action. But it is, in effect, a public telling off. Someone may have behaved very badly. It may be right to challenge them. Personally, I am yet to be convinced that public shaming frequently leads to genuine, deep transformation. It often exacerbates divisiveness. There are other, kinder ways of helping people to be more cognisant of their impact on others, which are more likely to transform their behaviour wholeheartedly, rather than to effect compliance driven by shaming. We could start by including ourselves in the foolish band of people who are getting things wrong. What a relief, I think. I may be a bimbling nicompoop but I'm not alone. I don't need to be incapacitated by shame. Maybe calling out could become "connecting in or helping each other out". That would be a bit kinder. We aren't always right. And accepting that we might sometimes be wrong, just like everyone else, might make for a less divided society.

So, kindness is needed. But if, as facilitators, we are really committed to change and transformation, we need to recognise that being lovely isn't enough on its own. When we are using the phrase *being human* as a defence it may justify being lovely but it keeps us away from a more three-dimensional view of being human, even if it isn't always lovely. As facilitators we need kindness, but we also need courage. Being supportive all the time, never challenging and never taking a risk might protect us from ever being accused of making a mistake. But we need to make mistakes so that we can also provide an experience for ourselves and others of rupture and repair. With my son's comment from the beginning of the book, I recognised my potential for interpersonal destructiveness. I learned something, and I mean truly learned something about myself, which had a profound and lasting impact on me. It led to the establishment of two organisations. Out of Picasso's mess, something creative emerged. Groups know that chaos can be destructive. But chaos doesn't need to be avoided. Chaos can be transformed into something productive.

5 Viewing the Frame as a Benign Enabler Not Just a Restrictive Constraint

The Pulitzer prize-winning author Annie Dillard (1989) says a writer needs to know her frame and know it intimately so that she can write all the way up to the edges. She can push the edges but she needs to know her limits. If she doesn't, she will lose her reader. That is what an effective group facilitator does too. If they are trusted, the facilitator holds the frame for the group. Once the group feels well held and contained, in a space that is safe enough yet dynamic, the facilitator can guide them towards the edges of the frame. The group can walk around within its limits and its bounds, contemplate, exchange thoughts, opinions and feelings, and carry away with them what they learn from the experience.

Unfortunately, people may have had experiences of frames or structures that were inhibiting and restricting. They may have had to deal with organising structures that consisted of a list of rules and regulations. That is not a benign frame. Or they may have had experiences of people in leadership positions whose behaviour has been authoritarian rather than authoritative. Throughout the book I have tried to show examples of authoritative facilitation and to examine closely how it is possible to become an authoritative facilitator. The frame can only be a benign and enabling frame, which can produce creative responses, if the facilitator is authoritative. This means a facilitator who knows how to collaborate, how to support, but also how to hold the line and, with courage, how to bear sometimes not being the most popular person in the room. They hold their nerve. They trust the group to think deeply and to act with fairness. They trust the group to behave with kindness and with courage.

6 Practice Makes the Theory Work: Walking the Talk

The principles of nonviolent communication Marshall Rosenberg (1999) align with the types of agreements about behaviour I have with the groups I facilitate. Non-violence was an approach used by Mahatma Gandhi as a form of resistance. I mention it now because I want to quote from Gandhi. He says we should keep non-violence: "in the heart, and it must be an inseparable part of our very being". Although he is referring to non-violence I think this principle applies to everything we say we believe in. That is what I understand by *walking the talk*. It is how we live our values, how we follow the three Confucian paths to wisdom I mentioned at the beginning of the book. Walking the talk is how we enact our practical wisdom and how we make theory come alive in our practice.

As a facilitator you are accountable. You may be accountable to any of the institutions in the outer concentric circles of the containing frame, described in Chapter 11. You are accountable to the members of groups you facilitate. And you are also accountable to yourself. To act with ethical maturity means that you don't just use external ethical guidelines to inform your behaviour and justify your practice. You trust in your integrity to make everyday ethical decisions in the moment. You model reflecting *in* action because you have spent the time reflecting *on* your action.

You don't have to do it all on your own though. In fact, ethical maturity implies an understanding that you can't do this on your own. You need another element in a concentric circle. In that surrounding circle is your supervisory structure, whatever form that takes. Sometimes for me that has been an individual supervisor, sometimes a group, sometimes a critical friend. They have held up a mirror for me so that we could see my reflection, contemplate it together, explore my underlying values and behaviour and try to make some sense of my experience and the implications for my future actions.

Reflecting in and on action yourself shows your commitment to walk the talk. Modelling what you are supporting group members to do is crucial, if they are going to trust you. It shows integrity. It's who you are and how you are that enables you to guide quietly, without unnecessary noise. What's the authoritative antidote to the authoritarian "Do as I say, not as I do"?

"Do as I do."

The Quiet Guide

I began this book by sharing my realisation about my own potential for destructive behaviour in relationships and group situations. My son's comment was a reminder to me of my responsibility to look at myself with a healthily critical eye and address the consequences. I also included a group member's depiction of me at the beginning of the book. She said I was like a pizza base. A pizza base isn't heroic, glamorous or brilliant, but it typifies the kind of quiet work in the background, and sometimes in the foreground, that goes into holding the frame for a group much of the time. It is work conducted with kindness and courage by a quiet guide who knows how to move slowly. Change can be slow, but its's worth the wait.

I started this concluding chapter by asking what has been the point of this book. At the start of the introductory chapter, I asked another, different question. The question was about what makes the difference between those groups that collapse and cause harm, and those groups that thrive and create new ideas, actions, products and even new ways of relating with each other. The answer to that question was unsurprisingly and fundamentally about the framing of the group. I proposed that the way in which the group's frame is held is a crucial component of productive groups. I also said, at the beginning of the book, that the aim was to look at the workings, the ingredients and methods involved in holding the frame, guiding, and facilitating groups. I hope you feel the book has delivered on that aim and that you have enough of a recipe to start cooking a simple meal. The meal may not be fancy. But there are many people who will welcome the nourishment, however basic it is to start with. If you dare to try, to fail, to keep going, fail again (Beckett, 1983) and learn as you go, you will find that increasingly more people benefit from your cooking. There is a hunger and a need for those who can hold the centre when it feels like things are falling apart all around. Many of us appreciate a good-quality, plain, firm, quiet pizza base. Don't underestimate it.

That's the point.

Note

1 See www.pasaloproject.org/colleagues-across-borders.html.

References

Beckett, S. (1983). *Worstward ho*. Grove Press.

Bregman, R. (2025). *Moral ambition: How to find your purpose*. Bloomsbury Publishing.

Dillard, A. (1989). Write till you drop. *The New York Times*, 28 March. https://archive.nytimes.com/www.nytimes.com/books/99/03/28/specials/dillard-drop.html.

Freire Institute. (2025). Concepts used by Paulo Freire. Retrieved from www.freire.org/paulo-freire/concepts-used-by-paulo-freire (accessed 26 July 2025).

Luxmoore, N. (2022). *Supporting young people through everyday chaos: Counselling when things fall apart*. Jessica Kingsley Publishers.

Mouffe, C. (2013). *Agonistics: Thinking the world politically.* Verso.

Pandya, A., & Lasley, M. (2025). *Facilitating authentic communication groups: Integrating process work, DEI, NVC, & IFS.* Discover Press.

Paredes, L. H., Riedy, C., Baumber, A., Robinson, H., Salignac, F., Matter, S., Spackman, C., Mason, S., Potts, M., & Wearne, S. (2025). Constructive discussion: Conceptualising a framework for productive communication across personal, conversational, institutional, and cultural spheres. *Global Social Challenges Journal.* Advance online publication. doi:10.1332/27523349Y2025D000000043.

Rosenberg, M. B. (1999). *Nonviolent communication: A language of compassion.* PuddleDancer Press.

Appendix: Resources for Practitioners

The resources provide templates, tips and a course outline for the foundational training of practitioner-facilitators.

Example of a Reflective Practice Support Group Information Sheet and FAQs

Information Sheet

Reflective practice support groups serve at least two functions. They support practitioners firstly to repair from cumulative, challenging and stressful experiences from their practice. Secondly, the groups support them to be reflective about their practice in order to maintain their professional standards and improve the quality of their work. Supportive reflective practice can be viewed as continuous professional development. It is a non-clinical activity.

When reflective practice is conducted within a group it helps us to take a broad view of a problem or issue. Groups transform solitary reflection into shared, relational learning. Attending to others' perspectives on an issue in our practice can develop our critical reflexivity. Reflecting with others is a way of holding ourselves to account. It supports us to transform knowledge into practical, useable wisdom. In a world of divisions, sharing together in groups has seldom been so necessary.

The following frequently asked questions and answers offer further information.

Frequently Asked Questions

1 What are the aims of a reflective practice support group?

To give participants a safe and confidential space where they have a chance to share their experiences that might have left them with a lot of feelings and emotions as a result of their work, or where they had to make an ethical decision. In the long term, it aims to offer participants a regular safe space to share their experiences, think in depth about their experiences, and learn from the experiences of others in order to develop as practitioners and as part of their continuing professional development (CPD).

2 Are reflective practice support groups a form of counselling?

No, reflective practice is not counselling or psychotherapy. The setting is not clinical. The groups are run by trained facilitators who are not usually therapists.

3 Who are the facilitators? And what training have they had?

*Facilitators are trained and experience. They have completed a training course on facilitating Reflective Practice Support Groups with the Pásalo Project (*www.pasaloproject.org).

4 Do I have to contribute?

Although you don't have to contribute immediately, this is not a suitable group for those who wish only to observe. As you participate in a session, you might find yourself able and willing to either support a colleague who has shared their dilemma, or to share a situation that has affected you or that might be relevant and helpful for everyone.

5 How long are the sessions and how many sessions will I need to attend?

The sessions last one and a half hours. There will be four sessions in total. The first session is a foundation session where the ground rules and expectations will be set. To fully benefit, you will be asked to attend all four sessions and you need to join in time. Late arrivals cannot be accepted.

6 How big are the groups?

Typically, a maximum of 8 people in a group.

7 Where are the sessions conducted? If online, are they recorded?

The sessions will be conducted remotely via an online platform. They will not be recorded and participants will be asked to find a safe space where they will not be overheard. Everyone is expected to have their camera on throughout the session. Those without the camera switched on will not be accepted to participate.

8 Are we all bound by confidentiality / GDPR and will anyone be informed of what's discussed?

What we discuss will be confidential – only in the event that there is a safeguarding issue which the facilitator thinks is so serious that it could reasonably be expected to pose a risk to you or others might the facilitator need to share it with someone with authority in the matter who is competent to assess such a situation. Otherwise, the content of the sessions will not be disclosed.

Example Points for Inclusion in a Working Agreement

- **Confidentiality and boundaries**

Clear agreements about confidentiality, including the extent and limitations of contact between group members and the facilitator outside of sessions.

- **Respect for difference**

A shared commitment to respect difference in identity, experience, perspective, and opinion.

- **Awareness of power and context**

Ongoing attention to social, cultural, and structural power dynamics, both within the group and in the wider context in which we live and work.

- **Personal responsibility and scope of the group**

Responsibility for one's own participation and wellbeing, with clarity about the limits of the group in processing individual psychological material in depth.

- **External support and signposting**

Identification of personal support structures outside the group, and agreement on appropriate signposting when additional support is needed.

- **Creating a space of acceptance**

A collective aim to create a space that minimises shame and supports exploration, compassion, and learning.

- **Learning from mistakes**

Encouragement to bring what has not gone well, recognising the learning potential of mistakes and unintentional clumsiness.

- **Time boundaries**

Commitment to starting and ending sessions on time, and to respecting agreed time limits within sessions.

- **Communication and metacommunication**

Agreement on how we communicate about the group process itself, including turn-taking, fairness in speaking time, supporting those who may need help to build confidence to speak, and permission for the facilitator to intervene, or even interrupt, in the interest of equity and containment.

Example of a Joining Email

Dear group member

I am very much looking forward to welcoming you to the taster *reflective practice support group (RPSG)* on Tuesday, 6th January, from 6 p.m. to 7.30 p.m. UK time.

Practical guidelines

The following will help the group to run as productively as possible. We would like to ask you to please:

- join the meeting from a laptop, computer or tablet rather than from a phone.
- make sure you have a stable internet connection which enables you to have the camera on.
- ensure in advance that the device is fully charged and that you can have your camera switched on throughout.
- make sure you are in a confidential space where no one can see or hear *you* as well as *anyone else* in the group.

Preparation

1 Although this is a RPSG, and we will usually be working with everyone's individual material, for this session I will facilitate a group conversation based on a fictionalised case example.

2 For the future, please note that reflective practice support groups do not have a set agenda. Their effectiveness is driven by the material that members of the group are willing to bring to discuss so I will ask you in future to think, in advance of the sessions, about something you want to bring that you would like the group to think about together. This can be, for example, about a session that may have left you with a lot of feelings and emotions; a situation where you had to make a difficult ethical decision; a concern that you may be burning out or becoming vicariously traumatised, or a general question or concern or observation you wish to share with the group, and to hear group members' thoughts about.
3 For the first part of the session, we will have some time for introductions, context and ground rules for the reflective group, and then we will focus on issues people bring. Time is dedicated to setting up the session so that people can feel safe to share sensitive issues. It is a key component of the sessions, which is why we cannot accept latecomers.
4 As you are all aware, this is not a clinical supervision session or personal therapy. It is therefore recommended that you know about other support structures in place besides this group.

Joining the call

Please log on the call between 5.45 and 5.55 p.m. so you are ready to be admitted to the room shortly before we start. You may be aware that Zoom occasionally updates automatically and this can take a few minutes. We will start promptly at 6.00 p.m. Please note that it may not be possible to admit anyone who tries to join the call after 6.05 p.m.

Best wishes, and see you on Tuesday, 6th January, at 6 p.m. (UK time),
Maria

Foundation Training in Skills for Practitioner-Facilitators of Reflective Practice Support Groups

Overview

The intensive course aims to prepare participants to facilitate RPSGs safely, ethically, and effectively. The course combines experiential learning, skills practice, and supervised facilitation to support participants in developing both competence and confidence in reflective group work.

The training begins with an introductory session, followed by **three days of trainer-led learning**, and concludes with a **supported practice phase** ("the plus" component).

The training begins with an introductory session, followed by three days of trainer-led learning, and concludes with a supported practice phase ("the plus" component).

During the three days of the trainer-led phase, participants:

- Take part in reflective practice groups
- Practise peer support
- Develop facilitation skills by leading reflective groups with fellow trainees.

Following the three training days, participants organise and facilitate **four additional practice group sessions** without the trainer present. Each practice session is followed by group supervision led by the trainer, enabling reflection, feedback, and continued skill development.

Throughout the programme, the emphasis is on creating ethically grounded and psychologically safe spaces in which group members feel able to share concerns, dilemmas, and uncertainties. Participants are introduced to reflective facilitation skills and to the role of the RPSG facilitator as a guide rather than an expert, supported by ongoing supervision as they put learning into practice.

Course Structure

1 Attending and Deconstructing a Reflective Practice Support Group

Duration: 3 hours (online)

DESCRIPTION

Participants attend a 3-hour online session in which they take part in Reflective Practice Support Groups facilitated by the trainer. The session includes guided deconstruction of the facilitation process, offering participants direct experience of the methodology alongside reflective analysis of how the group is held and guided.

2 Introduction to Group Facilitation

Duration: 3 days (in-person or online)
Schedule: Two consecutive days, followed by a third day four weeks later

DESCRIPTION

This module introduces the core principles and practices of group facilitation, providing a solid foundation in both theory and practice. Participants deepen their understanding of reflective group work while developing practical facilitation skills through experiential learning.

Content includes:

- Theoretical foundations of group facilitation
- Core facilitation skills

- Participation in reflective practice groups
- Common facilitation challenges
- Ethical considerations
- Feedback and reflective learning.

Self-study activities include:

- Reflective journalling
- Watching selected films and reading key papers
- Completing homework tasks such as developing facilitation scripts, learning structured sequences of activities, and engaging in self-evaluation exercises.

3 Practice and Supervision

Duration: 4 practice hours and 4 hours of online supervision

DESCRIPTION

After completing the three-day module, participants organise and lead **four online practice groups** as trainee facilitators. Fellow trainees act as group participants. Each practice group is followed by a one-hour online group supervision session facilitated by the trainer, supporting ongoing learning, feedback, and refinement of practice.

This stage marks the conclusion of the formal training input. While the course provides a clear and supportive structure, trainee and graduate facilitators are encouraged to build a growing bank of practical experience. Over time, this enables them to bring their own creativity and personal style to facilitation, to take thoughtful risks, develop new frames, and experience facilitation as a skilled and reflective practice—and, ultimately, as an art.

COURSE OUTCOMES

By the end of the course, participants will:

1 Understand the theory and process of Reflective Practice Support Group facilitation.
2 Have experience of—and confidence in—creating psychologically safe group spaces.
3 Be able to support ethical discussion of case work and dilemmas and facilitate productive responses.
4 Understand the concept of *intelligent empathy* and how to model it as a facilitator.

5 Recognise their professional limits and know when referral to other forms of support is required.
6 Have developed foundational group facilitation skills using the *Repair–Reflect–Response* model.

Teaching methods include:

- Lectures
- Discussions
- Roleplays
- Demonstrations
- Dismantling and critiquing of processes
- Discussing videoed material
- Self-evaluation questionnaires
- Creative apprenticeship/learning by doing

A filmed excerpt of an introductory training session in group facilitation (for people learning to facilitate reflexive practice support groups) can be found here: https://www.pasaloproject.org/resources.html#Facilitator

A Few Tips for Facilitators

The sections in italics are practice exercises for you to do if you wish.

- Have some *go-to* phrases e.g. "Who here connects with what X has just said?"
- One-minute exercise in silence for thinking.
- Online, use chat rather than verbal sharing at the end if time is pressured. Or use one-minute, one-word exercise.

Prepare some go-to phrases and techniques for managing the group especially when time is pressured. If you have the opportunity, practise them in your professional contexts.

- Work on your own conciseness as a model to the group

Keep practising this as much as possible and get feedback from friends and colleagues.

- Include your vulnerability for *yourself*. Don't exclude it. This takes commitment.

What activities help you to do this? What private, self-talk phrases (that are compassionate with, inclusive and containing of your vulnerability) can you have ready to hand?

Again, practise this in your own contexts. Make a note of what happens and how you feel.

- Advance preparation about power and authority.

Make a list of what may happen in a group if you don't use your power wisely.

How can group members overtly undermine your power as a facilitator? How can group members subtly undermine your power as a facilitator?

What if some people are annoyed with you? What happens to your vulnerable self? See if you can pay attention to this in your professional and social lives over the next months.

Think of ways you are going to manage this type of situation in a group you facilitate, that work for you.

Some Additional Tips for Creating and Maintaining the Potential for a Safe Enough Space

A safe space is a "place or environment in which a person or category of people can feel confident that they will not be exposed to discrimination, criticism, harassment, or any other emotional or physical harm" (Oxford Languages, 2025).

It is a space that is as shame-free as possible so that people feel able to take risks, be clumsy, make mistakes – ultimately to be creative and learn!

- Share ground rules about expectations, communication, respect, confidentiality, timing, personal responsibility etc.
- Allow group members to contribute. Avoid rushing in yourself but be prepared to step in if necessary to e.g., challenge disrespectful behaviour.
- Avoid isolating yourself. Keep checking with the group.
- Avoid isolating members of the group. After a person has shared, allow them some space. Discourage other members from asking lots of questions but encourage members to share something about themselves so that the sharer feels connected back in. Ask the sharer if they want to have the last word.
- Keep everything in the group. If individuals want to talk to you outside of the group *about the group*, for anything that is not just administrative, make sure they know that this will need to be fed back to the group.
- Avoid having special alliances with individual members. Avoid taking sides and if you find you don't like a member of the group (or you like them too much) take this to your own supervision!
- Notice and reflect on parallel processes, countertransference and projective identification occurring within the group.

- Keep to time. Begin when you said you would, and end when you said you would. Keep an eye on the time throughout the session and remind people of how much time is left at appropriate moments. Don't overrun with one person's sharing so that there is not enough time for someone else's. A sense of fairness is crucial if people are going to feel safe.
- Do what you say you are going to do. Be consistent and committed.
- Be honest if you forget something or make a mistake.
- Avoid talking about yourself. If you really feel you need to share something then this session may not be the appropriate time and place for you to do it. As the facilitator you need to avoid getting so absorbed with the material that you lose your ability to provide a steady anchor for the group. This isn't your session. Only share about yourself if you feel that a) the group would benefit *significantly* to hear about your personal experience, b) you can stay in role as the facilitator.

Go-to Phrases

In emotionally charged situations it can be useful to have a phrase or a sentence that you can use to help to anchor yourself and the group. It is difficult to be creative in the midst of anxiety and tension. Having a way to take down the emotional temperature can help in the moment.

Nothing is completely safe but here are some phrases that are suitable for less experienced and more experienced facilitators.

Reasonably Safe

Let's just stop for a moment. I think it is possible that some people are feeling quite hurt, judged, and misunderstood. Is that right? (Check with group but don't invite further comment.) Before we go any further, could I suggest that we take a moment to remind ourselves why we are here, what is the task we have set ourselves for this group, and the agreement we made about communication?

A Bit More Risky

Make an empathic connection with each party. Suggest the speaker takes some time to compose what they want to say, so that we can truly hear them without being defensive.

Potentially Very Helpful but Reasonably High Risk

- Name and acknowledge difficult situations: "I notice there's a bit of hesitation or discomfort as we talk about difference. That makes sense—

these are difficult topics. That's why people don't get much practice to talk about them. Can we try to practice talking about them here?"

- One-minute exercise.
- Transparency: Acknowledge your own limits without abdicating responsibility: "I'm learning how to hold these conversations. I may not always get it right, but I want to try even if it's difficult. And the reason why I want to try is that these conversations may be difficult but they are vitally important. Can we try and help each other out in our attempts, here?"

The Stages of a Reflective Practice Support Group

A reflective practice support group has various phases.

1 Reparative, supportive, or restorative – empathic connection.
2 Reflective, formative – developing thinking and learning.
3 Responsive:

   a making a bridge between the discussion and action (i.e. what are participants going to *do* differently because of their reflections?).
   b applying systemic change at the organisational level and across professions.

(Costa, 2020; Hawkins & Shohet, 2012; Inskipp & Proctor, 1994; Page & Wosket, 2001)

Practitioner Stories and Testimonies: The Impact

The following accounts—drawn from different professional contexts—illustrate the value and impact of reflective practice.

We begin with perspectives from arts practitioners. In *The Work Hurts*, Alison O'Connor (2022) reports on her research into the emotional impact on arts practitioners working in health, social care, and participatory settings, and on the potential role of supervision or reflective practice. One interviewee emphasised the importance of supervision:

> supervision needs to be valued and understood... it's not about just having a natter, it's actually needed to support your practice. It's not quite CPD but it underpins what you do and it's a cushion. And how on earth can you go around delivering some intensive projects without having that there for you?
>
> (O'Connor, 2022, p. 162)

A second perspective comes from a trainee psychologist who took part in a reflective practice group co-facilitated by Arabella Kurtz (2019). The trainee psychologist describes how the group's reflections influenced her therapeutic approach and impacted on her practice. The perspective of her peers helped her to gain distance from her immediate experience and find compassion for the client:

> I was coming at a different point from the rest of the group because I was so in it and they were able to take that step back ... after I came back from reflective practice it's like another sort of filter had been put in those lenses... I could see her differently ...which I think led to different things in therapy.
>
> (Kurtz, 2019, p. 73)

Insights from education professionals offer a third context. Banegas and Glatigny's (2021) study of teachers found that participants valued the *ateneo* as a collaborative, interactive space where an inclusive community of practice could form. One teacher reflected:

> Talking to peers, seeing that we have the same issues has reduced my stress and anxiety about teaching and I feel ok ... Every time I attend the meetings, I go back home with new strategies and ideas and we can even share resources.
>
> (Banegas & Glatigny, 2021, p. 370)

Finally, the following testimonies come from postgraduate researchers and interpreters who participated in reflective practice support groups that I facilitated. One postgraduate researcher wrote:

> It is possible, and also necessary, to take time to reflect on my research process and to reflect in a group with other postgraduate researchers, who have shown they share some of my experiences and also provide their own unique insights. The three sessions have all been very helpful in these respects, and the dates set have provided a kind of "safety net" in which I know I will be able to continue that self-reflexive process.
>
> I really appreciated the space as a quiet, slow reflective opportunity. I also appreciated the freedom and flexibility of the sessions, there were no pre-set topics or themes, which allowed us to bring our own ideas or speak spontaneously about what was on our minds. It was valuable to hear about others' experiences and reassuring to see that we are not alone. As a postgraduate researcher, the experience of research (with sensitive/personal subjects) can feel daunting and lonely. Having room for these feelings to exist, be acknowledged, and held space for/responded to made me feel heard and like I wasn't alone in this. Having a

> smaller and consistent group also meant we could build shared language to describe our experiences and learn not just from presenting what was on top for us, but also from how we responded to others/ourselves. I would very much recommend this as a conscious practice … as a way for postgrad researchers to find ways to develop their work and thinking around it.

Interpreters echoed similar themes after attending a taster session:

> Despite not being the norm, it is very important to be able to reflect about personal experiences, share challenges openly, and understand how others in similar situations feel. All in a place where you know you are going to be fully understood by someone else or at least provided with a kind listening ear. I've found this session very interesting and I think it's a great initiative to prevent long term problems for interpreters. It reminded me of the importance of having a safe space to reflect, and how valuable it is to pause, think, and process what we go through in our work. I would definitely join a regular group like this, if it was on offer.

References

Banegas, D. L., & Glatigny, R. (2021). The ateneo as an effective model of continuing professional development: Findings from southern Argentina. *Pedagogies*, 16(4), 363–377. doi:10.1080/1554480X.2021.1897012.

Costa, B. (2020). *Other tongues: Psychological therapies in a multilingual world: A guide for qualified practitioners, trainers and supervisors*. PCCS Books.

Hawkins, P., & Shohet, R. (2012). *Supervision in the helping professions: An individual, group and organizational approach* (4th ed.). Open University Press.

Inskipp, F., & Proctor, B. (1994). *The art, craft and tasks of supervision, part 1: Making the most of supervision*. Cascade.

Kurtz, A. (2019). *How to run reflective practice groups: A guide for healthcare professionals*. Routledge. doi:10.4324/9781351112994.

O'Connor, A. (2022). The work hurts. *Journal of Applied Arts & Health*, 13(2), 153. doi:10.1386/jaah_00096_1.

Oxford Languages. (2025). Safe space. Retrieved from https://languages.oup.com/google-dictionary-en. (accessed 18 October 2025).

Page, S., & Wosket, V. (2001). *Supervising the counsellor: A cyclical model* (2nd edition). Brunner-Routledge.

Index

Note: Locators in *italic* refer figures.

For Product Safety Concerns and Information please contact our EU representative GPSR@taylorandfrancis.com Taylor & Francis Verlag GmbH, Kaufingerstraße 24, 80331 München, Germany

"This is the type of book I want to have on my desk and look through it every now and then, to remind myself, to reassure myself, and to look for ideas."

Zora Jackman, *MCIL CL MITI DPSI, Tutor on the public service interpreting programme, Cardiff University*

"At a time when division and disconnection are increasingly visible, the book offers something both modest and radical: a workable approach to collective reflection that supports professional integrity, resilience, and ethical judgement, while helping groups remain engaged with difference, disagreement, and complexity in ways that deepen understanding and sustain meaningful change."

Professor Andrew Reeves, *Emeritus Professor in Counselling Professions and Mental Health*

"*The Art of Group Facilitation: Difficult Conversations and Reflective Practice* is an exceptional guide for any group facilitator interested in holding difficult and deeply reflective conversations."

Mamood Ahmad, *UKCP Psychotherapist, tutor and author*

In this insightful book, Beverley Costa explores the crucial role of the group facilitator in shaping reflective groups that can move beyond disorganised and stagnant group dynamics, contain anxiety and foster meaningful change.

How can we create spaces where people can truly think together – especially when emotions run high, voices are unequal, and disagreement feels risky? Facilitating such spaces requires skill, ethical courage, attentiveness to power and boundaries, and a willingness to stay present when conversations become difficult. This practical, ethically grounded guide shows how reflective groups can be facilitated with care, confidence, and fairness, even in complex or divided contexts. Drawing on real cases examined from multiple perspectives, it invites readers to reflect on voice, power, positionality, and collective responsibility. Not everyone in a group feels equally entitled to speak. Some hesitate, unsure whether their voice is welcome; others may assert a strong right to be heard. These dynamics influence whose knowledge is valued and how power takes shape. The book explores how such tensions can be recognised and worked with compassionately, without reinforcing inequality. Groups tend to return to familiar ideas, mistaking repetition for insight. *The Art of Group Facilitation* shows how facilitators can raise awareness of this drift, hold uncertainty, and keep reflective practice alive.

Drawing on decades of real-world experience, the book offers clear frameworks, case examples, and practical tools for professionals in education, healthcare, social care, law, journalism, community and humanitarian work, and other relational fields – anyone who recognises the power of people thinking together.

Beverley Costa is a psychotherapist, trainer, supervisor, and founder of Mothertongue and the Pásalo Project. For over three decades she has facilitated reflective groups, pioneering therapeutic work across languages, and training thousands of professionals internationally. She is a senior practitioner fellow at Birkbeck, University of London and a senior visiting research fellow at the University of Reading.

Routledge
Taylor & Francis Group
www.routledge.com

an **informa** business

ISBN 978-1-041-11231-0

9 781041 112310

Routledge titles are available as eBook editions in a range of digital formats

"This is the type of book I want to have on my desk and look through it every now and then, to remind myself, to reassure myself, and to look for ideas."

Zora Jackman, *MCIL CL MITI DPSI, Tutor on the public service interpreting programme, Cardiff University*

"At a time when division and disconnection are increasingly visible, the book offers something both modest and radical: a workable approach to collective reflection that supports professional integrity, resilience, and ethical judgement, while helping groups remain engaged with difference, disagreement, and complexity in ways that deepen understanding and sustain meaningful change."

Professor Andrew Reeves, *Emeritus Professor in Counselling Professions and Mental Health*

"*The Art of Group Facilitation: Difficult Conversations and Reflective Practice* is an exceptional guide for any group facilitator interested in holding difficult and deeply reflective conversations."

Mamood Ahmad, *UKCP Psychotherapist, tutor and author*

In this insightful book, Beverley Costa explores the crucial role of the group facilitator in shaping reflective groups that can move beyond disorganised and stagnant group dynamics, contain anxiety and foster meaningful change.

How can we create spaces where people can truly think together – especially when emotions run high, voices are unequal, and disagreement feels risky? Facilitating such spaces requires skill, ethical courage, attentiveness to power and boundaries, and a willingness to stay present when conversations become difficult. This practical, ethically grounded guide shows how reflective groups can be facilitated with care, confidence, and fairness, even in complex or divided contexts. Drawing on real cases examined from multiple perspectives, it invites readers to reflect on voice, power, positionality, and collective responsibility. Not everyone in a group feels equally entitled to speak. Some hesitate, unsure whether their voice is welcome; others may assert a strong right to be heard. These dynamics influence whose knowledge is valued and how power takes shape. The book explores how such tensions can be recognised and worked with compassionately, without reinforcing inequality. Groups tend to return to familiar ideas, mistaking repetition for insight. *The Art of Group Facilitation* shows how facilitators can raise awareness of this drift, hold uncertainty, and keep reflective practice alive.

Drawing on decades of real-world experience, the book offers clear frameworks, case examples, and practical tools for professionals in education, healthcare, social care, law, journalism, community and humanitarian work, and other relational fields – anyone who recognises the power of people thinking together.

Beverley Costa is a psychotherapist, trainer, supervisor, and founder of Mothertongue and the Pásalo Project. For over three decades she has facilitated reflective groups, pioneering therapeutic work across languages, and training thousands of professionals internationally. She is a senior practitioner fellow at Birkbeck, University of London and a senior visiting research fellow at the University of Reading.

an **informa** business

ROUTLEDGE Routledge
Taylor & Francis Group
www.routledge.com

Routledge titles are available as eBook editions in a range of digital formats

ISBN 978-1-041-11231-0

9 781041 112310